DESCENDING STORIES

SHOWA GENROKU RAKUGO SHINJU

Haruko Kumota

THE STORY SO FAR

YOTARO'S ODYSSEY

Yotaro falls in love with Yakumo Yurakutei's *rakugo* when he hears it in prison. Once free, he becomes Yakumo's apprentice and is soon made a *zenza*. As his appreciation for *rakugo* grows, the incredible *rakugo* of the late Sukeroku takes hold of him and he commits an unthinkable faux pas at a solo recital by his teacher. Facing expulsion, Yotaro begs forgiveness. Yakumo relents, but extracts three promises from his student. Then he begins to tell the tale of his own promise with Sukeroku...

YAKUMO AND SUKEROKU

Yakumo Yurakutei VII takes two apprentices on the same day: Kikuhiko and Hatsutaro. Promoted to *shin'uchi* together, the two are soon popular *rakugo* artists, with Hatsutaro adopting the name "Sukeroku," and Kikuhiko finding his own style at last.

But Sukeroku argues with his shisho and is expelled from the lineage. Wounded, he disappears with Miyokichi, Kikuhiko's former lover. Not long after, Yakumo makes a deathbed confession to Kikuhiko of his secret connection to the Sukeroku name. Bereaved and alone, Kikuhiko goes in search of Sukeroku at a hot springs town in the countryside, in order to make him inherit the Yakumo name. Sukeroku has abandoned *rakugo*, but, at Kikuhiko's insistence, the two Yurakutei disciples put on a successful joint show.

CAST OF CHARACTERS

Yakumo and Sukeroku

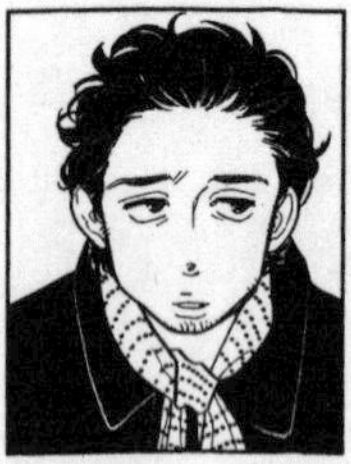

Sukeroku
Apprentice of Yakumo VII, making him a brother apprentice to Kikuhiko, until his expulsion.

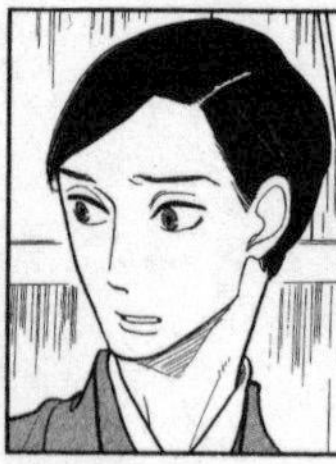

Kikuhiko
Yakumo Yurakutei VIII as a young *zenza*. The same age as Sukeroku.

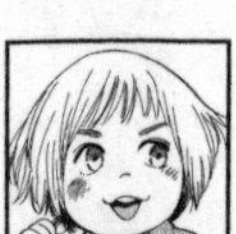

Konatsu
Konatsu in her youth. Daughter of Sukeroku and Miyokichi.

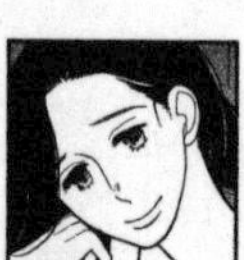

Miyokichi (Yurie)
Konatsu's mother. Dies falling from a window with Sukeroku.

Yotaro's Odyssey

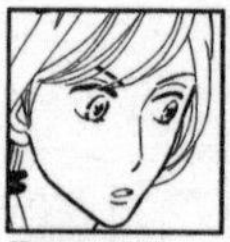

Konatsu
Sukeroku's only daughter, taken in by Yakumo.

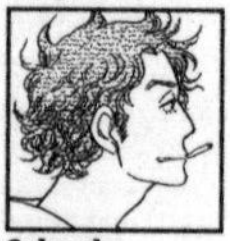

Sukeroku Yurakutei
Legendary *rakugo* artist hailed as a genius before his untimely death.

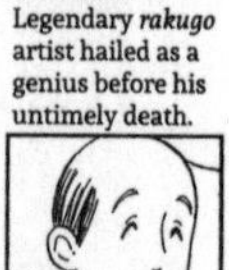

Matsuda-san
Faithful servant and driver of Yakumo VIII, and Yakumo VII before him.

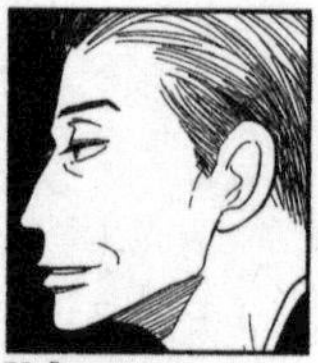

Yakumo Yurakutei VIII
Renowned as the Showa period's last great master of *rakugo*.

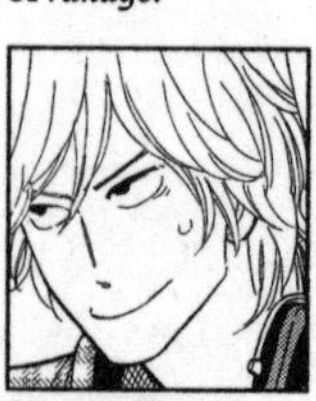

Yotaro (Kyoji)
Reformed street tough who became Yakumo's apprentice.

That night, however, Miyokichi reappears, hinting at a joint suicide with Kikuhiko. Driven by a hunch, Sukeroku bursts in to stop them, and the scene ends in tragedy as he and Miyokichi fall to their deaths together.

Taking in their child Konatsu in memory of the two, Kikuhiko inherits the Yakumo name himself, in order to put an end to the story...

SUKEROKU AGAIN

Taking the promises he made to Yakumo to heart, Yotaro diligently polishes his craft. With the *rakugo* world fading and only one yose left in Tokyo, he is finally promoted to *shin'uchi*—adopting the name "Sukeroku III." Meanwhile, Konatsu reveals that she is pregnant. Yotaro marries her, becoming father to her child.

Suspecting, however, that the child's biological father is a yakuza boss, Yotaro confronts his past and resolves things once and for all.
Still in search of his own *rakugo*, Yotaro is admonished by Yakumo to put his self into his work. Yakumo agrees to a father-and-son recital—but only if Yotaro performs "*Inokori.*"

Can Yotaro make this difficult story his own?

Cast of Characters

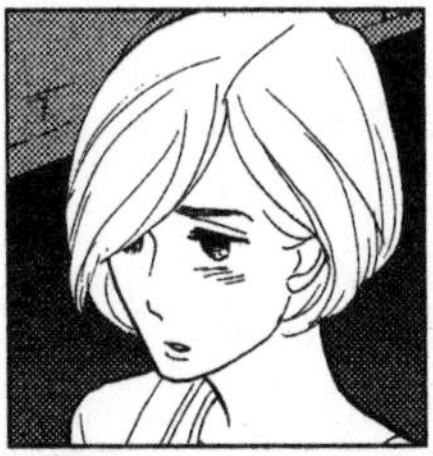

Konatsu
Only daughter of the late Sukeroku II, taken in by Yakumo. Had a child without revealing the father. Now married to Yotaro.

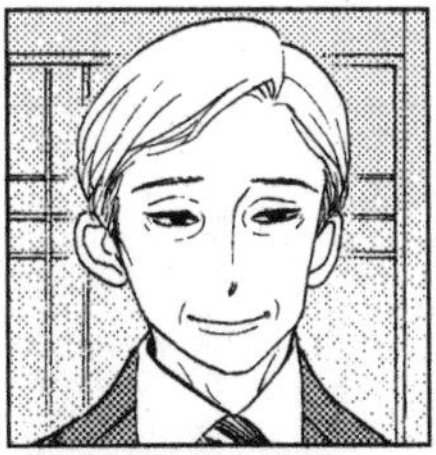

Yakumo Yurakutei VIII
Now the most powerful figure in the world of *rakugo* and president of the *Rakugo* Association. Accepted no apprentices except Yotaro, leaving nobody to inherit the Yakumo name.

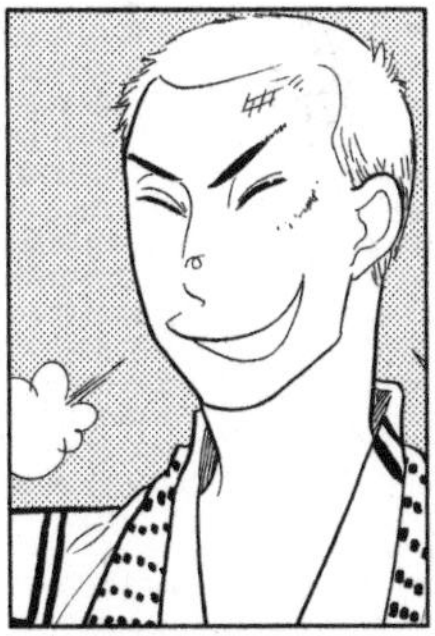

Sukeroku Again

Sukeroku Yurakutei III (a.k.a. Yotaro)
Promoted to *shin'uchi*, Yotaro inherits the Sukeroku name and marries Konatsu to form a family. Loves *rakugo* with all his heart.

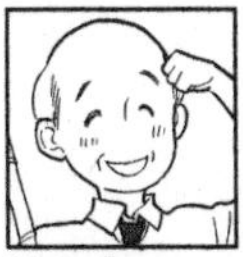

Matsuda-san
Faithful servant and driver of Yakumo VIII. Part of the Yurakutei family in all but name.

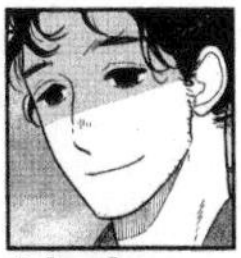

Sukeroku Yurakutei II
Konatsu's deceased father, whose *rakugo* remains legendary.

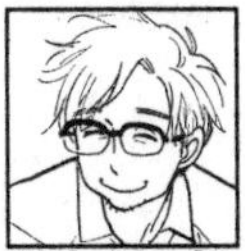

Eisuke Higuchi
A.k.a. "Sensei." Popular writer and fan of Yotaro.

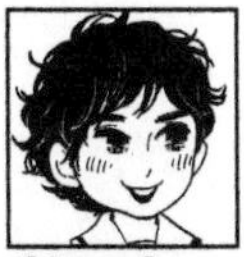

Shinnosuke
Yotaro and Konatsu's son, whose real father remains a secret.

DESCENDING STORIES

SHOWA GENROKU RAKUGO SHINJU

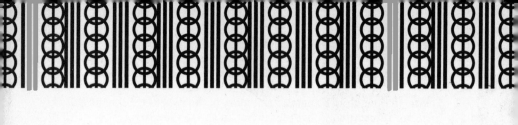

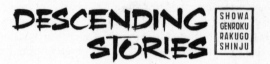

Contents

Sukeroku Again

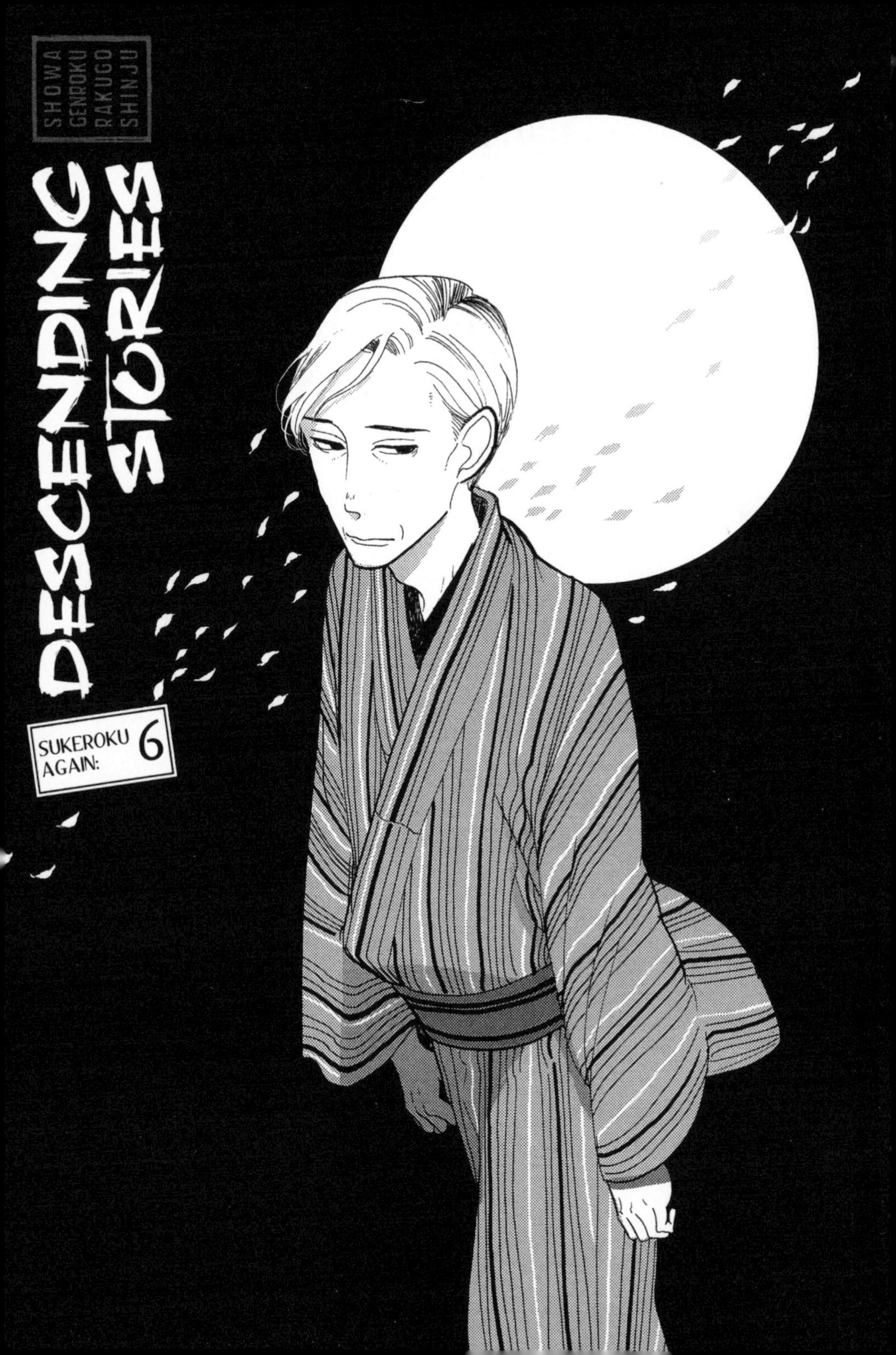
SHOWA GENROKU RAKUGO SHINJU
DESCENDING STORIES
SUKEROKU AGAIN: 6

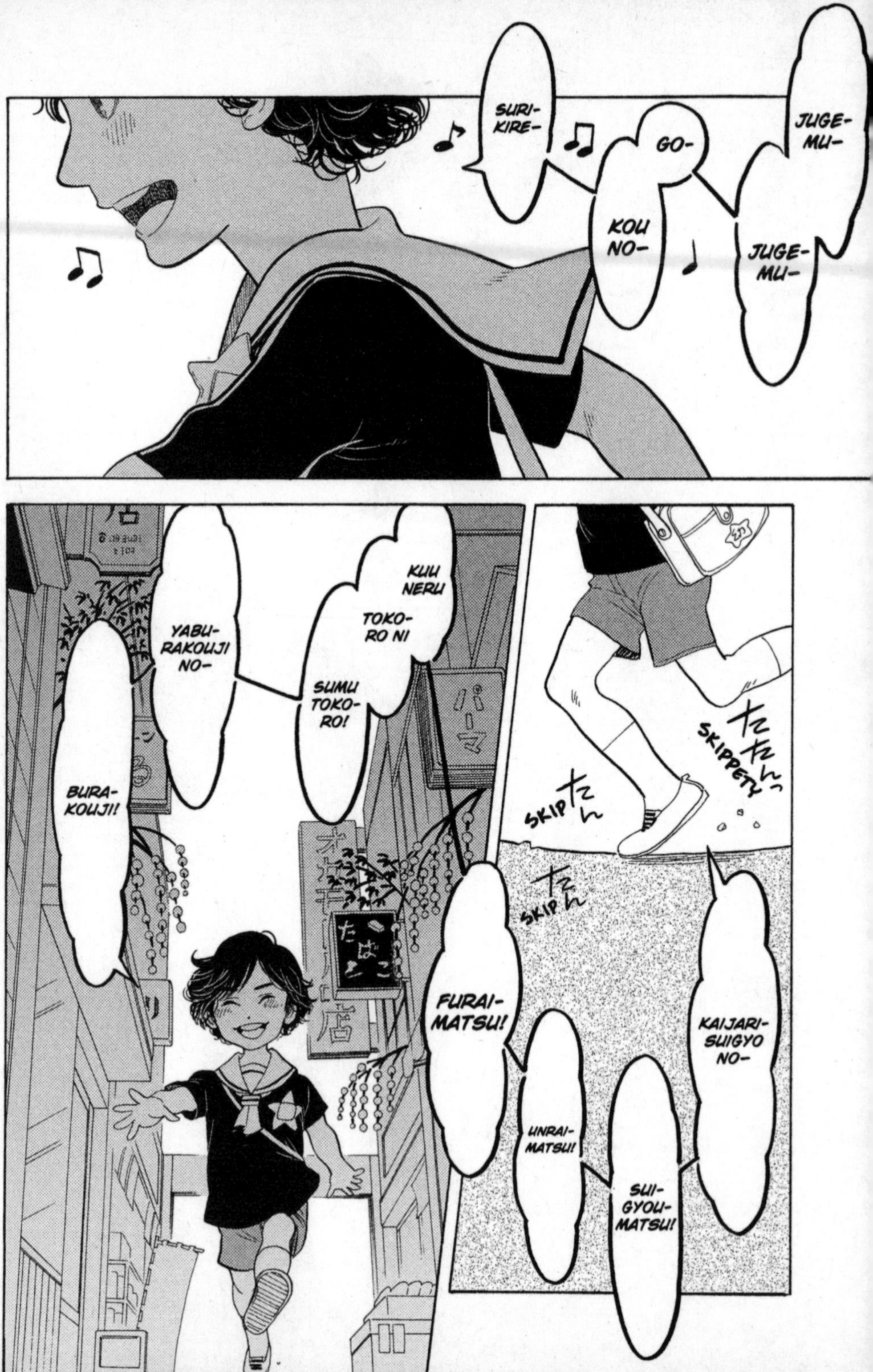
JUGE-MU-
JUGE-MU-
GO-
KOU NO-
SURI-KIRE-
SKIPPETY
SKIP
SKIP
KAIJARI-SUIGYO NO-
SUI-GYOU-MATSU!
UNRAI-MATSU!
FURAI-MATSU!
KUU NERU
TOKO-RO NI
SUMU TOKO-RO!
YABU-RAKOUJI NO-
BURA-KOUJI!
たばこ

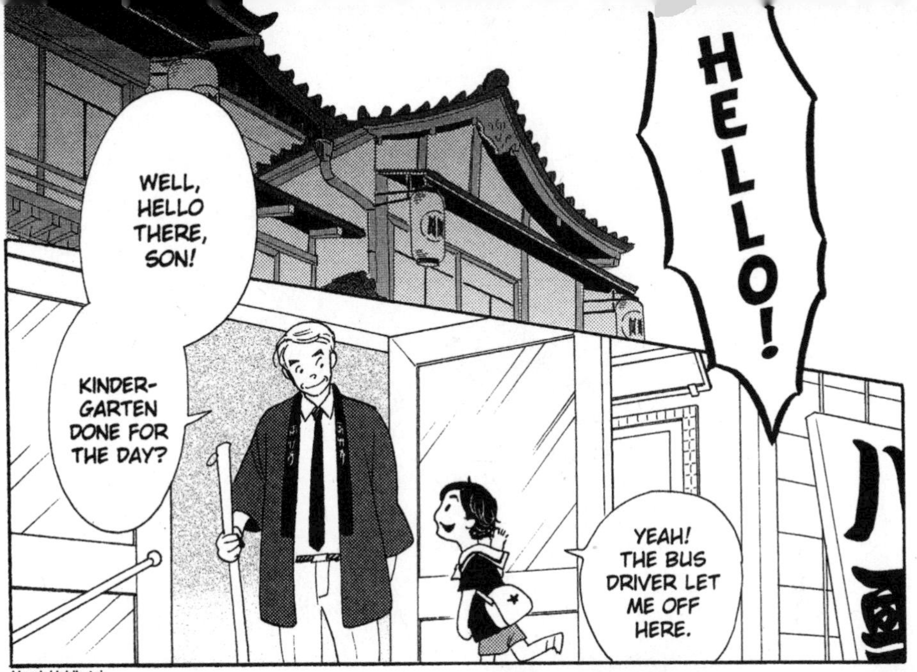
HELLO!
WELL, HELLO THERE, SON!
KINDER-GARTEN DONE FOR THE DAY?
YEAH! THE BUS DRIVER LET ME OFF HERE.

Haori: Uchikutei

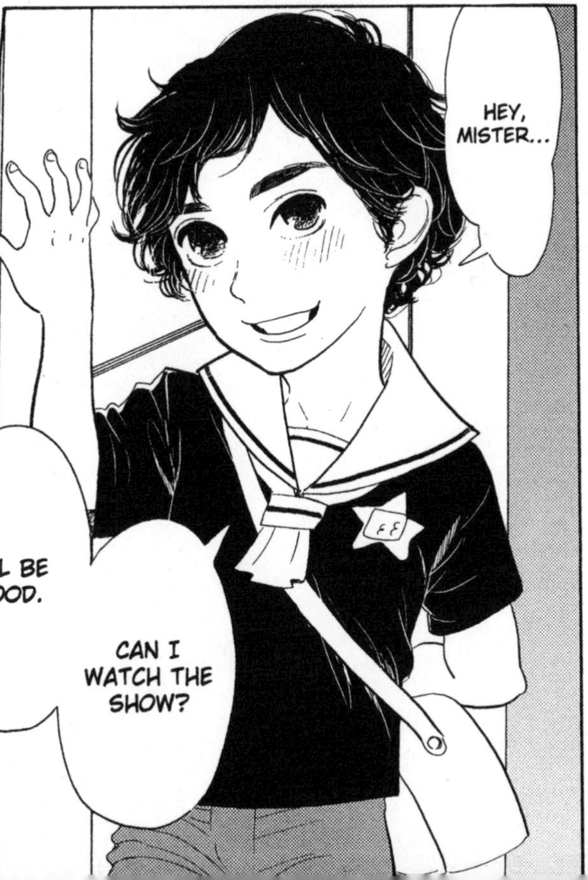
HEY, MISTER...
I'LL BE GOOD.
CAN I WATCH THE SHOW?

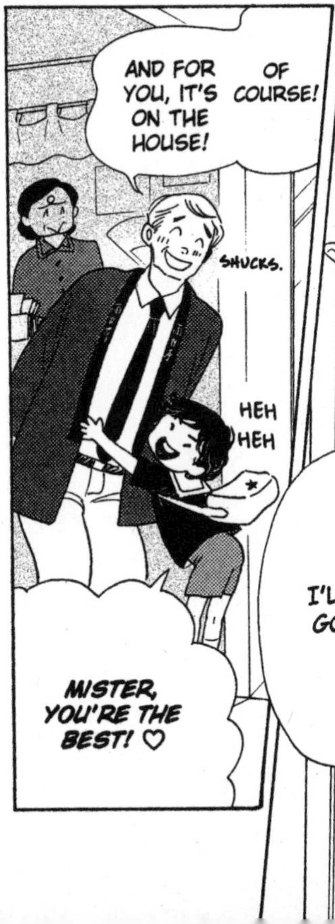
OF COURSE!
AND FOR YOU, IT'S ON THE HOUSE!
SHUCKS.
HEH HEH
MISTER, YOU'RE THE BEST! ♡

Sign: *Dorayaki* 100 yen

Package: Full House *Yose dorayaki*

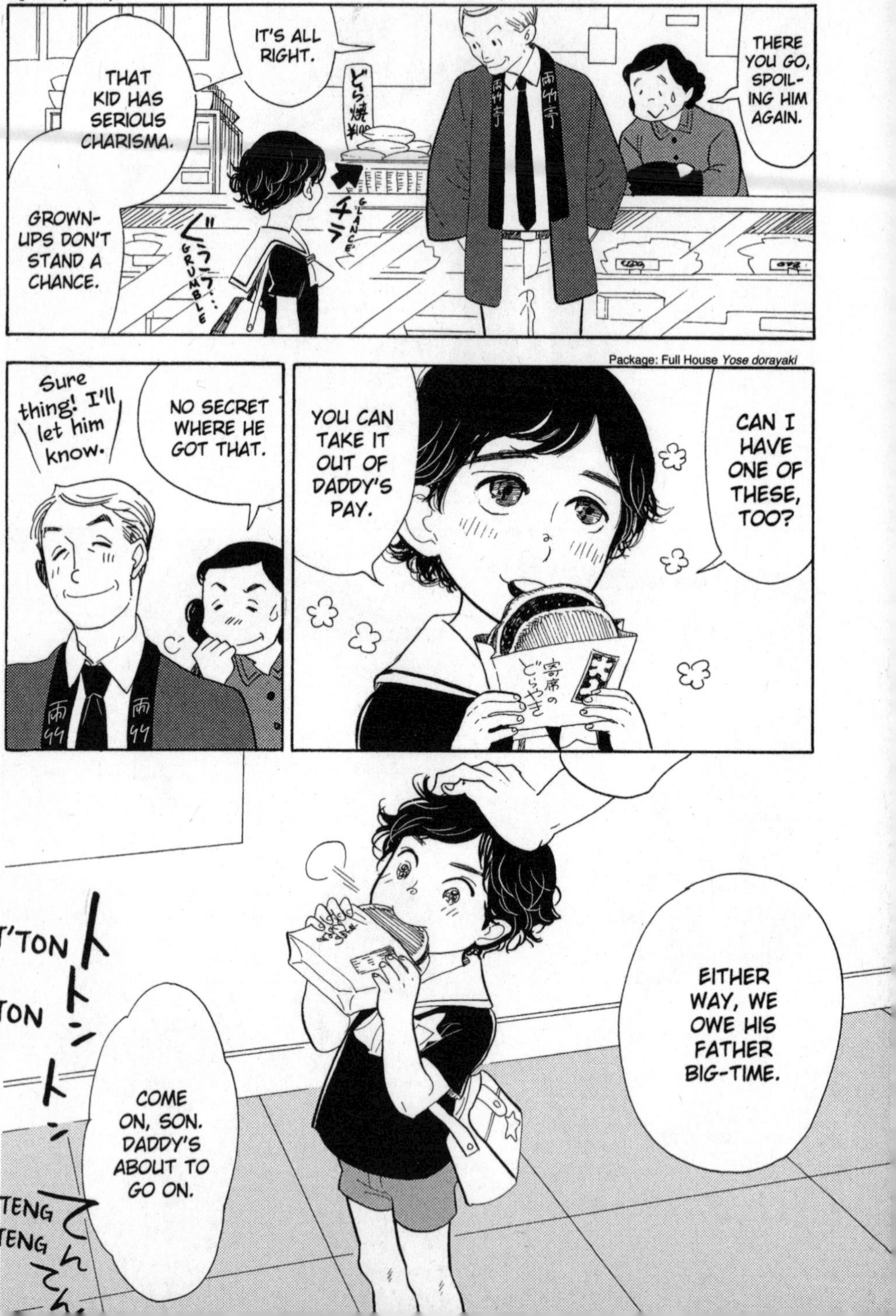
THERE YOU GO, SPOIL-ING HIM AGAIN.
IT'S ALL RIGHT.
どら焼 ¥100
GLANCE
チラ
THAT KID HAS SERIOUS CHARISMA.
GROWN-UPS DON'T STAND A CHANCE.
GRUMBLE
CAN I HAVE ONE OF THESE, TOO?
YOU CAN TAKE IT OUT OF DADDY'S PAY.
寄席のどらやき
NO SECRET WHERE HE GOT THAT.
Sure thing! I'll let him know.
EITHER WAY, WE OWE HIS FATHER BIG-TIME.
COME ON, SON. DADDY'S ABOUT TO GO ON.
T'TON
TON
TENG TENG

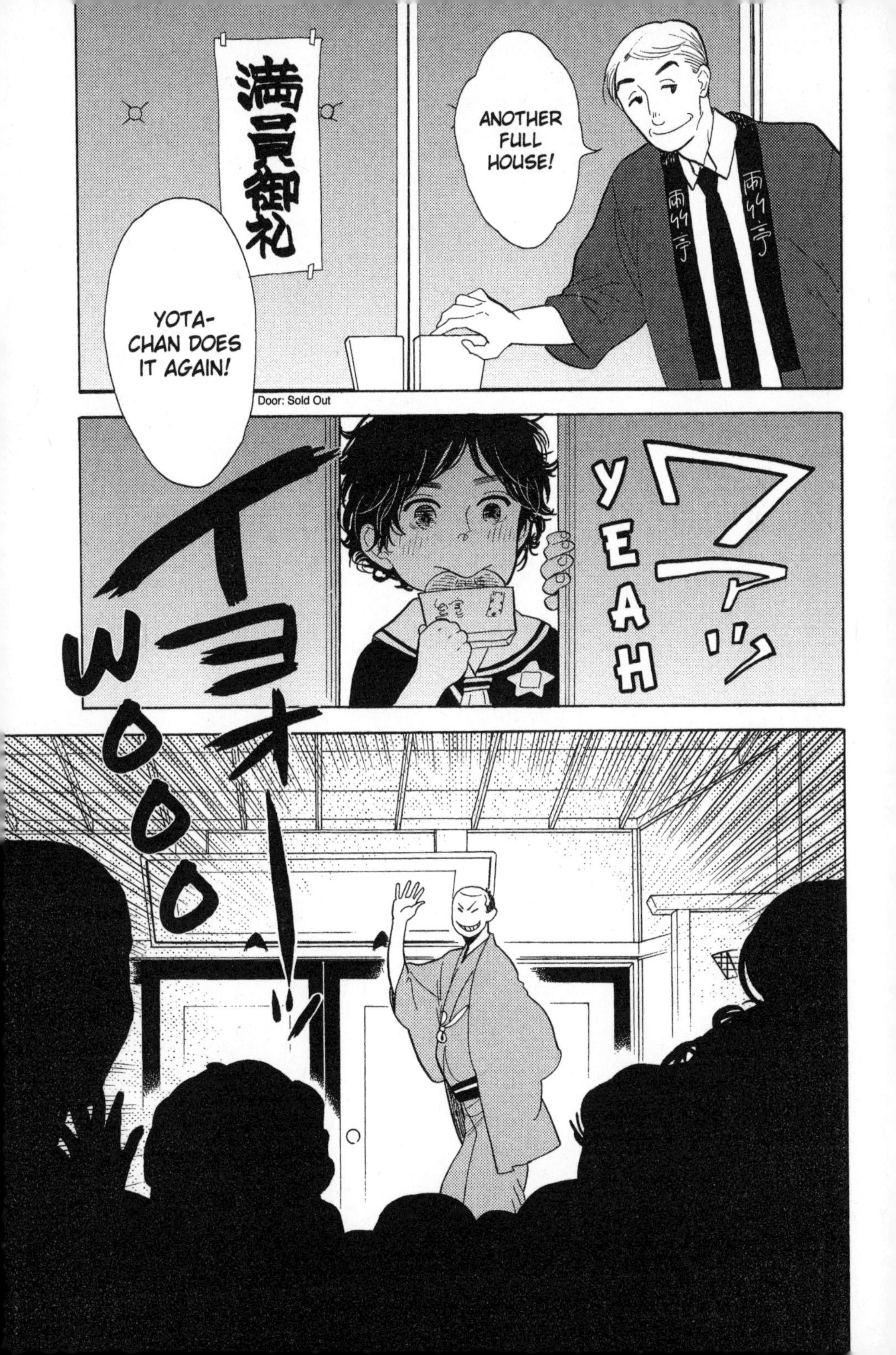

満員御礼
ANOTHER FULL HOUSE!
雨竹亭
YOTA-CHAN DOES IT AGAIN!
Door: Sold Out
YEAH
WOOOO!!

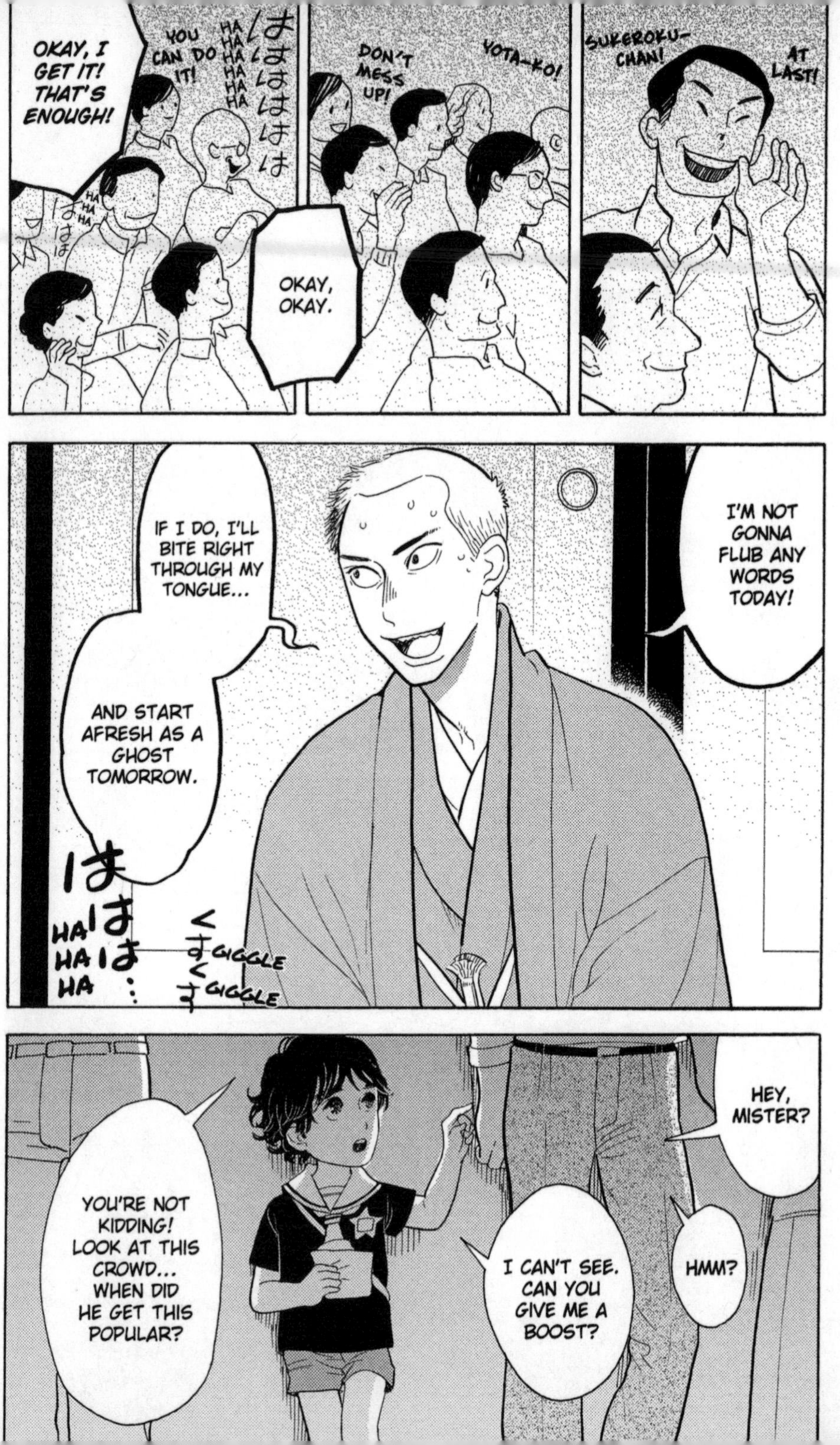

SUKEROKU-CHAN!
AT LAST!
YOTA-KO!
DON'T MESS UP!
OKAY, OKAY.
HA HA HA HA HA HA
YOU CAN DO IT!
OKAY, I GET IT! THAT'S ENOUGH!
HA HA HA
I'M NOT GONNA FLUB ANY WORDS TODAY!
IF I DO, I'LL BITE RIGHT THROUGH MY TONGUE...
AND START AFRESH AS A GHOST TOMORROW.
くすくす GIGGLE GIGGLE
ははは… HA HA HA
HEY, MISTER?
HMM?
I CAN'T SEE. CAN YOU GIVE ME A BOOST?
YOU'RE NOT KIDDING! LOOK AT THIS CROWD... WHEN DID HE GET THIS POPULAR?

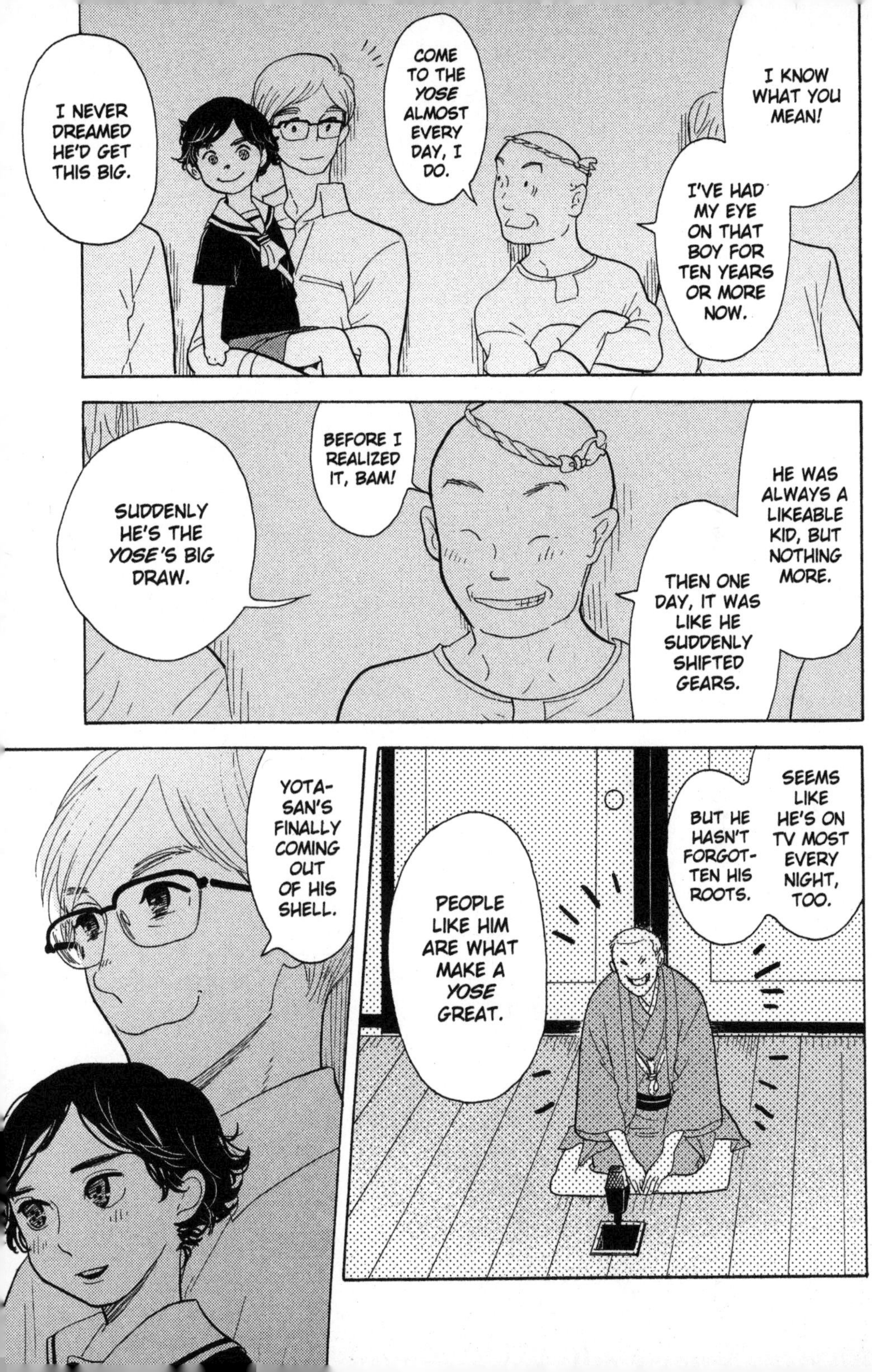
I KNOW WHAT YOU MEAN!
I'VE HAD MY EYE ON THAT BOY FOR TEN YEARS OR MORE NOW.
COME TO THE *YOSE* ALMOST EVERY DAY, I DO.
I NEVER DREAMED HE'D GET THIS BIG.
HE WAS ALWAYS A LIKEABLE KID, BUT NOTHING MORE.
THEN ONE DAY, IT WAS LIKE HE SUDDENLY SHIFTED GEARS.
BEFORE I REALIZED IT, BAM!
SUDDENLY HE'S THE *YOSE*'S BIG DRAW.
SEEMS LIKE HE'S ON TV MOST EVERY NIGHT, TOO.
BUT HE HASN'T FORGOT-TEN HIS ROOTS.
PEOPLE LIKE HIM ARE WHAT MAKE A *YOSE* GREAT.
YOTA-SAN'S FINALLY COMING OUT OF HIS SHELL.

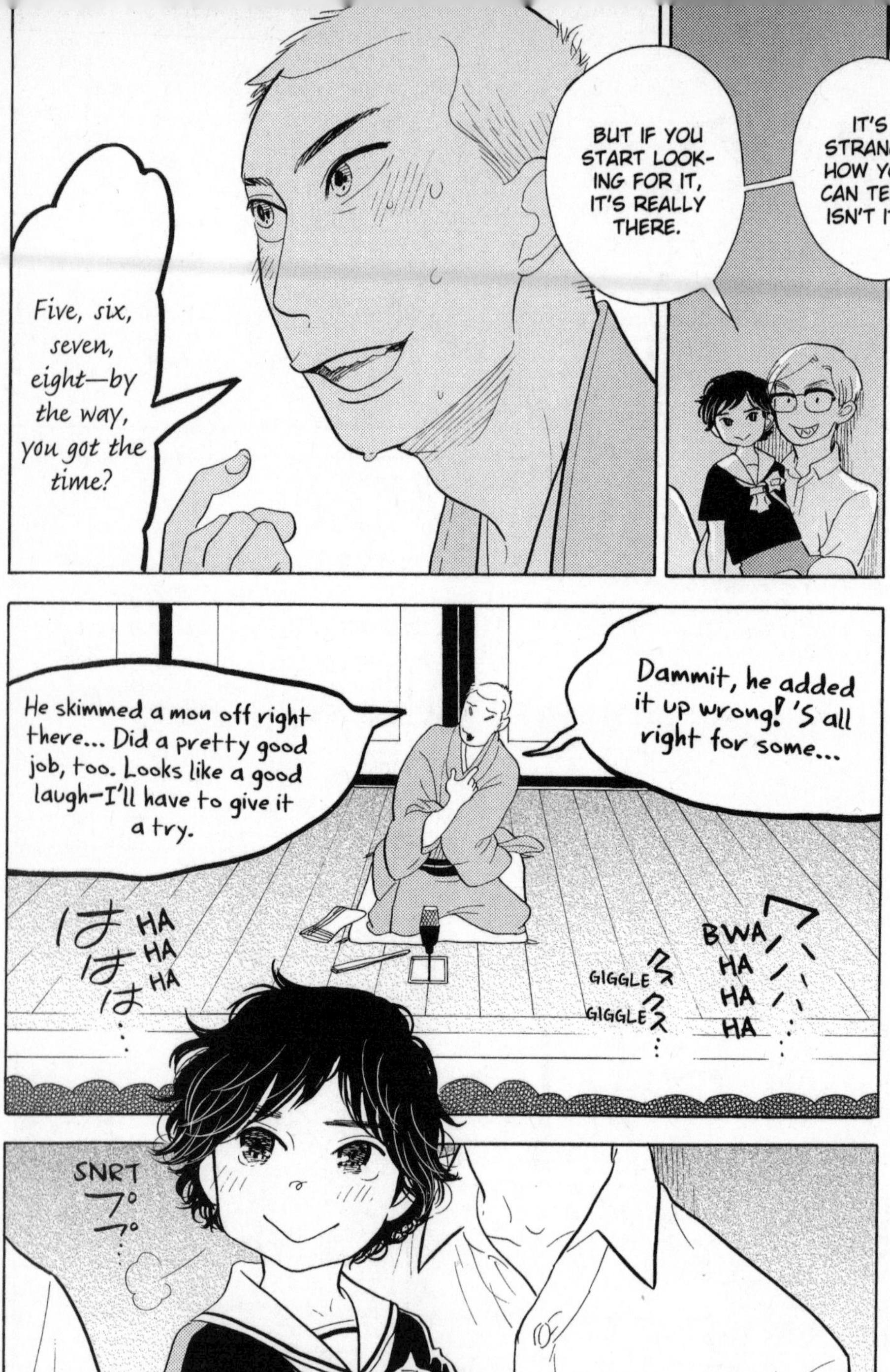
IT'S STRANGE HOW YOU CAN TELL, ISN'T IT?
BUT IF YOU START LOOKING FOR IT, IT'S REALLY THERE.
Five, six, seven, eight—by the way, you got the time?
Dammit, he added it up wrong! 'S all right for some...
He skimmed a mon off right there... Did a pretty good job, too. Looks like a good laugh—I'll have to give it a try.
BWA HA HA HA
GIGGLE GIGGLE
HA HA HA
SNRT

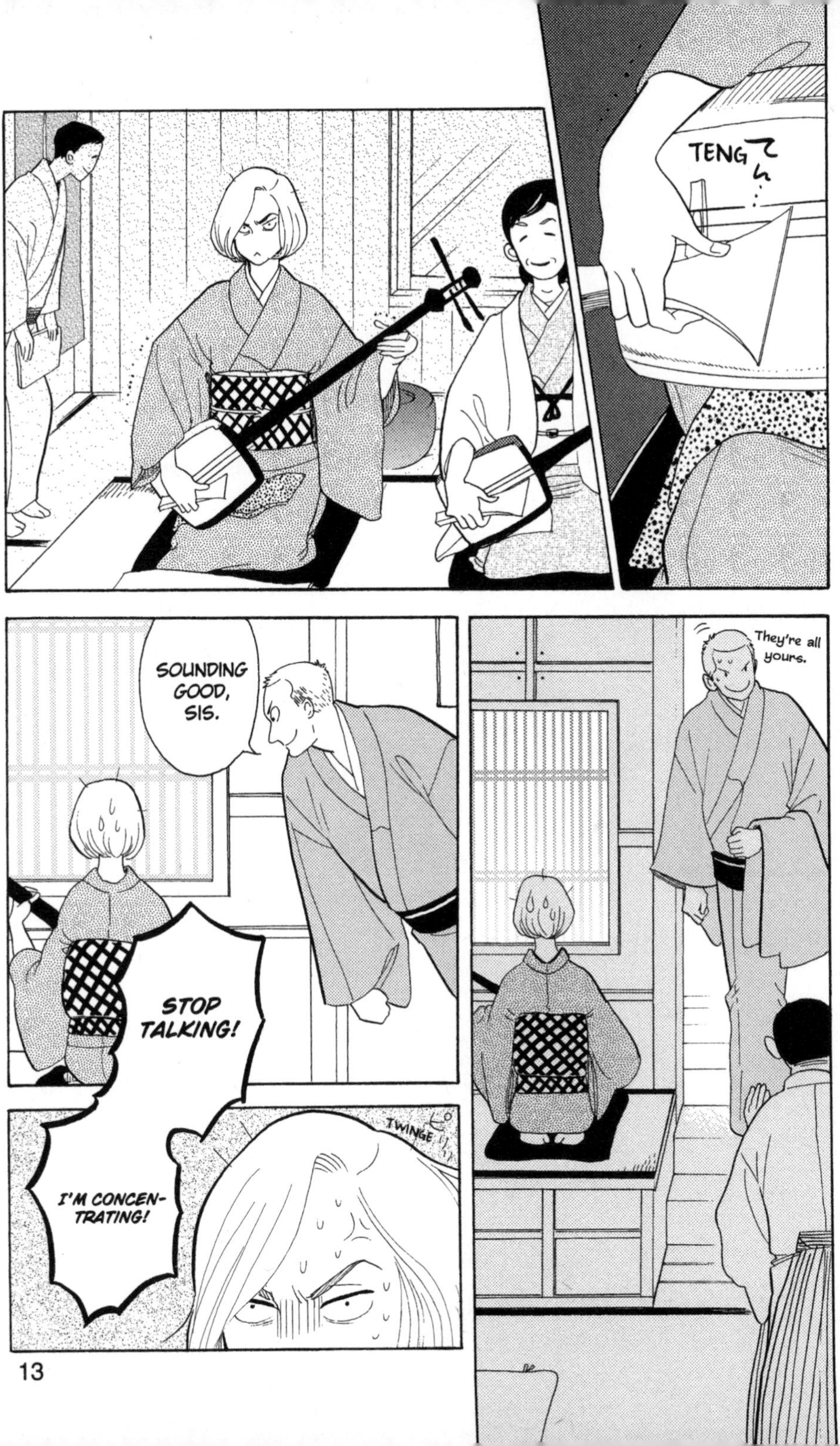
TENG てん…
They're all yours.
SOUNDING GOOD, SIS.
STOP TALKING!
I'M CONCEN-TRATING!
TWINGE

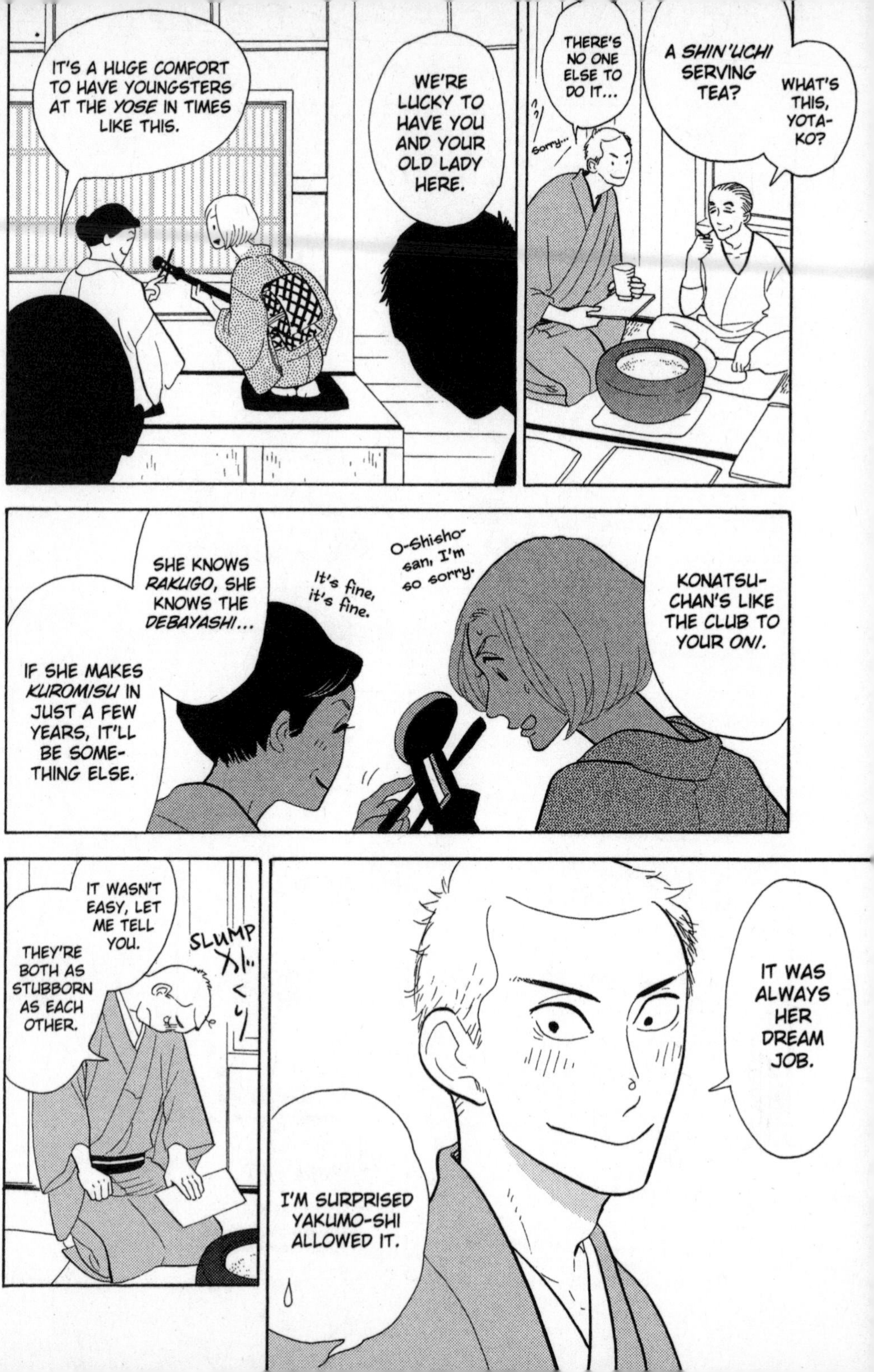
A *SHIN'UCHI* SERVING TEA?
WHAT'S THIS, YOTAKO?
THERE'S NO ONE ELSE TO DO IT...
Sorry...
WE'RE LUCKY TO HAVE YOU AND YOUR OLD LADY HERE.
IT'S A HUGE COMFORT TO HAVE YOUNGSTERS AT THE *YOSE* IN TIMES LIKE THIS.
KONATSU-CHAN'S LIKE THE CLUB TO YOUR *ONI*.
O-Shisho-san, I'm so sorry.
It's fine, it's fine.
SHE KNOWS *RAKUGO*, SHE KNOWS THE *DEBAYASHI*...
IF SHE MAKES *KUROMISU* IN JUST A FEW YEARS, IT'LL BE SOMETHING ELSE.
IT WAS ALWAYS HER DREAM JOB.
I'M SURPRISED YAKUMO-SHI ALLOWED IT.
IT WASN'T EASY, LET ME TELL YOU.
SLUMP
THEY'RE BOTH AS STUBBORN AS EACH OTHER.

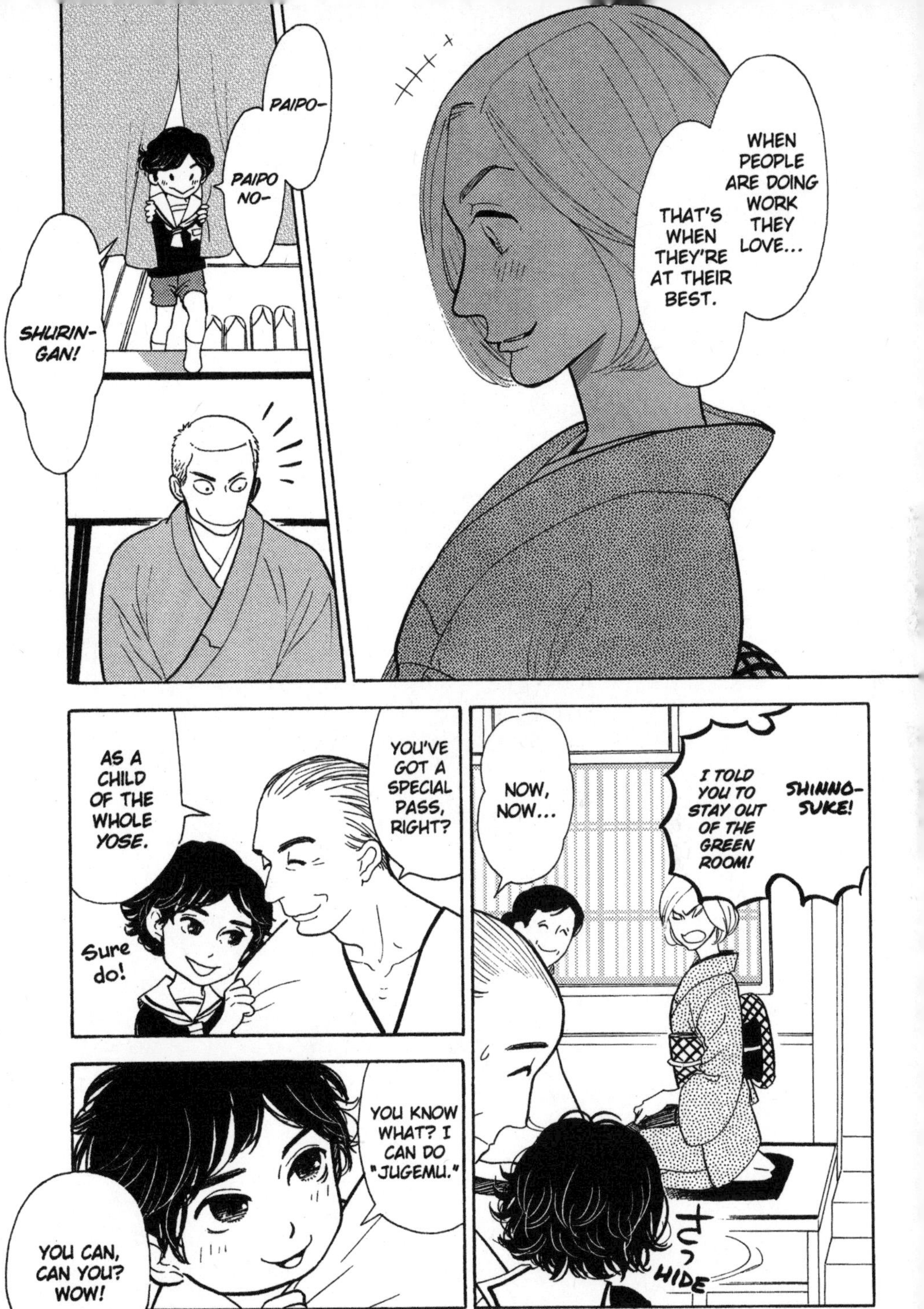
WHEN PEOPLE ARE DOING WORK THEY LOVE...
THAT'S WHEN THEY'RE AT THEIR BEST.
PAIPO-
PAIPO NO-
SHURIN-GAN!
SHINNO-SUKE!
I TOLD YOU TO STAY OUT OF THE GREEN ROOM!
NOW, NOW...
HIDE
YOU'VE GOT A SPECIAL PASS, RIGHT?
AS A CHILD OF THE WHOLE YOSE.
Sure do!
YOU KNOW WHAT? I CAN DO "JUGEMU."
YOU CAN, CAN YOU? WOW!

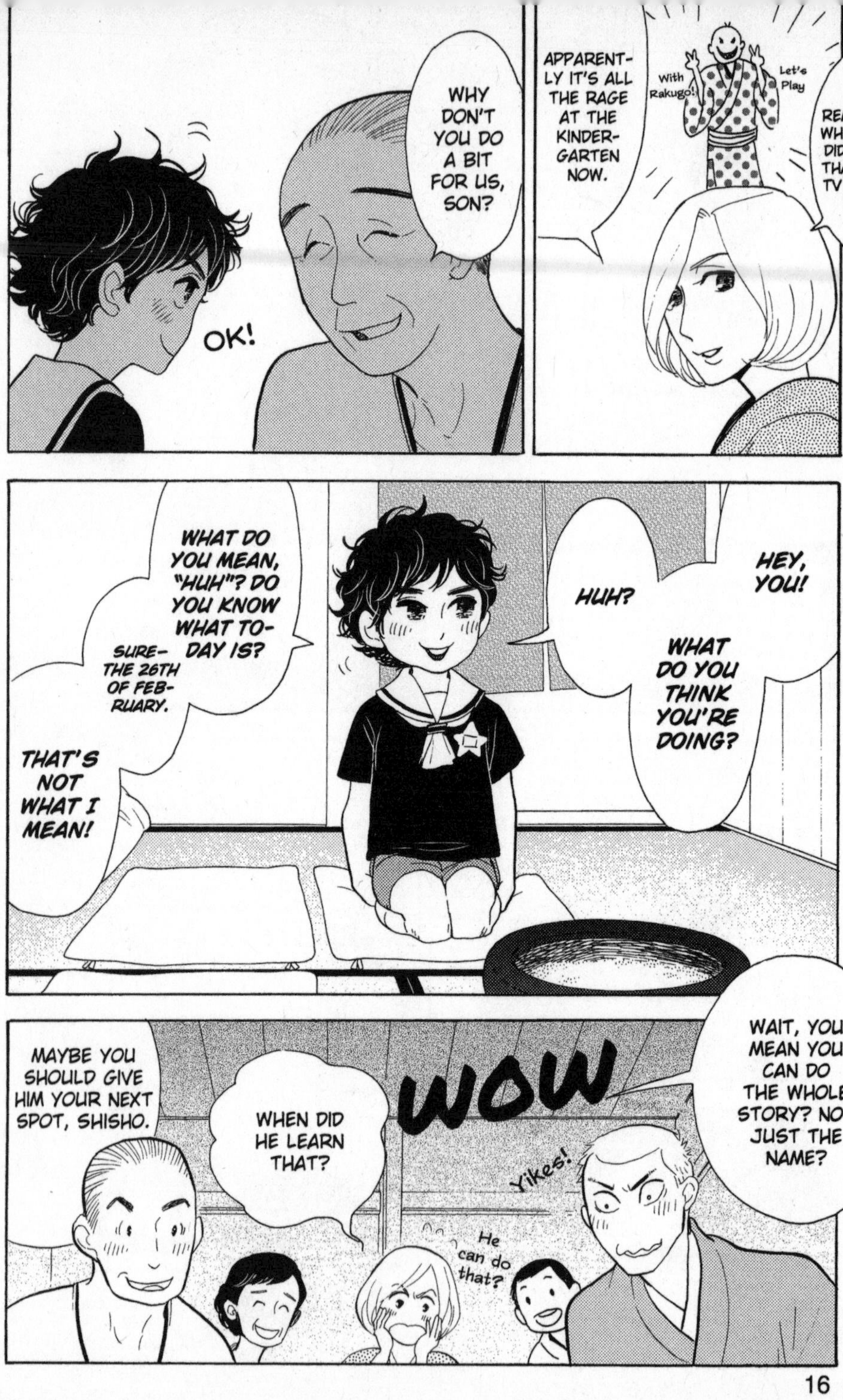
REMEMBER WHEN YOTA DID IT FOR THAT KIDS' TV SHOW?
Let's Play With Rakugo!
APPARENT-LY IT'S ALL THE RAGE AT THE KINDER-GARTEN NOW.
WHY DON'T YOU DO A BIT FOR US, SON?
OK!
HEY, YOU!
WHAT DO YOU THINK YOU'RE DOING?
HUH?
WHAT DO YOU MEAN, "HUH"? DO YOU KNOW WHAT TO-DAY IS?
SURE— THE 26TH OF FEB-RUARY.
THAT'S NOT WHAT I MEAN!
WAIT, YOU MEAN YOU CAN DO THE WHOLE STORY? NOT JUST THE NAME?
WOW
Yikes!
WHEN DID HE LEARN THAT?
He can do that?
MAYBE YOU SHOULD GIVE HIM YOUR NEXT SPOT, SHISHO.

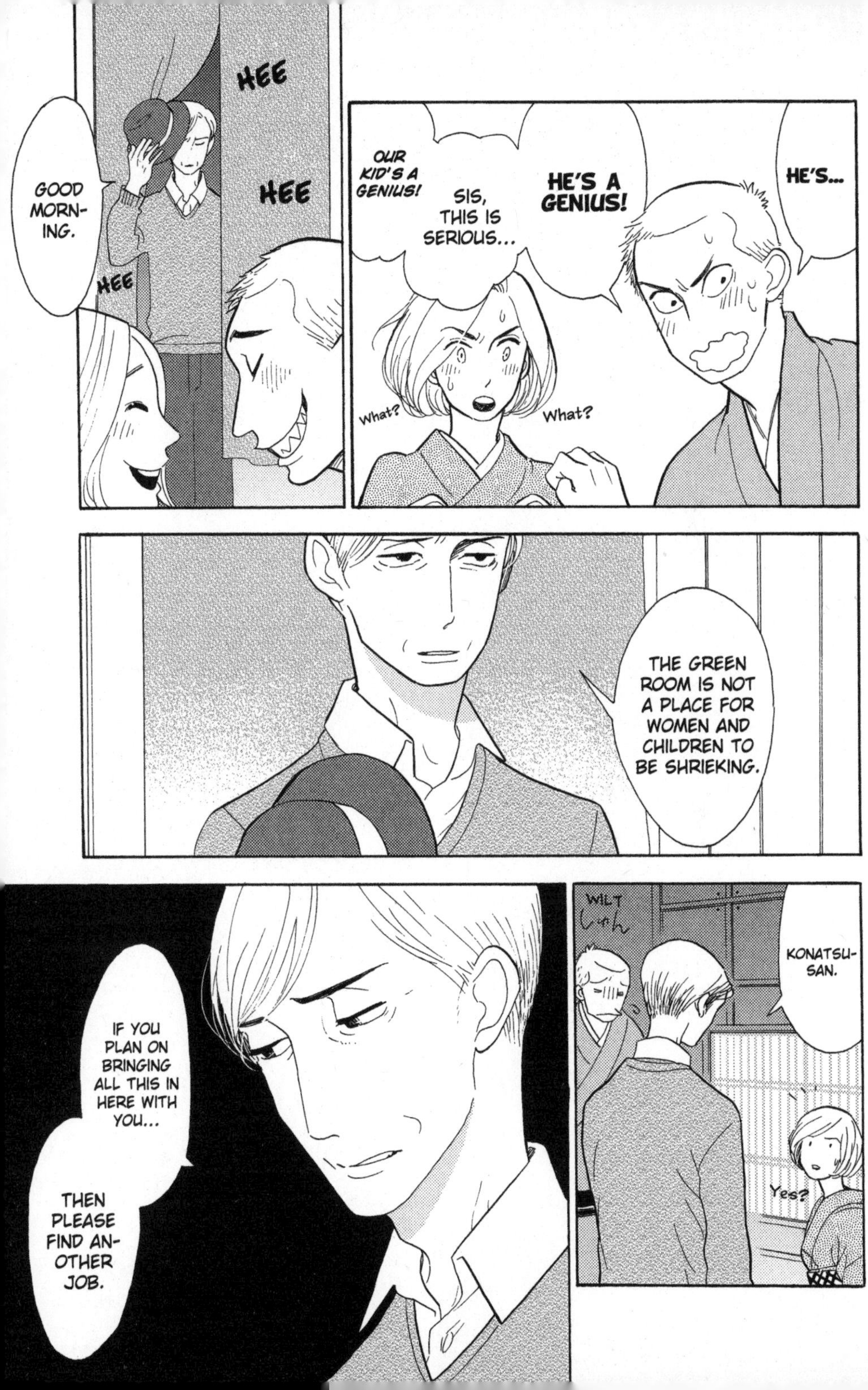
HE'S...
HE'S A GENIUS!
SIS, THIS IS SERIOUS...
OUR KID'S A GENIUS!
What?
What?
HEE
HEE
HEE
GOOD MORNING.
THE GREEN ROOM IS NOT A PLACE FOR WOMEN AND CHILDREN TO BE SHRIEKING.
WILT
KONATSU-SAN.
Yes?
IF YOU PLAN ON BRINGING ALL THIS IN HERE WITH YOU...
THEN PLEASE FIND ANOTHER JOB.

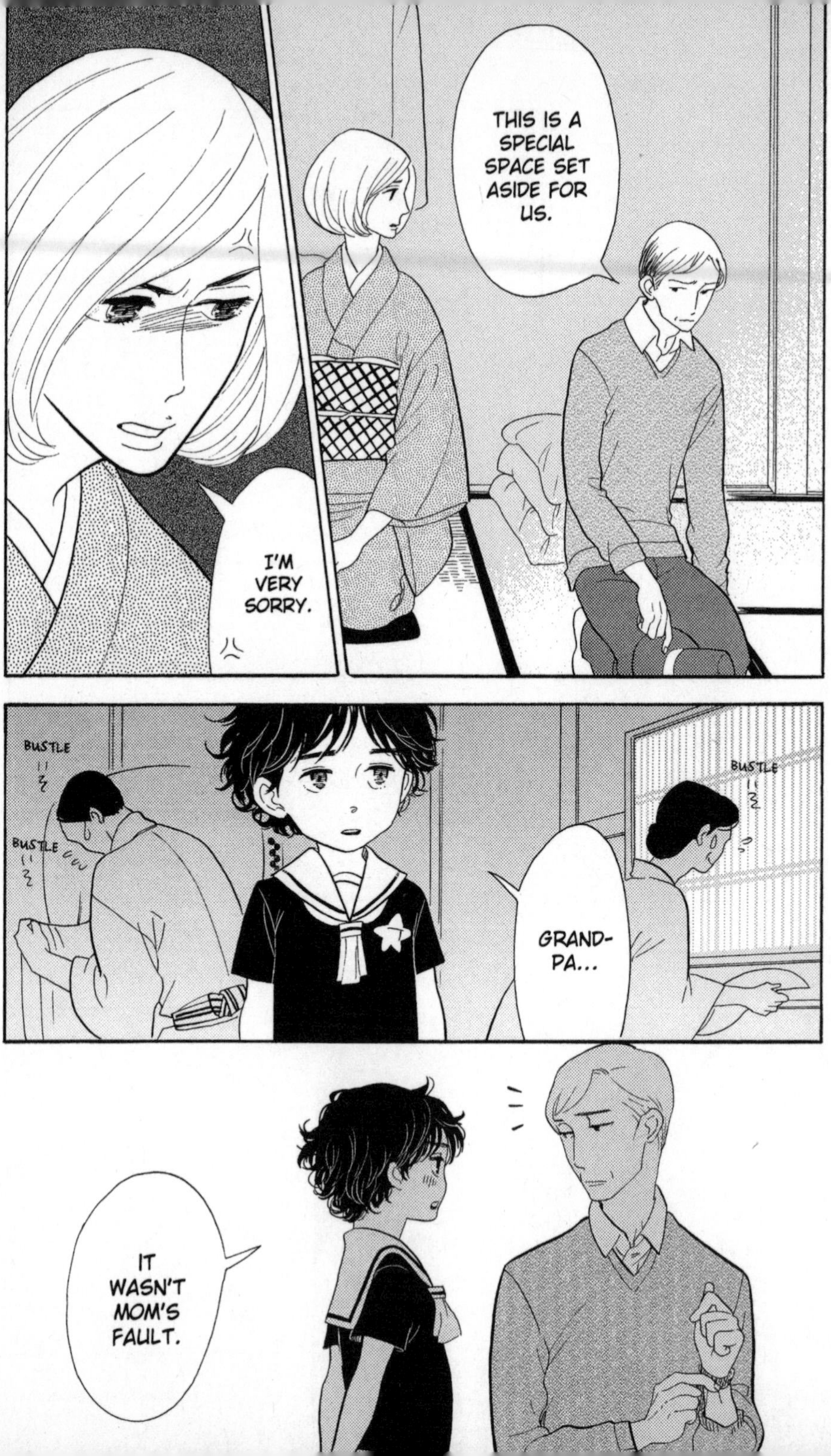
THIS IS A SPECIAL SPACE SET ASIDE FOR US.
I'M VERY SORRY.
BUSTLE
GRAND-PA...
BUSTLE
BUSTLE
IT WASN'T MOM'S FAULT.

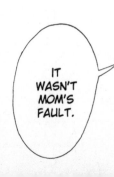

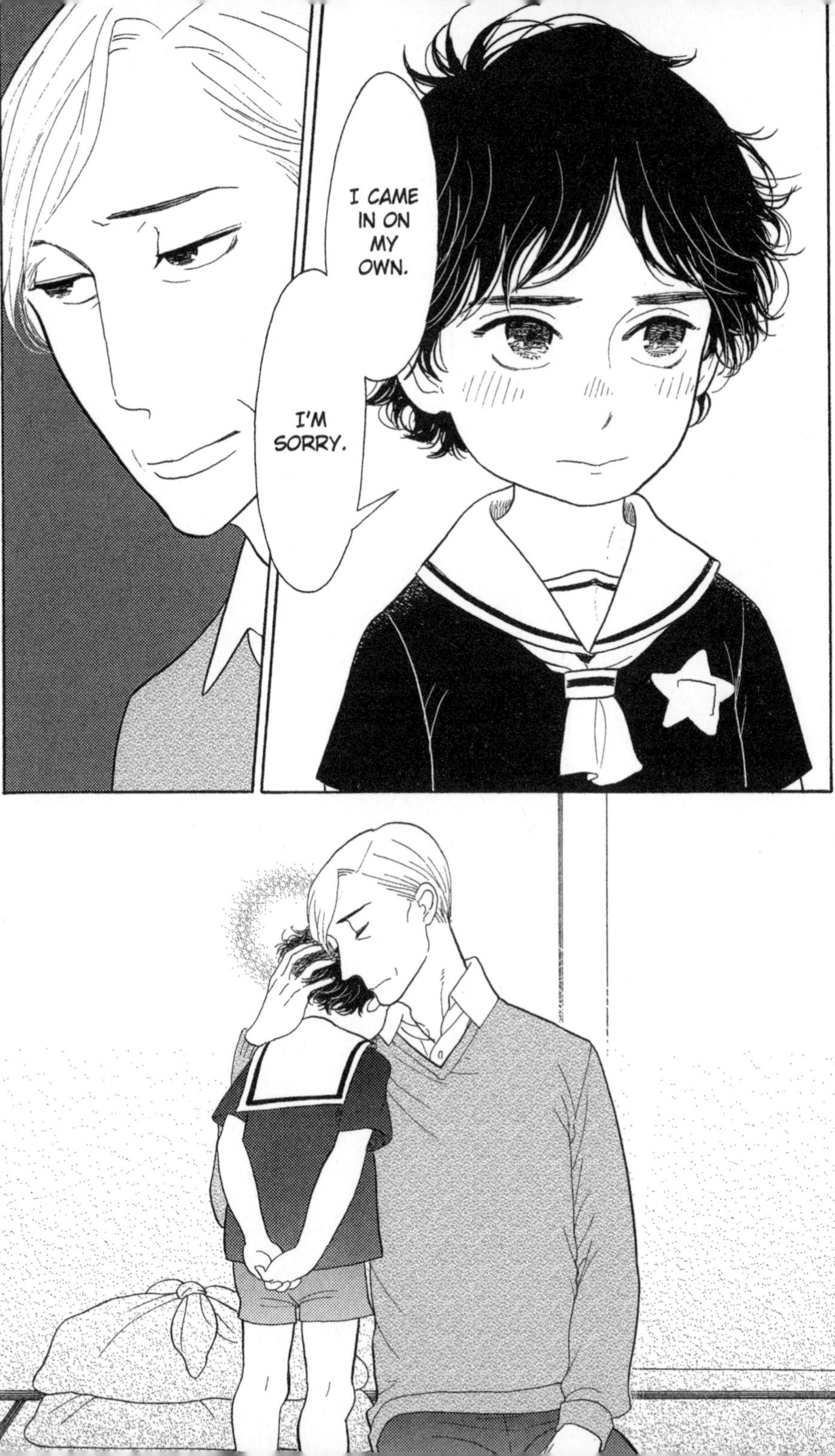
I CAME IN ON MY OWN.
I'M SORRY.

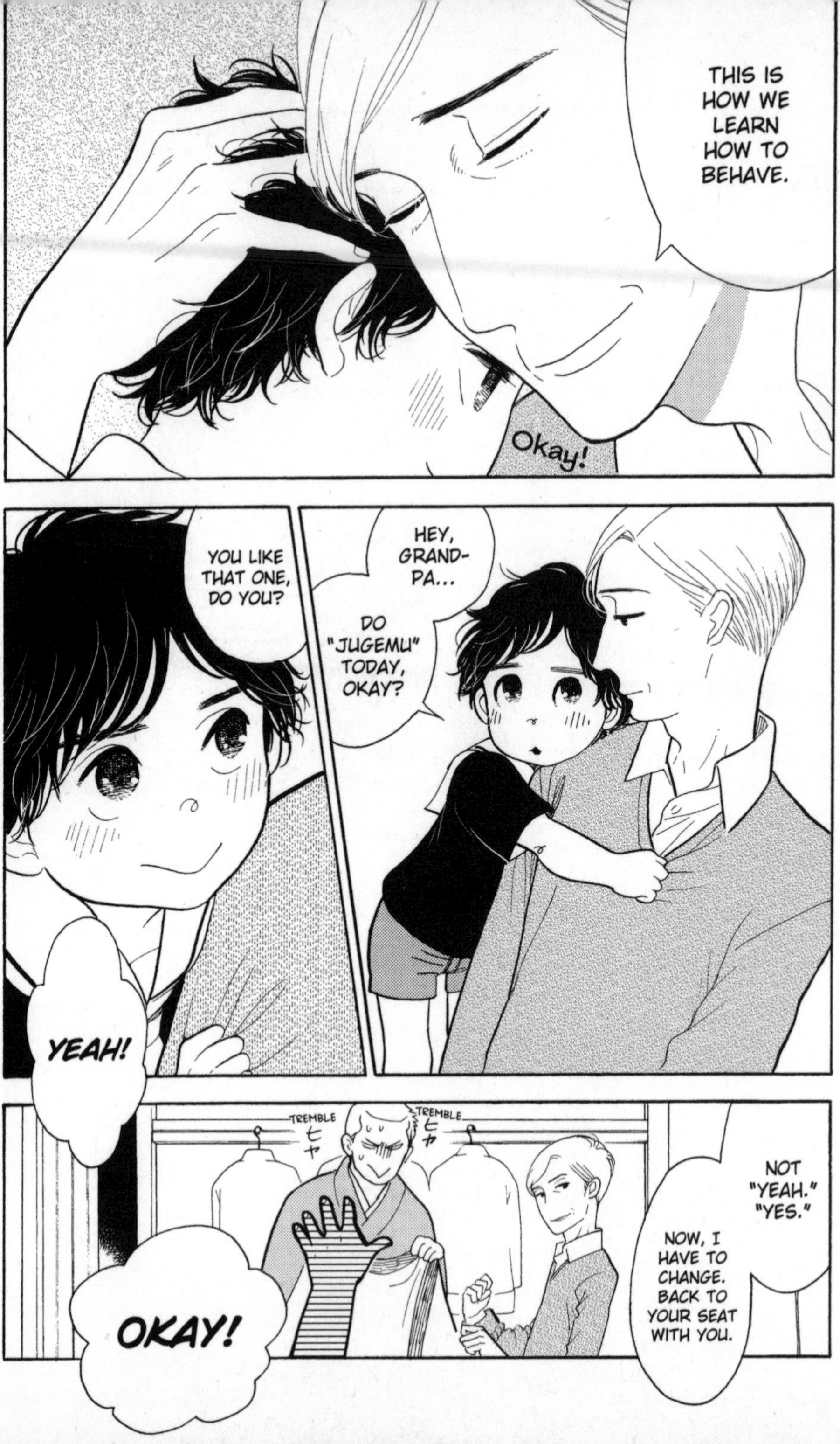
THIS IS HOW WE LEARN HOW TO BEHAVE.
Okay!
HEY, GRAND-PA...
DO "JUGEMU" TODAY, OKAY?
YOU LIKE THAT ONE, DO YOU?
YEAH!
NOT "YEAH." "YES."
NOW, I HAVE TO CHANGE. BACK TO YOUR SEAT WITH YOU.
TREMBLE ヒヤ
TREMBLE ヒヤ
OKAY!

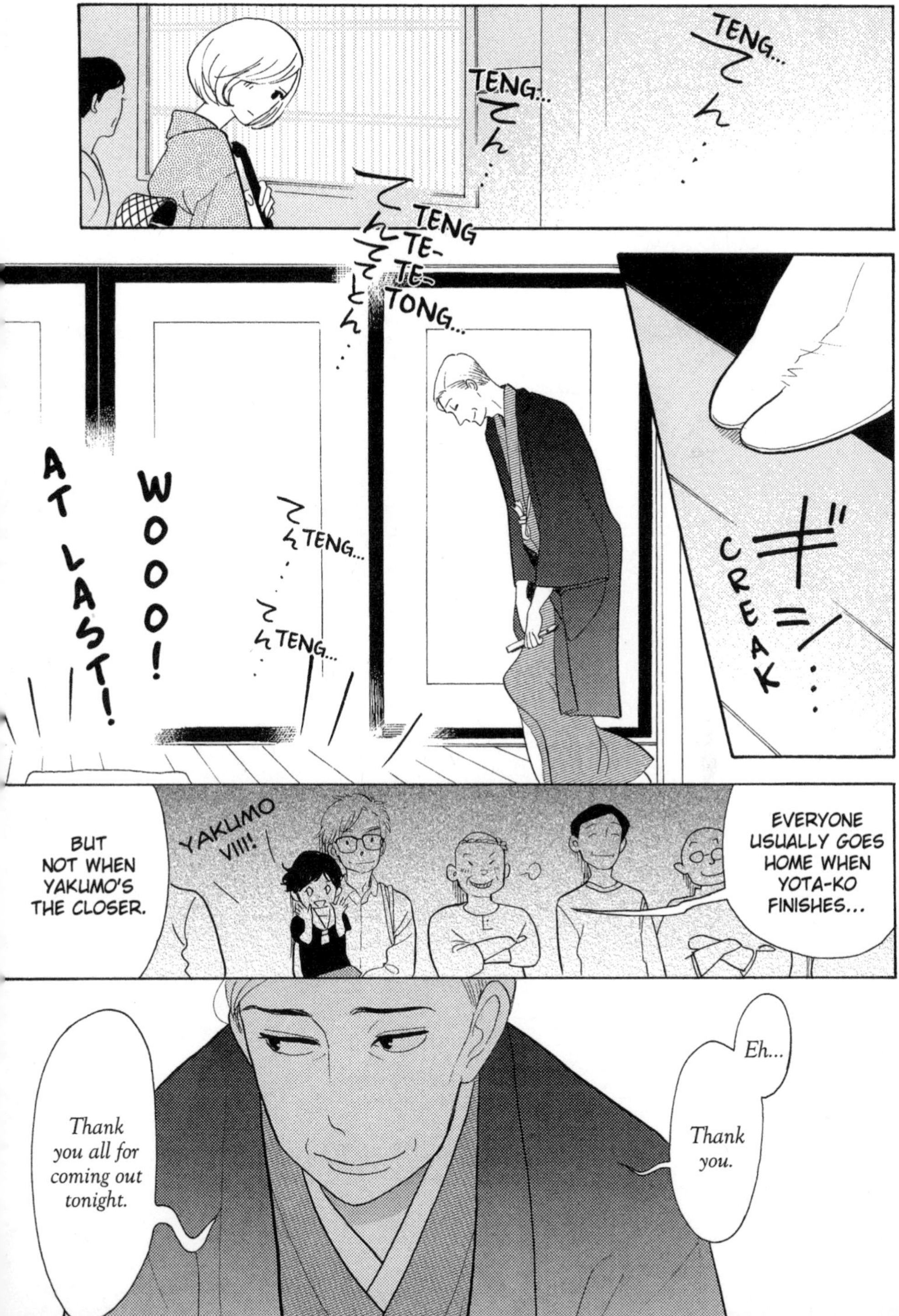

TENG...
てん...
TENG...
てん...
TENG TE-TE-TONG...
てんてててとん...
CREAK
ギ
TENG...
TENG...
WOOOO!
AT LAST!
EVERYONE USUALLY GOES HOME WHEN YOTA-KO FINISHES...
YAKUMO VIII!
BUT NOT WHEN YAKUMO'S THE CLOSER.
Eh...
Thank you.
Thank you all for coming out tonight.

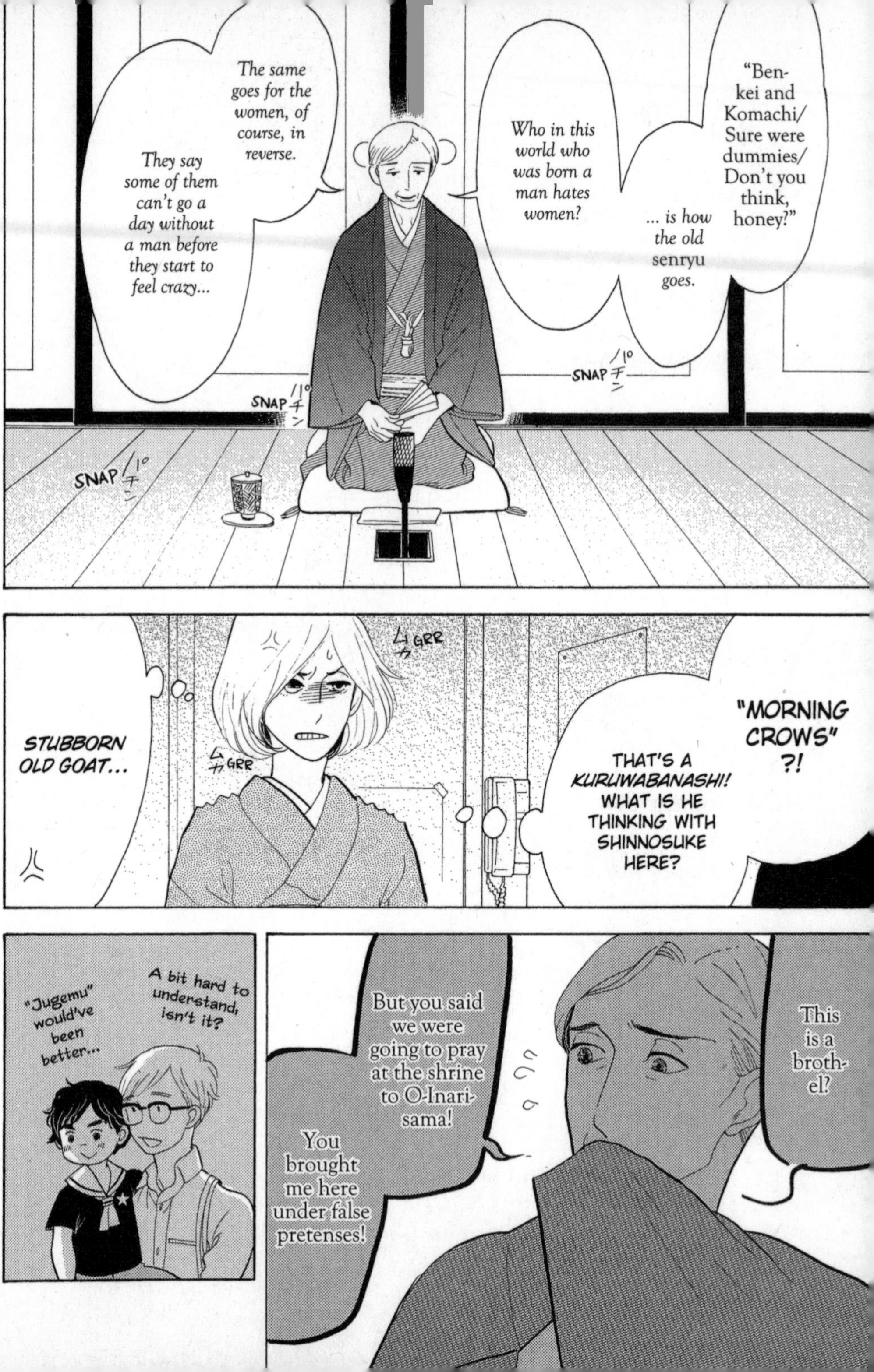
"Ben-kei and Komachi/ Sure were dummies/ Don't you think, honey?"
... is how the old senryu goes.
Who in this world who was born a man hates women?
They say some of them can't go a day without a man before they start to feel crazy...
The same goes for the women, of course, in reverse.
SNAP
SNAP
SNAP
"MORNING CROWS"?!
THAT'S A KURUWABANASHI! WHAT IS HE THINKING WITH SHINNOSUKE HERE?
GRR
GRR
STUBBORN OLD GOAT...
This is a broth-el?
But you said we were going to pray at the shrine to O-Inari-sama!
You brought me here under false pretenses!
A bit hard to understand, isn't it?
"Jugemu" would've been better...

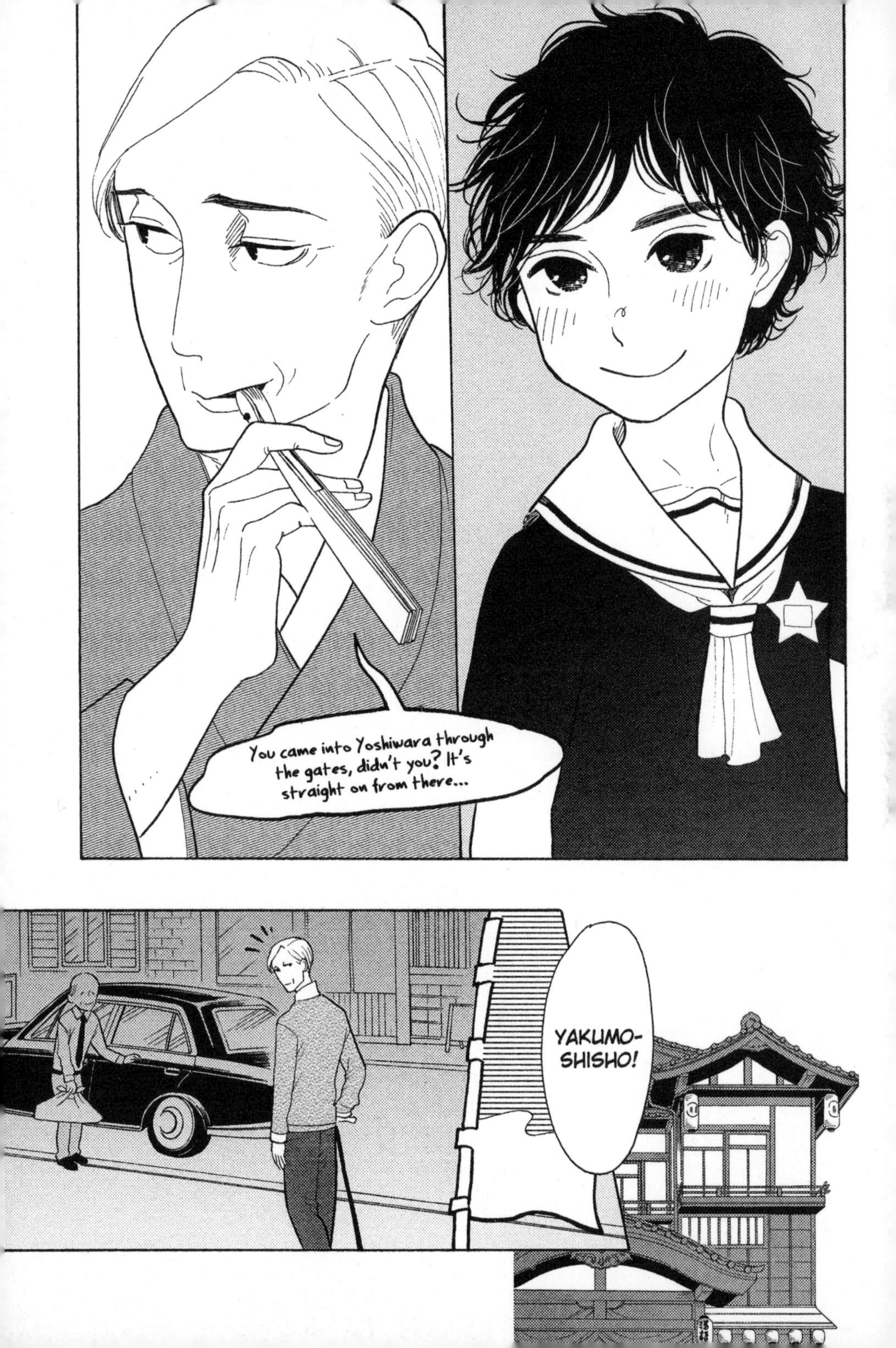
You came into Yoshiwara through the gates, didn't you? It's straight on from there...
YAKUMO-SHISHO!

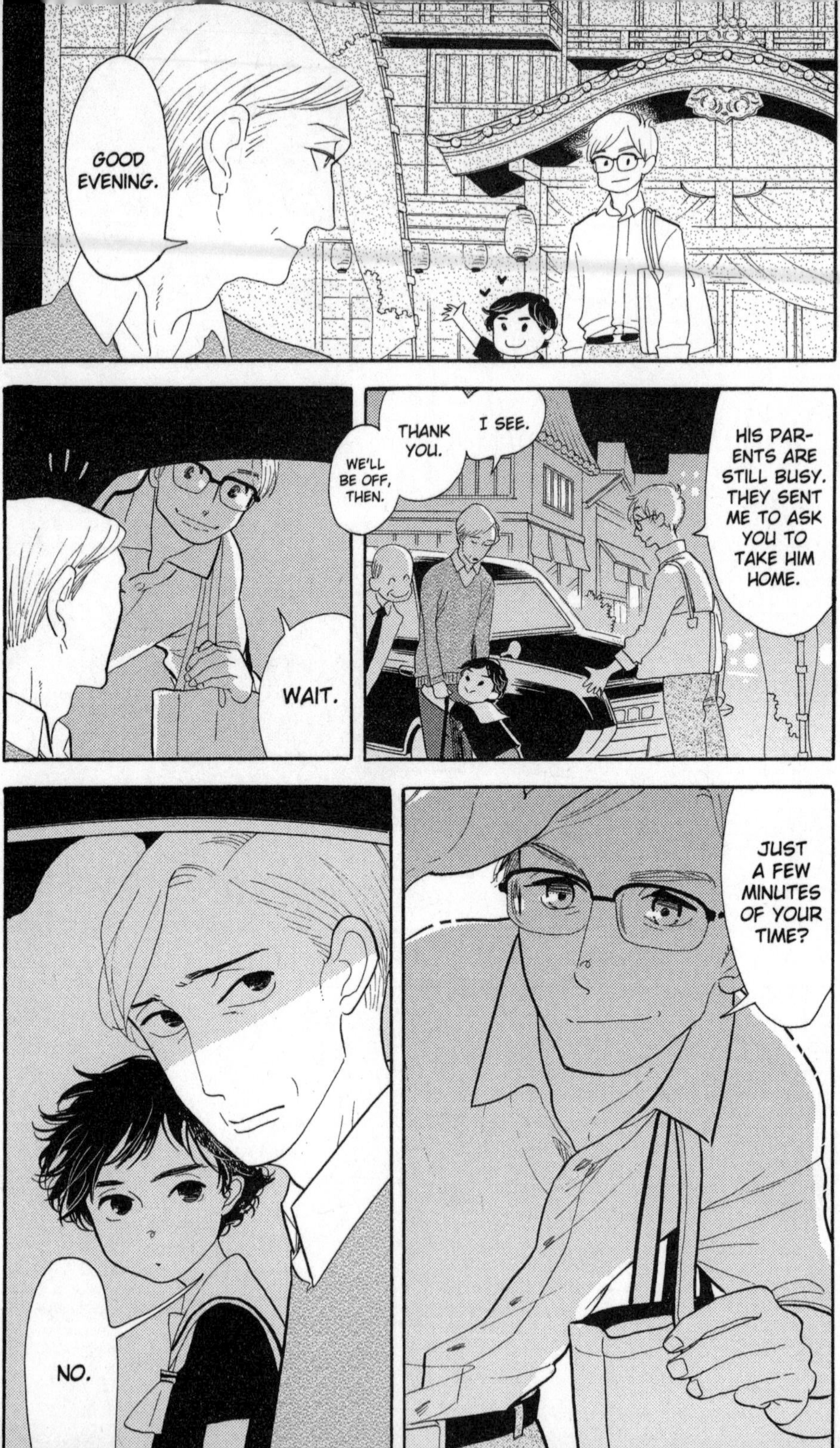
GOOD EVENING.
HIS PARENTS ARE STILL BUSY. THEY SENT ME TO ASK YOU TO TAKE HIM HOME.
I SEE.
THANK YOU.
WE'LL BE OFF, THEN.
WAIT.
JUST A FEW MINUTES OF YOUR TIME?
NO.

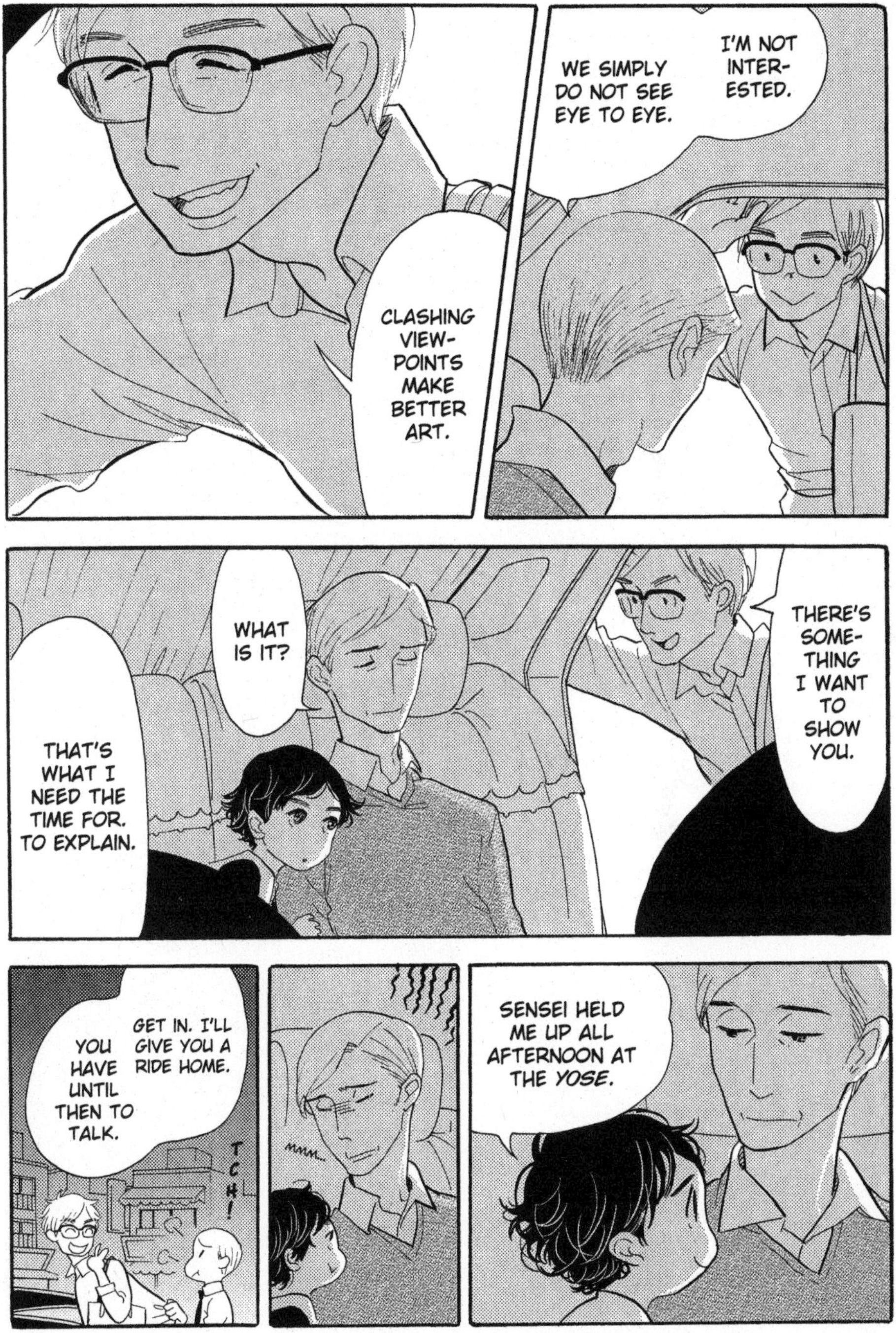
I'M NOT INTER-ESTED.
WE SIMPLY DO NOT SEE EYE TO EYE.
CLASHING VIEW-POINTS MAKE BETTER ART.
THERE'S SOME-THING I WANT TO SHOW YOU.
WHAT IS IT?
THAT'S WHAT I NEED THE TIME FOR. TO EXPLAIN.
SENSEI HELD ME UP ALL AFTERNOON AT THE *YOSE*.
MMM...
GET IN. I'LL GIVE YOU A RIDE HOME.
YOU HAVE UNTIL THEN TO TALK.
TCH!

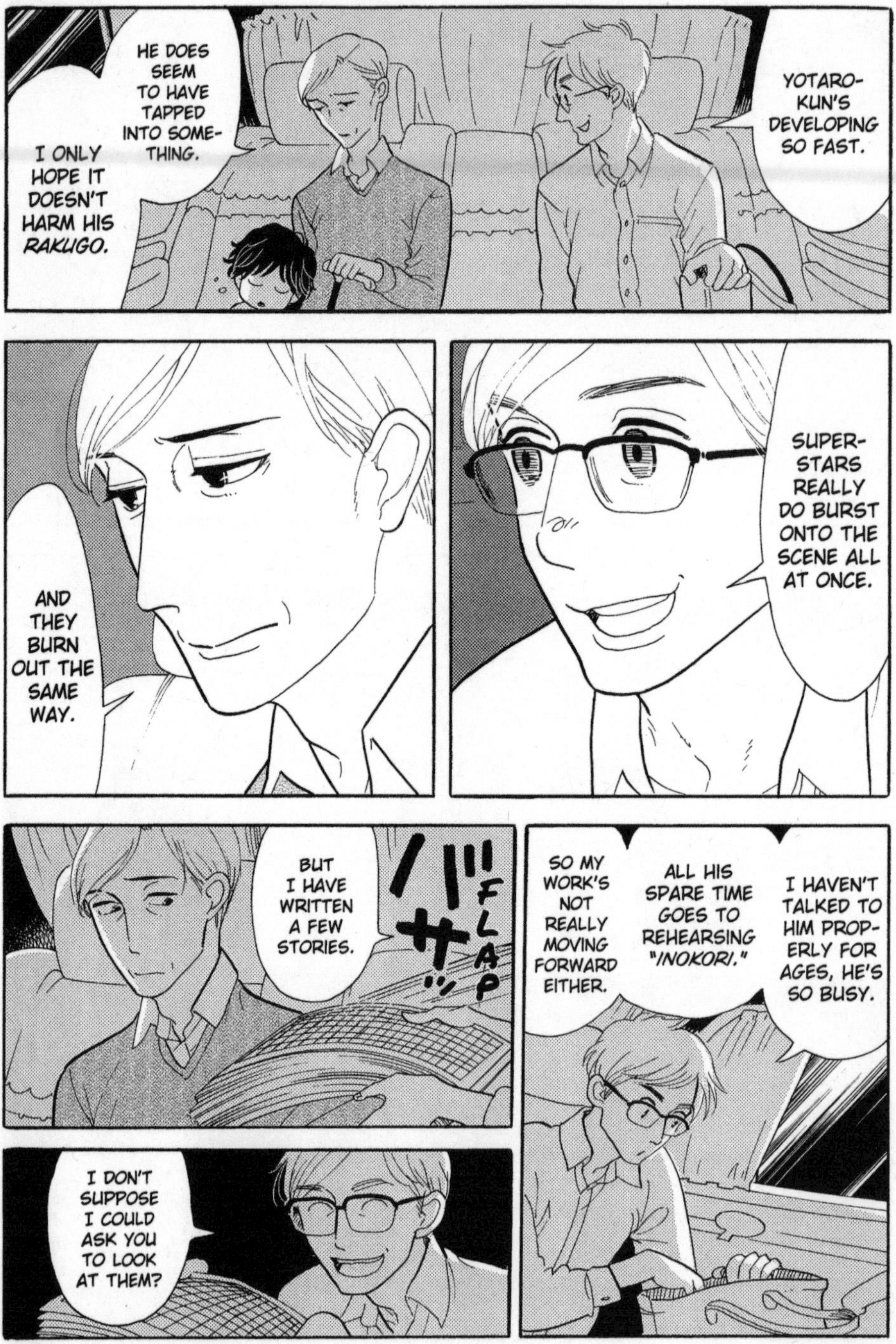
YOTARO-KUN'S DEVELOPING SO FAST.
HE DOES SEEM TO HAVE TAPPED INTO SOME-THING.
I ONLY HOPE IT DOESN'T HARM HIS *RAKUGO.*
SUPER-STARS REALLY DO BURST ONTO THE SCENE ALL AT ONCE.
AND THEY BURN OUT THE SAME WAY.
I HAVEN'T TALKED TO HIM PROP-ERLY FOR AGES, HE'S SO BUSY.
ALL HIS SPARE TIME GOES TO REHEARSING "*INOKORI.*"
SO MY WORK'S NOT REALLY MOVING FORWARD EITHER.
FLAP
BUT I HAVE WRITTEN A FEW STORIES.
I DON'T SUPPOSE I COULD ASK YOU TO LOOK AT THEM?

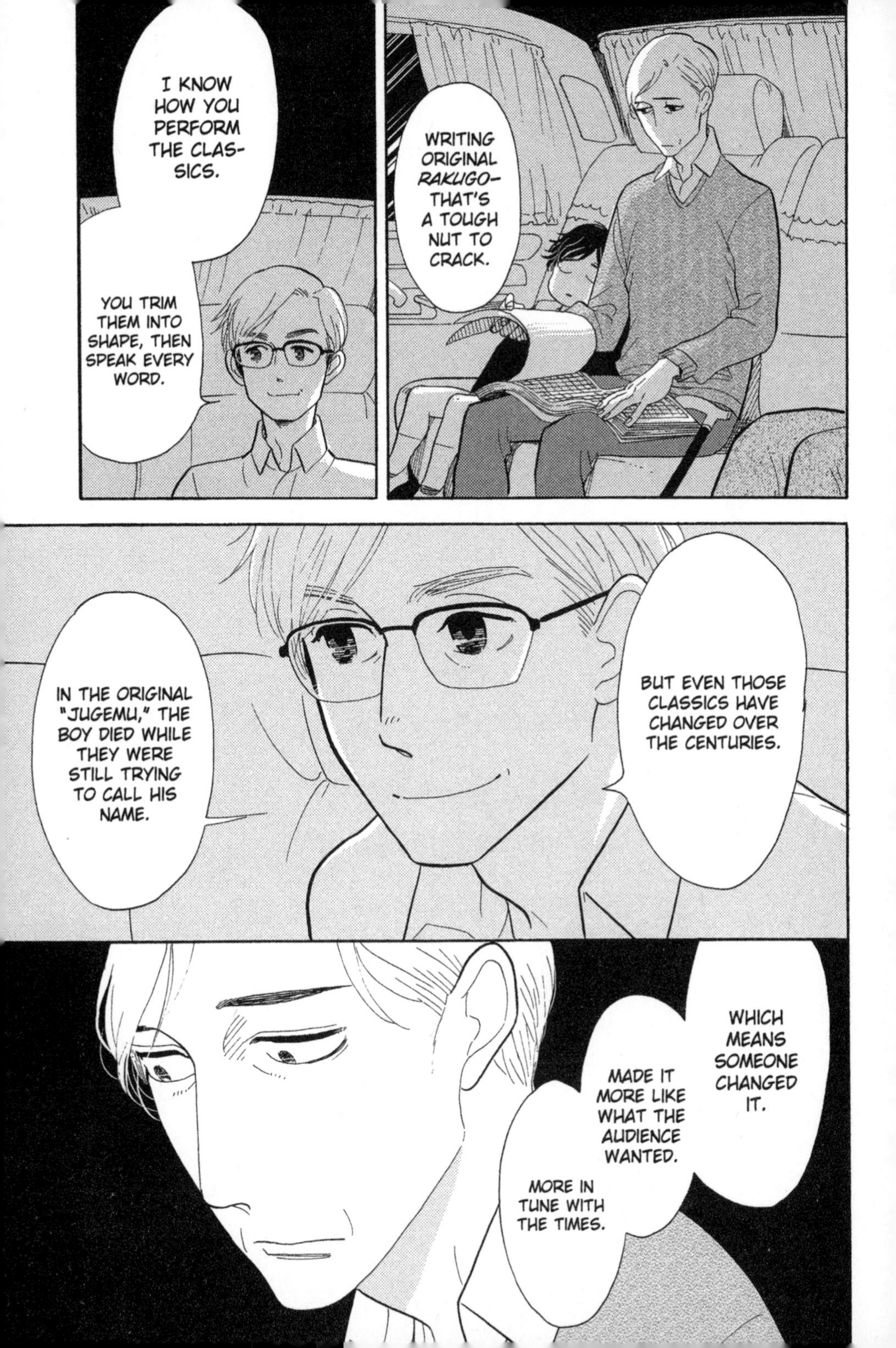
WRITING ORIGINAL *RAKUGO*—THAT'S A TOUGH NUT TO CRACK.
I KNOW HOW YOU PERFORM THE CLAS-SICS.
YOU TRIM THEM INTO SHAPE, THEN SPEAK EVERY WORD.
BUT EVEN THOSE CLASSICS HAVE CHANGED OVER THE CENTURIES.
IN THE ORIGINAL "JUGEMU," THE BOY DIED WHILE THEY WERE STILL TRYING TO CALL HIS NAME.
WHICH MEANS SOMEONE CHANGED IT.
MADE IT MORE LIKE WHAT THE AUDIENCE WANTED.
MORE IN TUNE WITH THE TIMES.

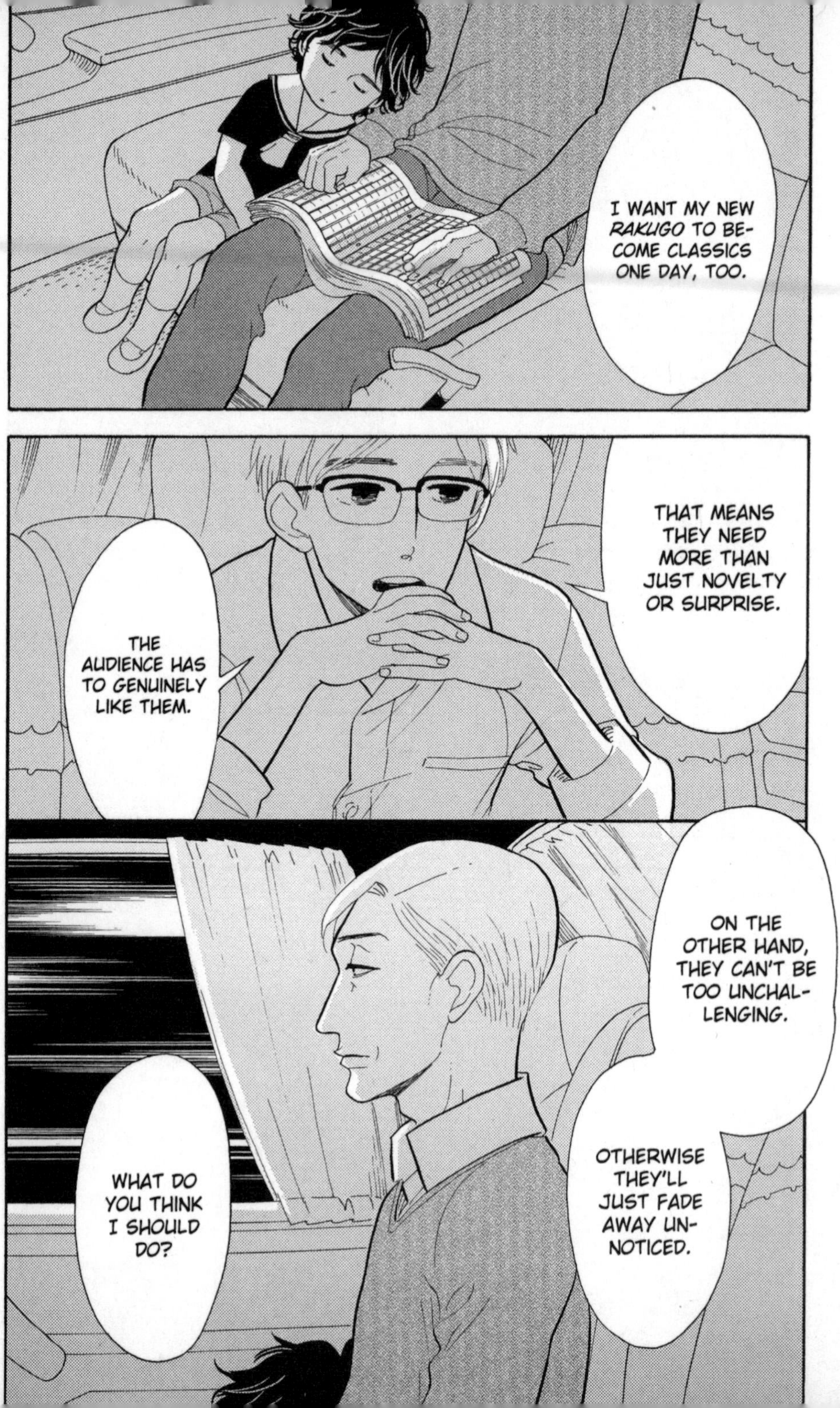
I WANT MY NEW *RAKUGO* TO BECOME CLASSICS ONE DAY, TOO.
THAT MEANS THEY NEED MORE THAN JUST NOVELTY OR SURPRISE.
THE AUDIENCE HAS TO GENUINELY LIKE THEM.
ON THE OTHER HAND, THEY CAN'T BE TOO UNCHALLENGING.
OTHERWISE THEY'LL JUST FADE AWAY UNNOTICED.
WHAT DO YOU THINK I SHOULD DO?

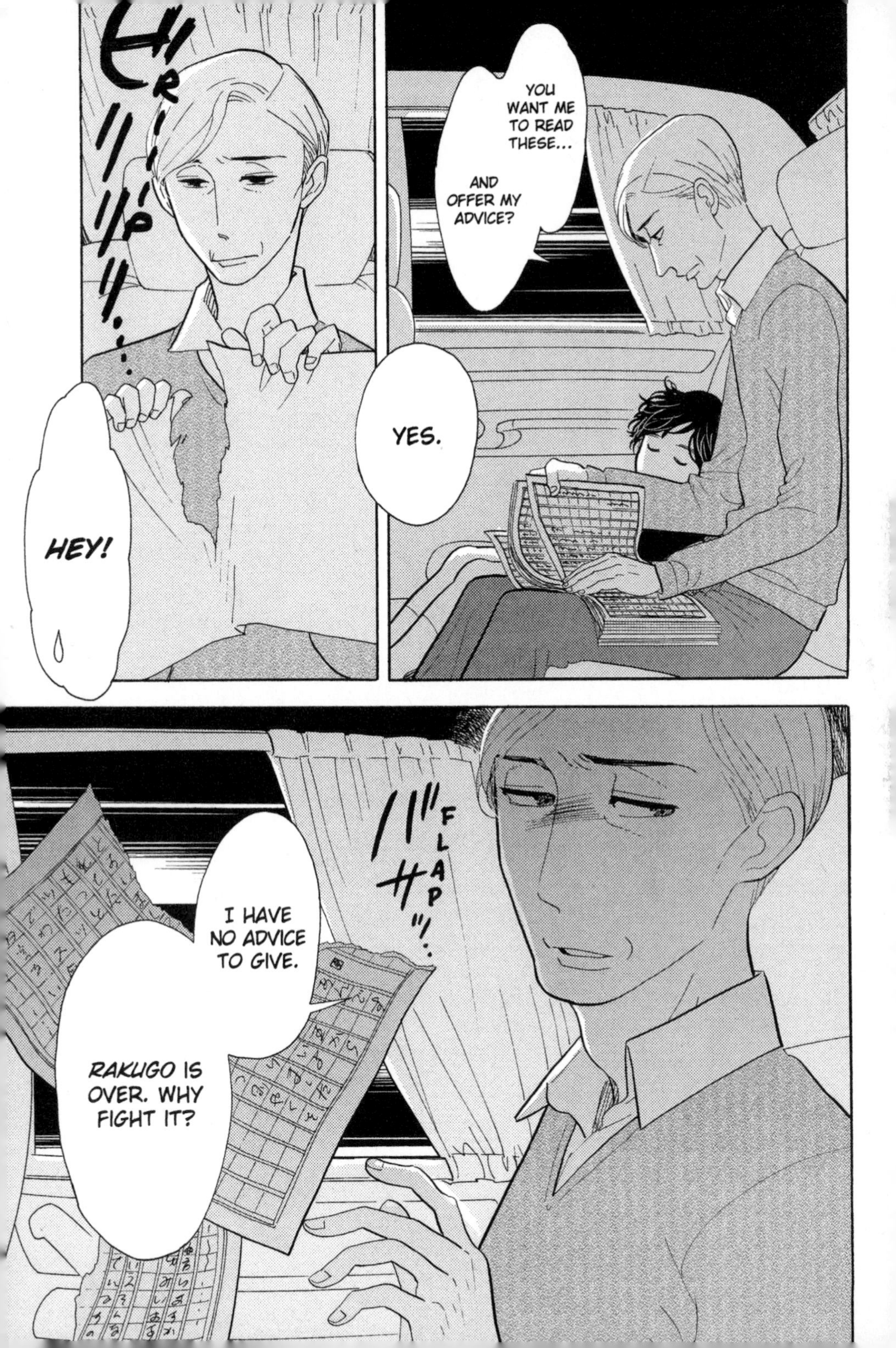
YOU WANT ME TO READ THESE...
AND OFFER MY ADVICE?
YES.
RIIIP...
HEY!
FLAP...
I HAVE NO ADVICE TO GIVE.
RAKUGO IS OVER. WHY FIGHT IT?

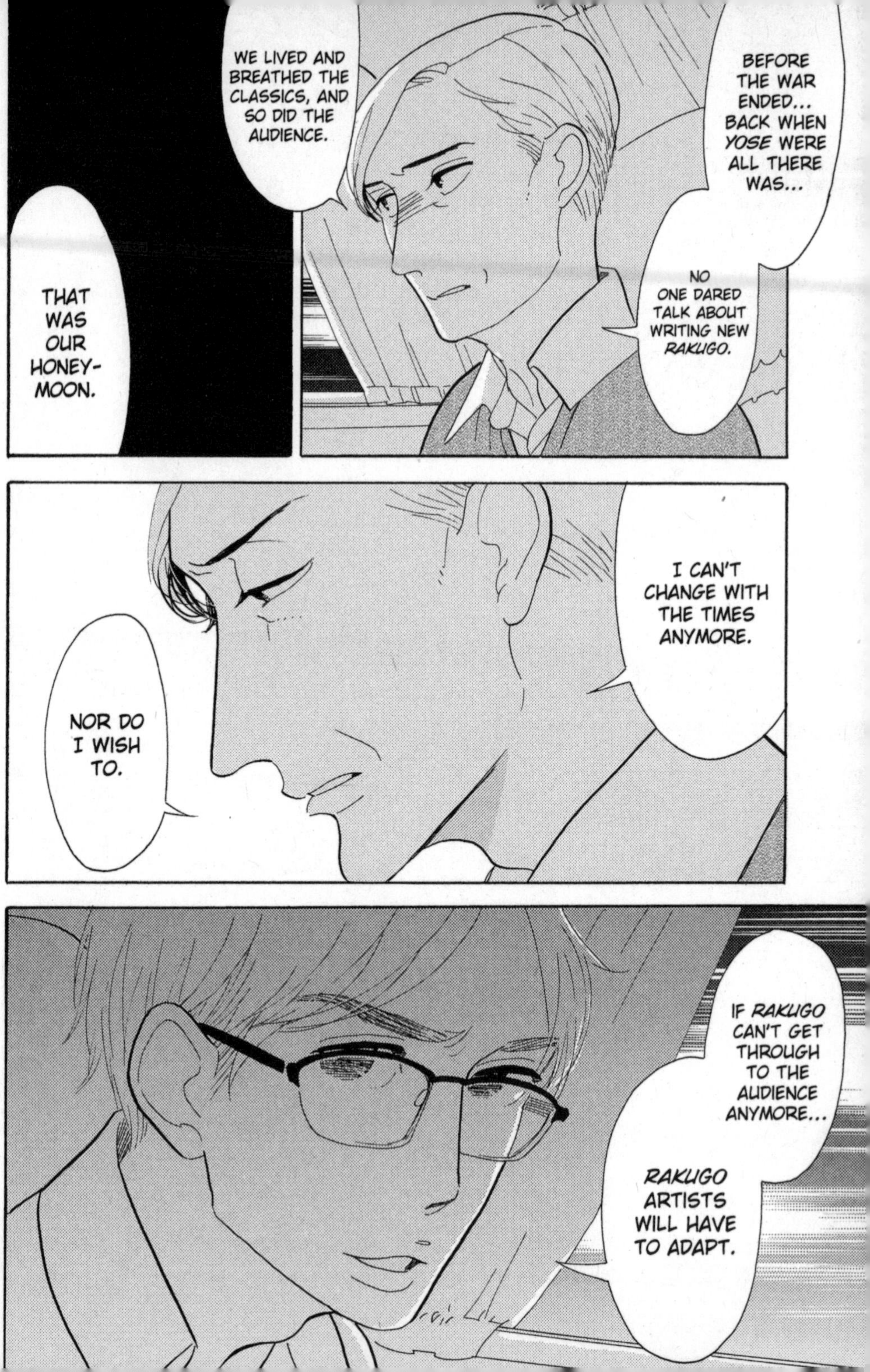
BEFORE THE WAR ENDED... BACK WHEN YOSE WERE ALL THERE WAS...
NO ONE DARED TALK ABOUT WRITING NEW RAKUGO.
WE LIVED AND BREATHED THE CLASSICS, AND SO DID THE AUDIENCE.
THAT WAS OUR HONEY-MOON.
I CAN'T CHANGE WITH THE TIMES ANYMORE.
NOR DO I WISH TO.
IF RAKUGO CAN'T GET THROUGH TO THE AUDIENCE ANYMORE...
RAKUGO ARTISTS WILL HAVE TO ADAPT.

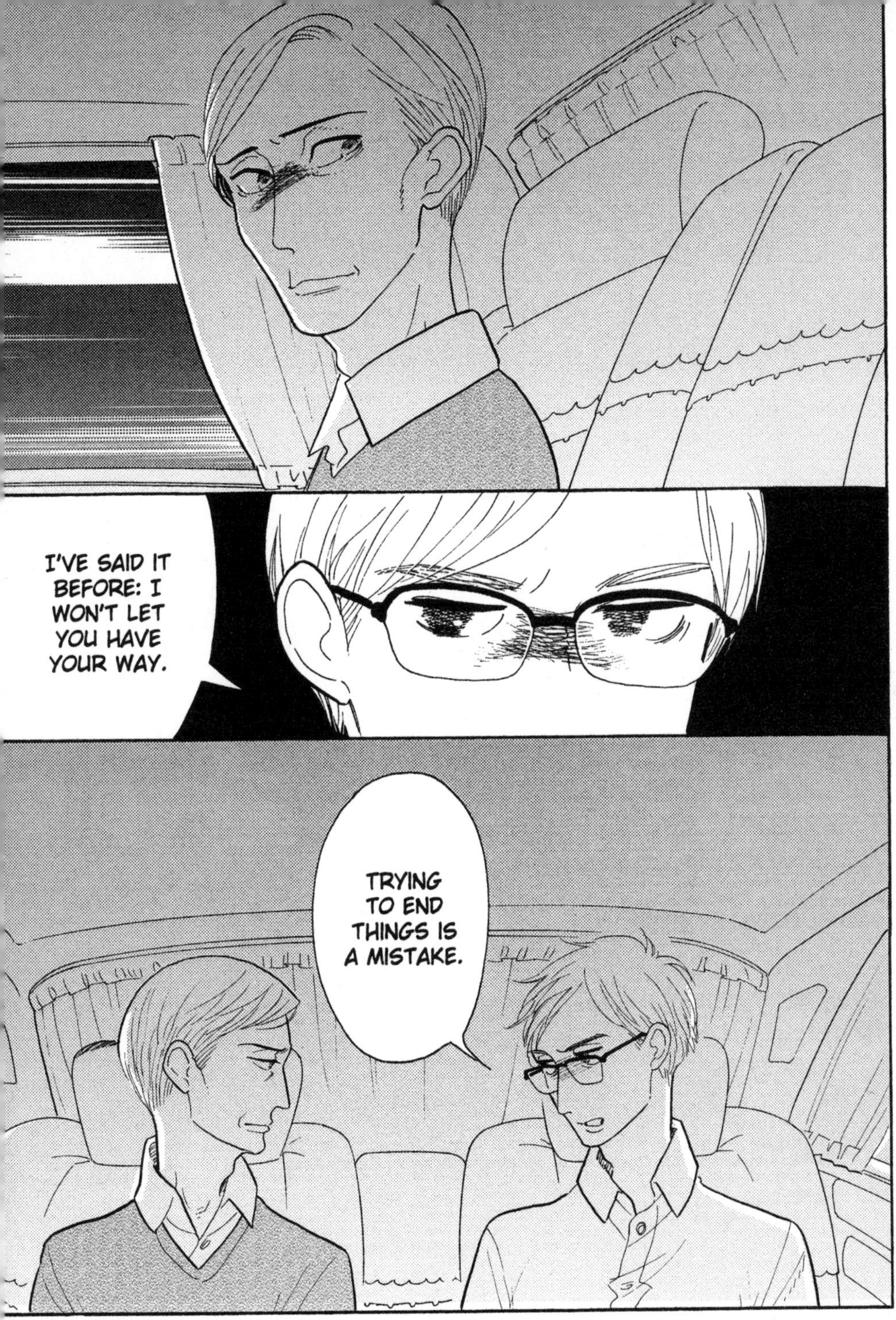
I'VE SAID IT BEFORE: I WON'T LET YOU HAVE YOUR WAY.
TRYING TO END THINGS IS A MISTAKE.

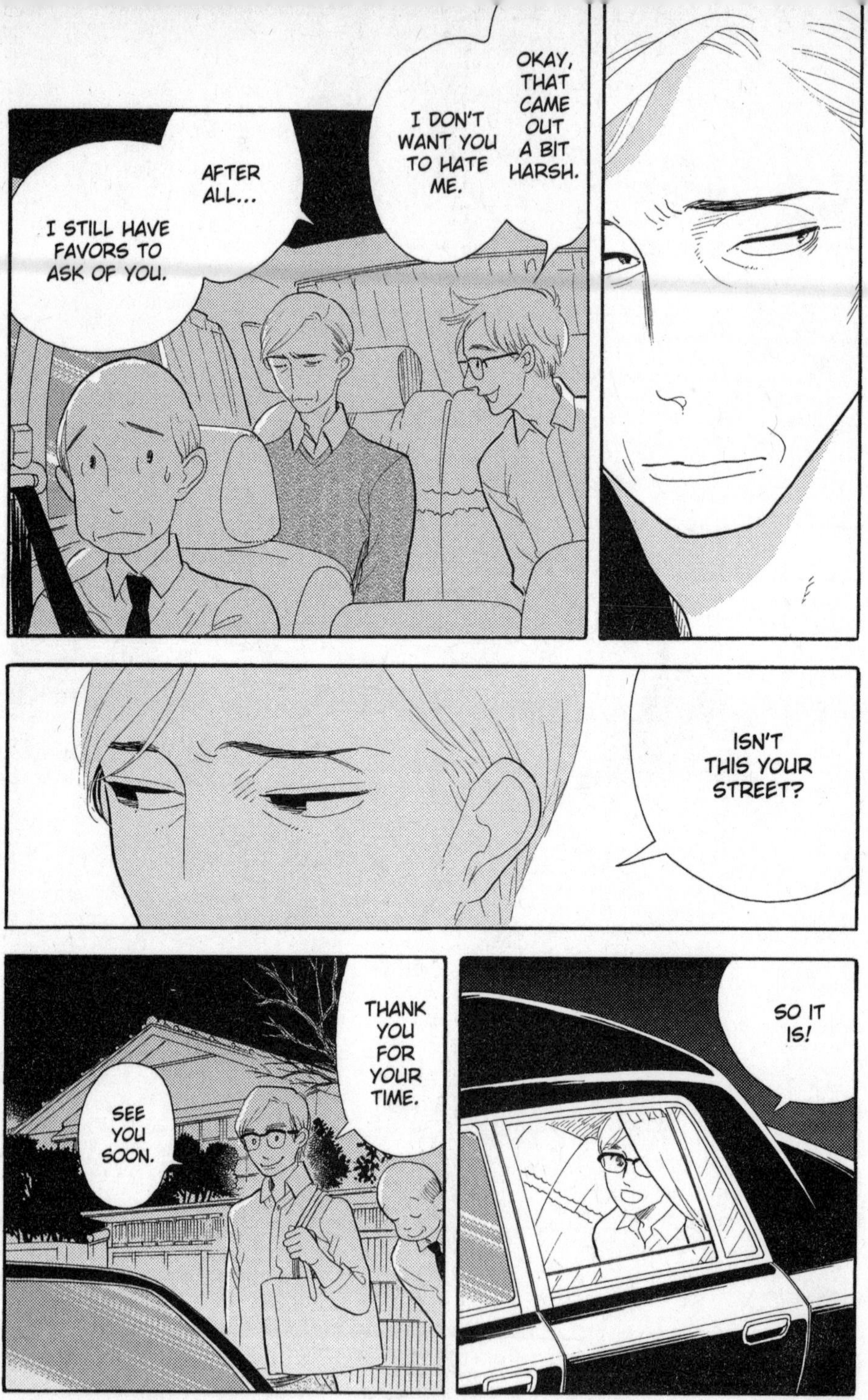
OKAY, THAT CAME OUT A BIT HARSH.
I DON'T WANT YOU TO HATE ME.
AFTER ALL...
I STILL HAVE FAVORS TO ASK OF YOU.
ISN'T THIS YOUR STREET?
SO IT IS!
THANK YOU FOR YOUR TIME.
SEE YOU SOON.

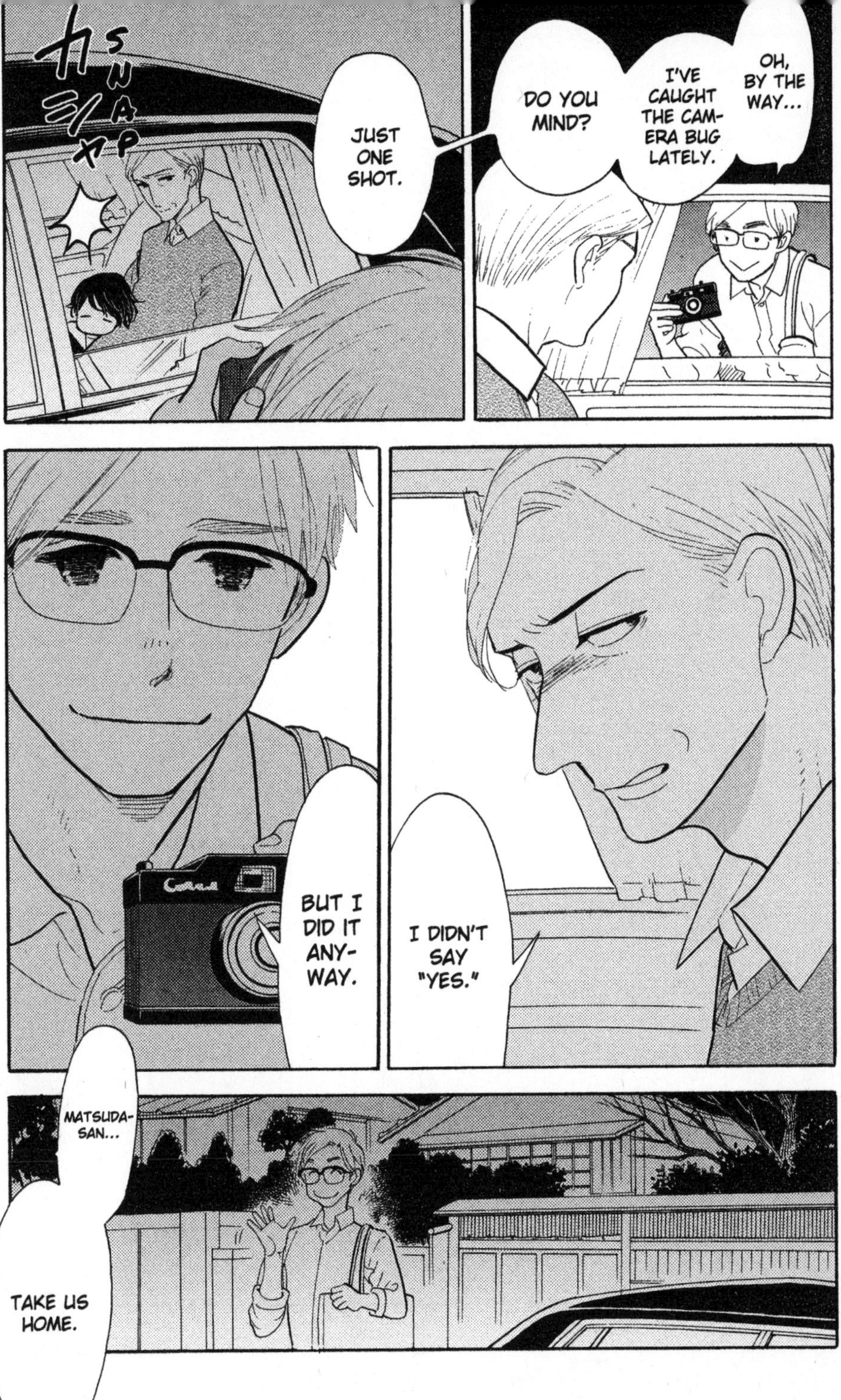
OH, BY THE WAY...
I'VE CAUGHT THE CAM-ERA BUG LATELY.
DO YOU MIND?
カシャ
SNAP
JUST ONE SHOT.
I DIDN'T SAY "YES."
BUT I DID IT ANY-WAY.
MATSUDA-SAN...
TAKE US HOME.

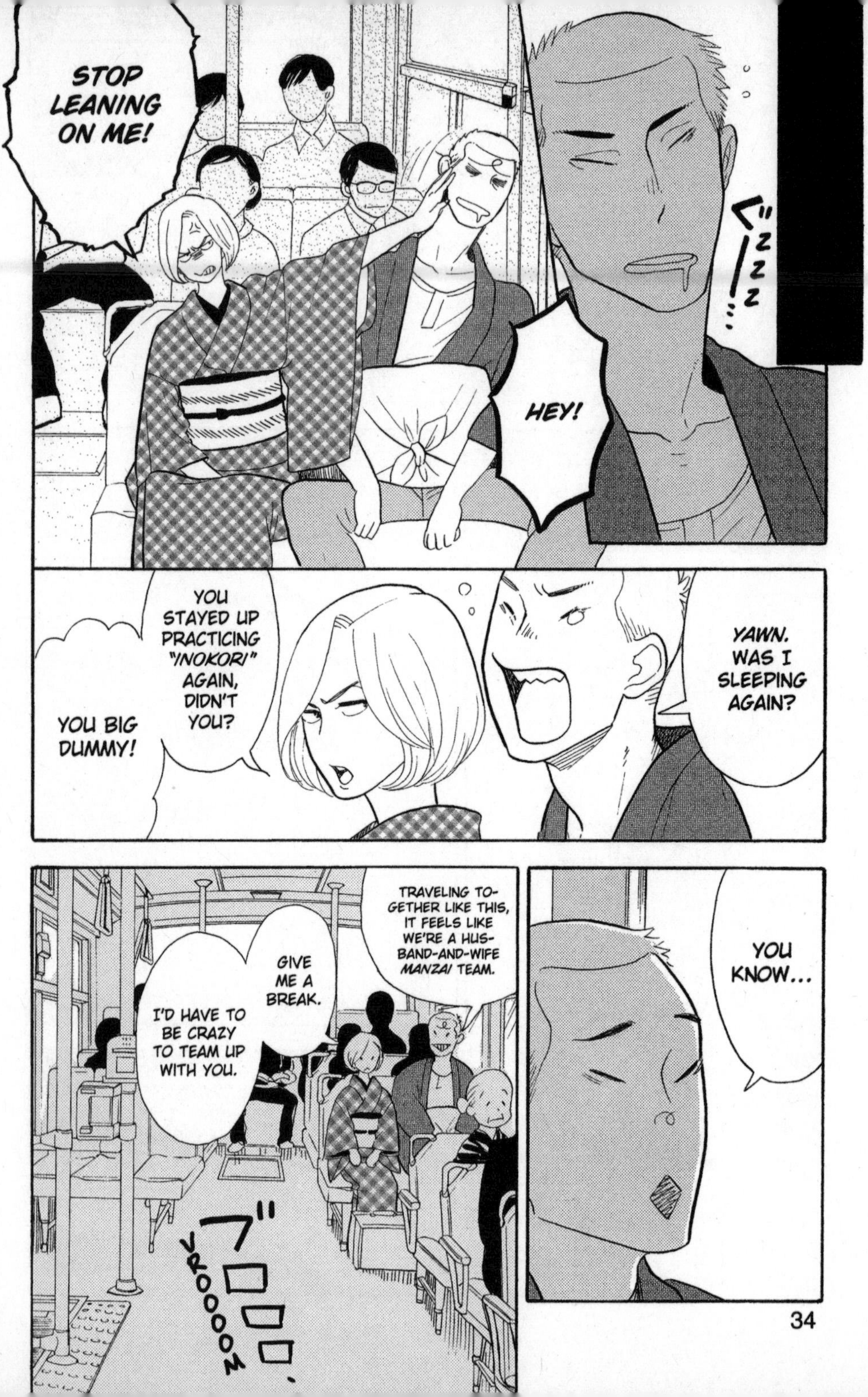
ZZZ
HEY!
STOP LEANING ON ME!
YAWN. WAS I SLEEPING AGAIN?
YOU STAYED UP PRACTICING "INOKORI" AGAIN, DIDN'T YOU?
YOU BIG DUMMY!
YOU KNOW...
TRAVELING TOGETHER LIKE THIS, IT FEELS LIKE WE'RE A HUSBAND-AND-WIFE MANZAI TEAM.
GIVE ME A BREAK.
I'D HAVE TO BE CRAZY TO TEAM UP WITH YOU.
VROOOOOM

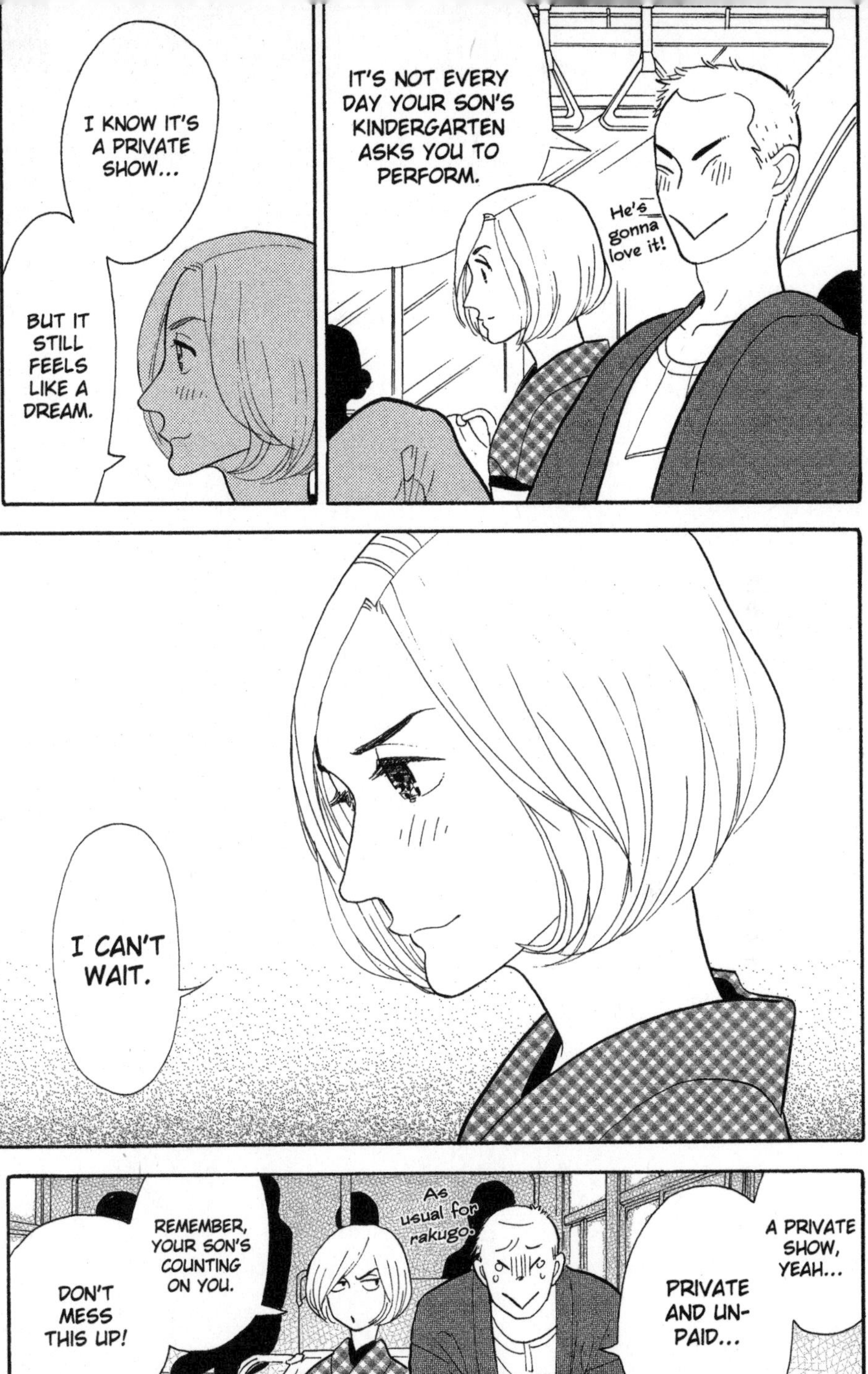
IT'S NOT EVERY DAY YOUR SON'S KINDERGARTEN ASKS YOU TO PERFORM.
He's gonna love it!
I KNOW IT'S A PRIVATE SHOW...
BUT IT STILL FEELS LIKE A DREAM.
I CAN'T WAIT.
A PRIVATE SHOW, YEAH...
PRIVATE AND UN-PAID...
As usual for rakugo.
REMEMBER, YOUR SON'S COUNTING ON YOU.
DON'T MESS THIS UP!

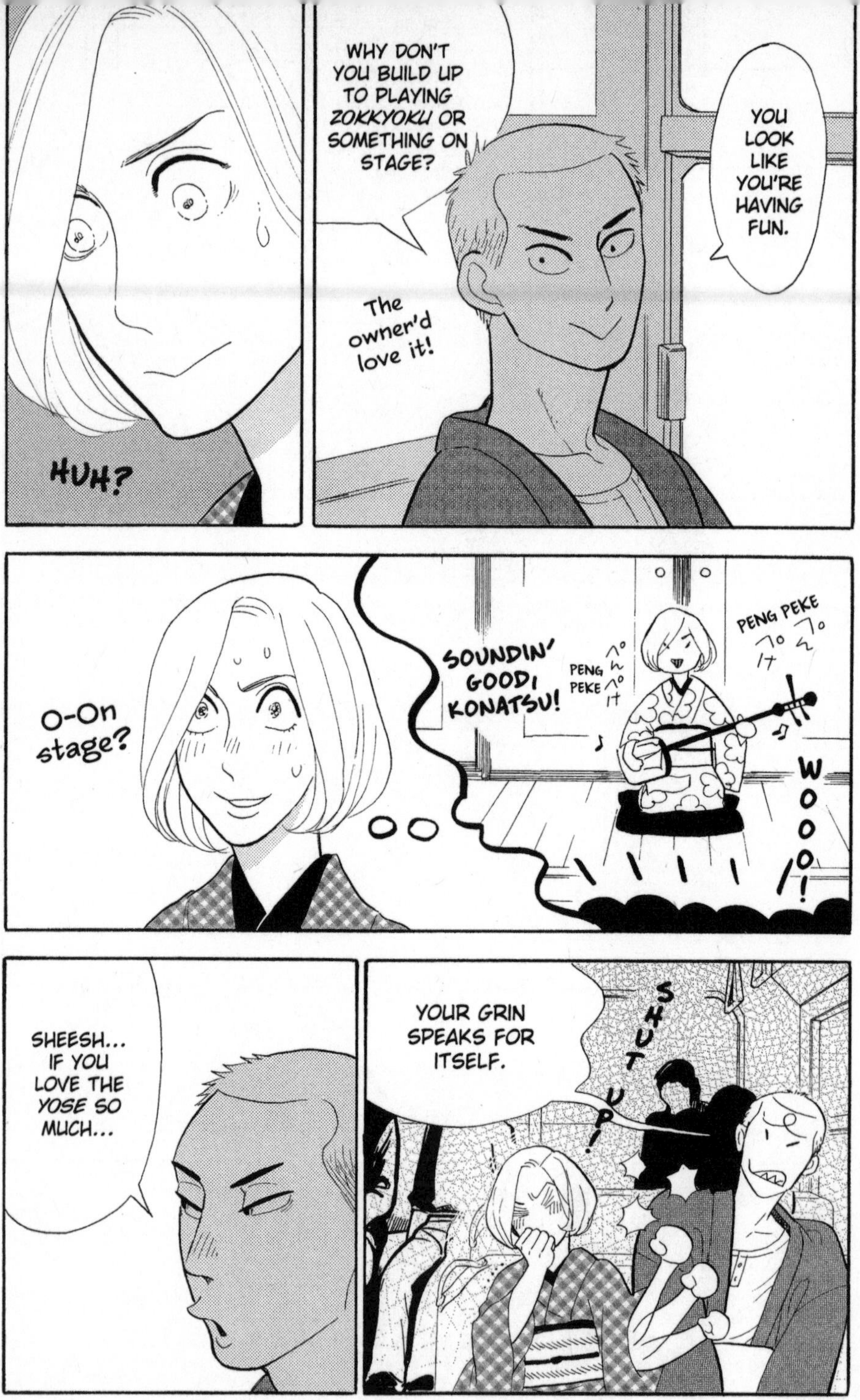
YOU LOOK LIKE YOU'RE HAVING FUN.
WHY DON'T YOU BUILD UP TO PLAYING *ZOKKYOKU* OR SOMETHING ON STAGE?
The owner'd love it!
HUH?
PENG PEKE
ぺんぺけ
WOOOO!
SOUNDIN' GOOD, KONATSU!
PENG PEKE
ぺんぺけ
O-On stage?
SHUT UP!
YOUR GRIN SPEAKS FOR ITSELF.
SHEESH... IF YOU LOVE THE *YOSE* SO MUCH...

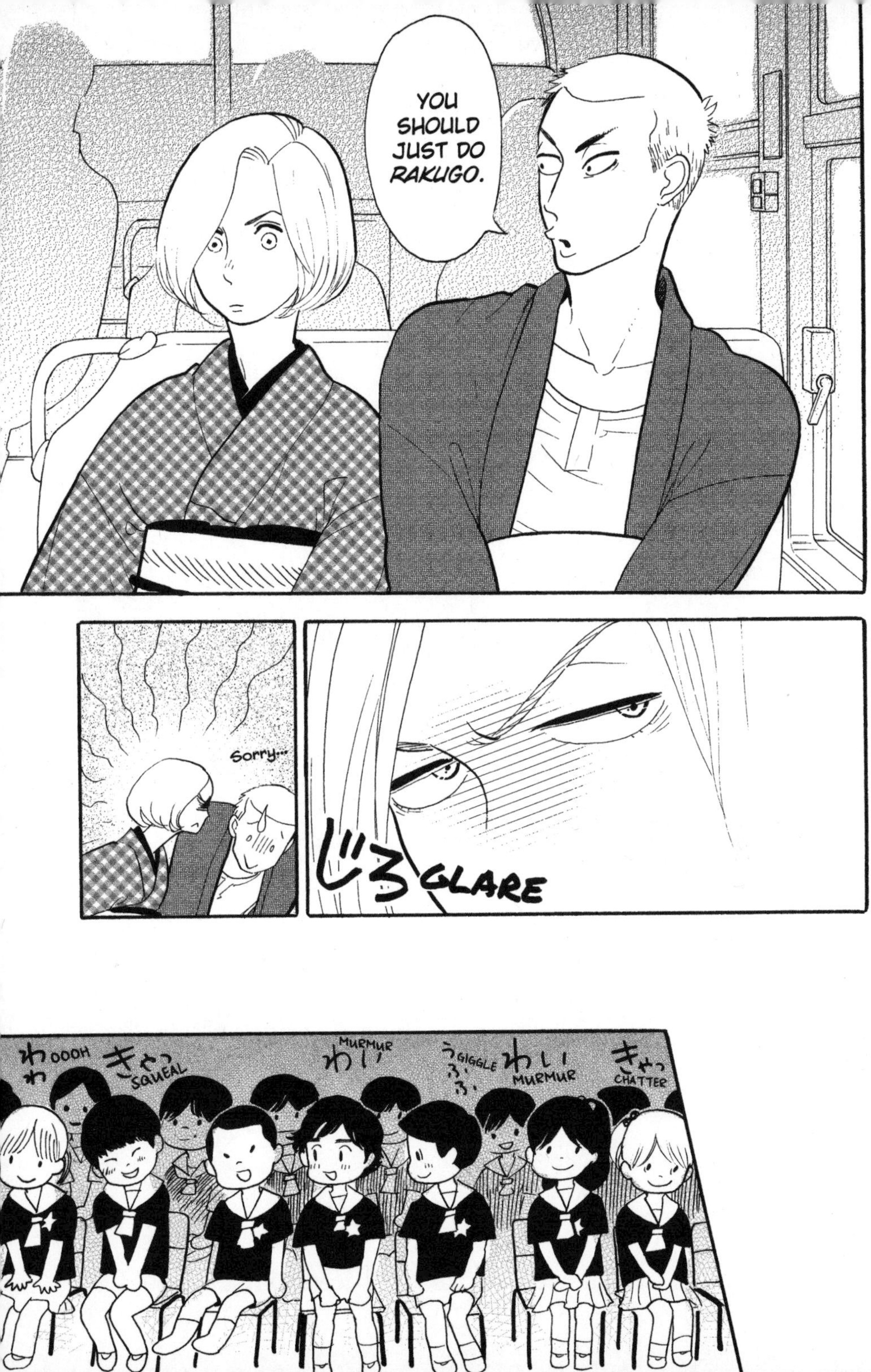
YOU SHOULD JUST DO RAKUGO.
じろ GLARE
Sorry...
きゃっ CHATTER
わい MURMUR
うふふ GIGGLE
わい MURMUR
きゃっ SQUEAL
わわ OOOH

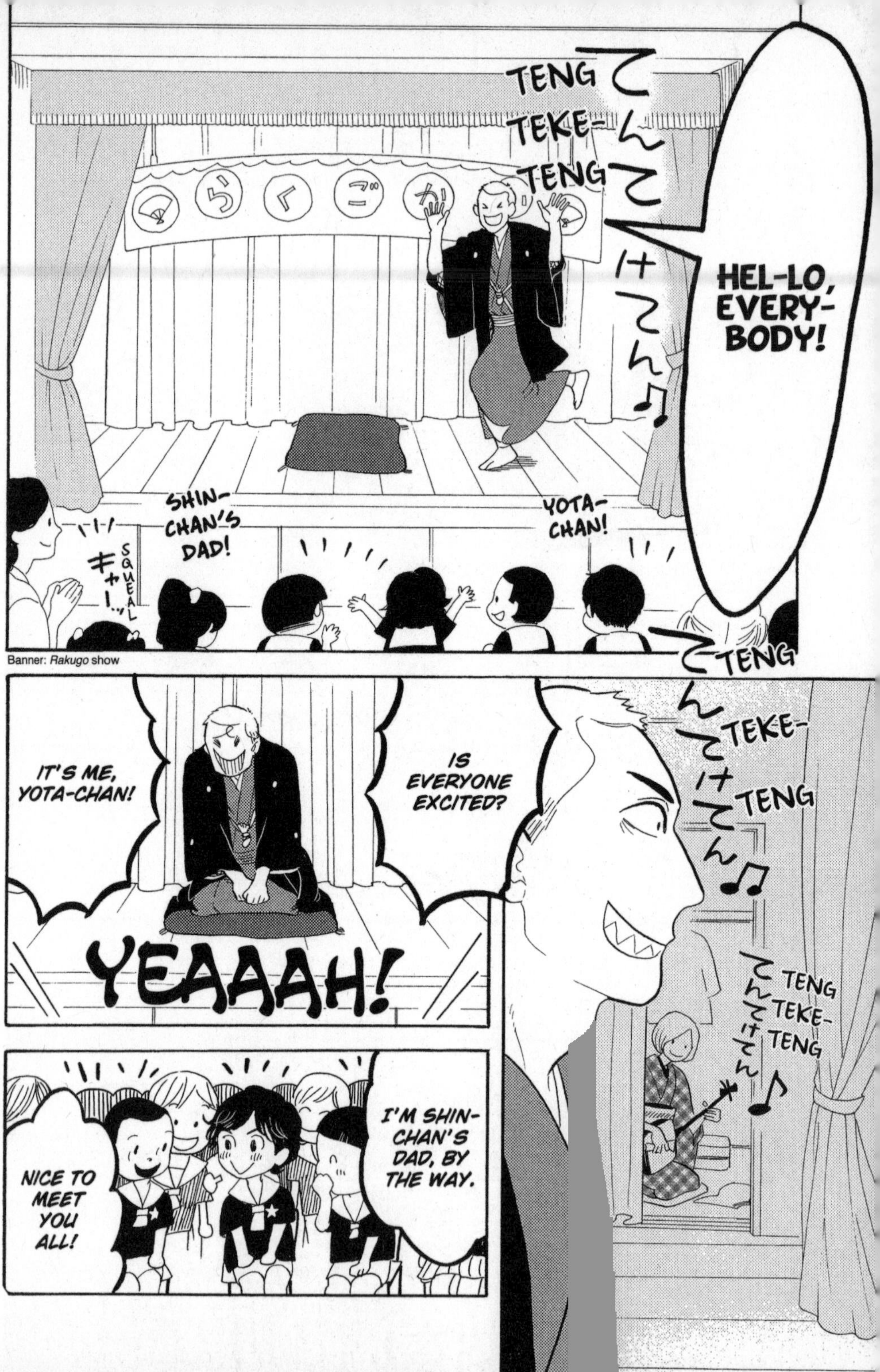
TENG TEKE-TENG
てんてけてん♪
HEL-LO, EVERY-BODY!
YOTA-CHAN!
SHIN-CHAN'S DAD!
SQUEAL
キャー…
らくごかい
TENG TEKE-TENG
てんてけてん♪
TENG TEKE-TENG
てんてけてん♪
IS EVERYONE EXCITED?
IT'S ME, YOTA-CHAN!
YEAAAH!
I'M SHIN-CHAN'S DAD, BY THE WAY.
NICE TO MEET YOU ALL!
Banner: *Rakugo* show

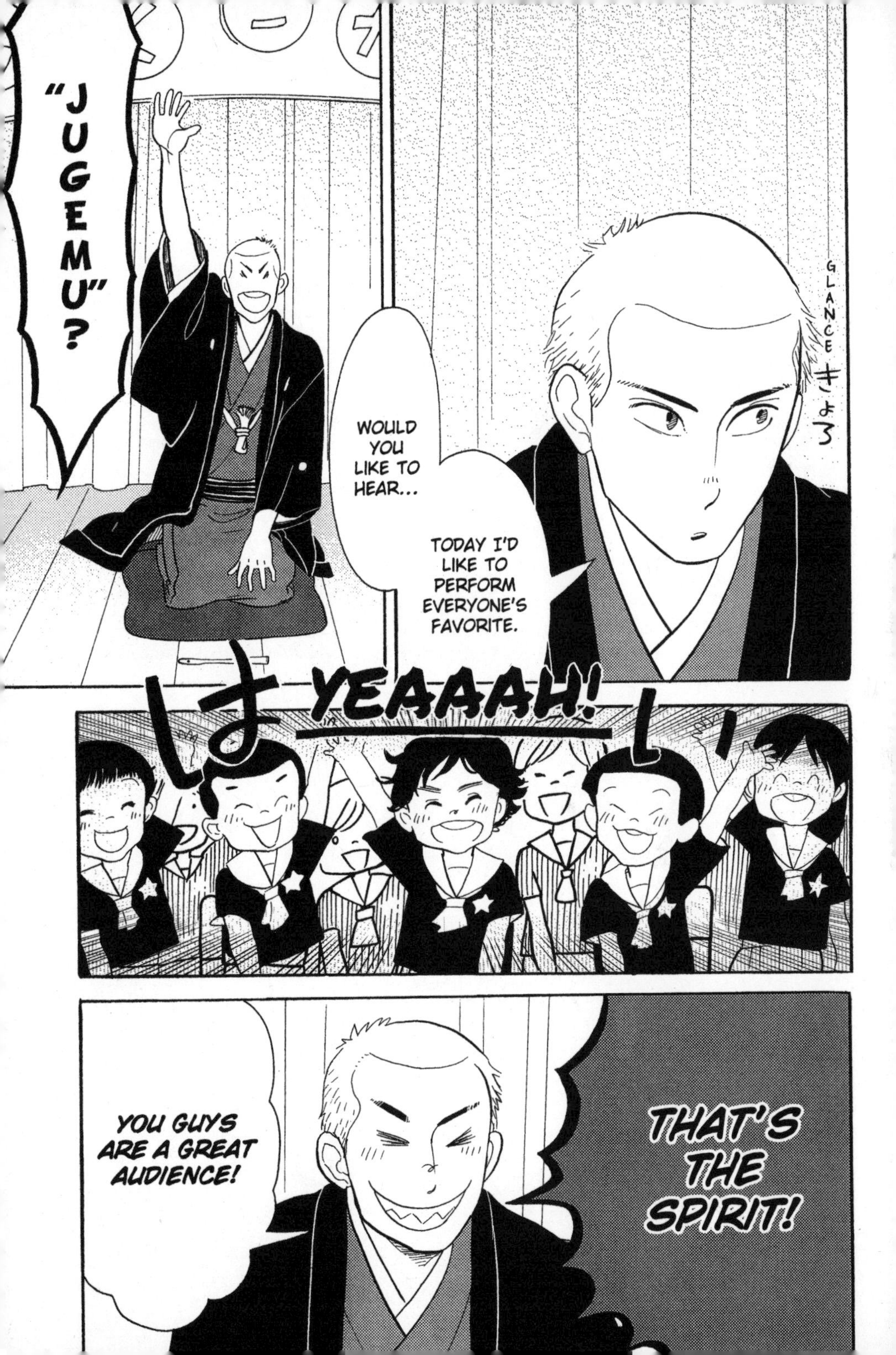
GLANCE
きょろ
TODAY I'D LIKE TO PERFORM EVERYONE'S FAVORITE.
WOULD YOU LIKE TO HEAR...
"JUGEMU"?
はい
YEAAAH!
THAT'S THE SPIRIT!
YOU GUYS ARE A GREAT AUDIENCE!

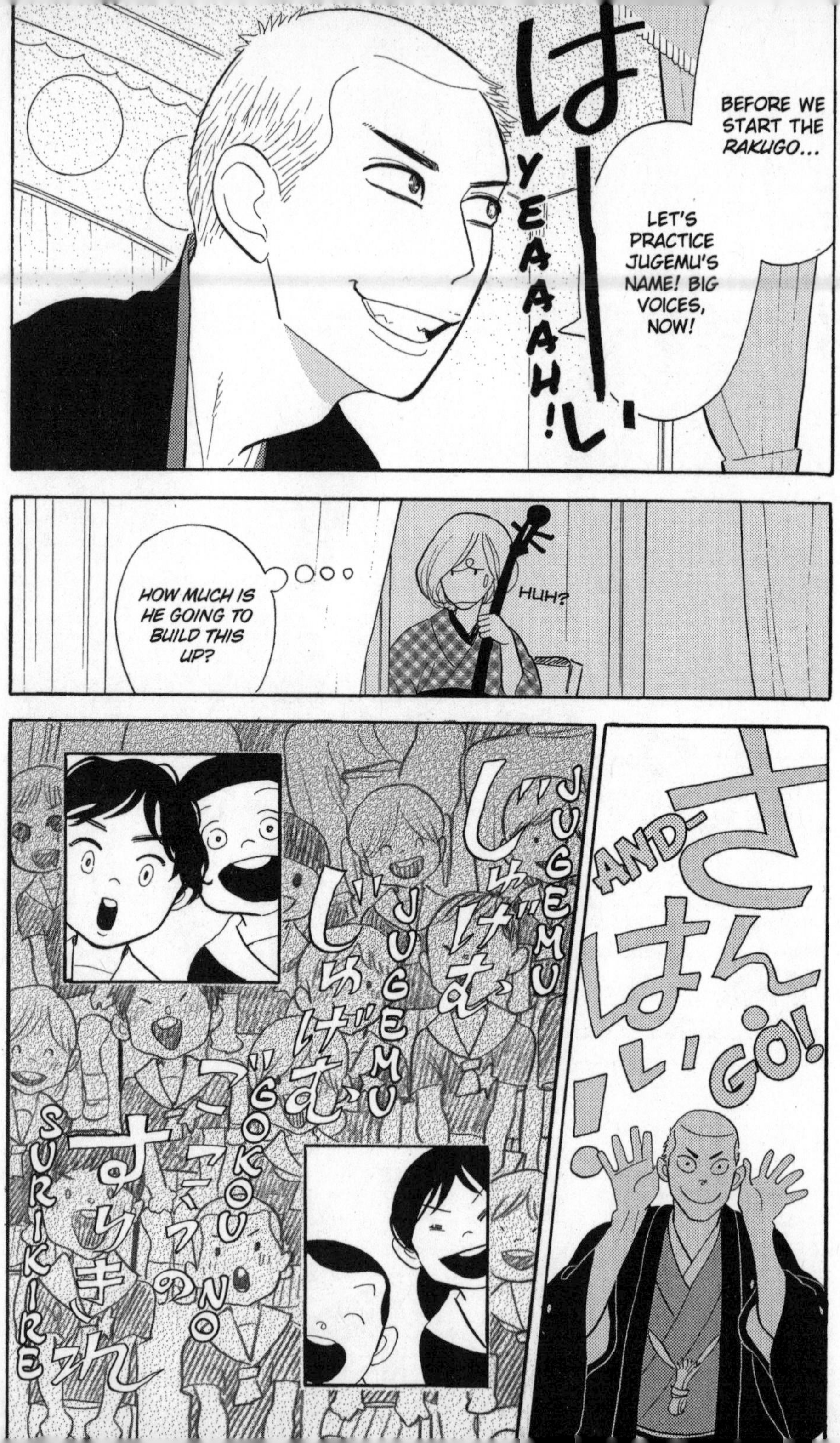
BEFORE WE START THE *RAKUGO*...
LET'S PRACTICE JUGEMU'S NAME! BIG VOICES, NOW!
はーい
YEAAAH!
HUH?
HOW MUCH IS HE GOING TO BUILD THIS UP?
さんはい
AND-GO!
じゅげむ
JUGEMU
じゅげむ
JUGEMU
ごこうのすりきれ
GOKOU NO SURIKIRE

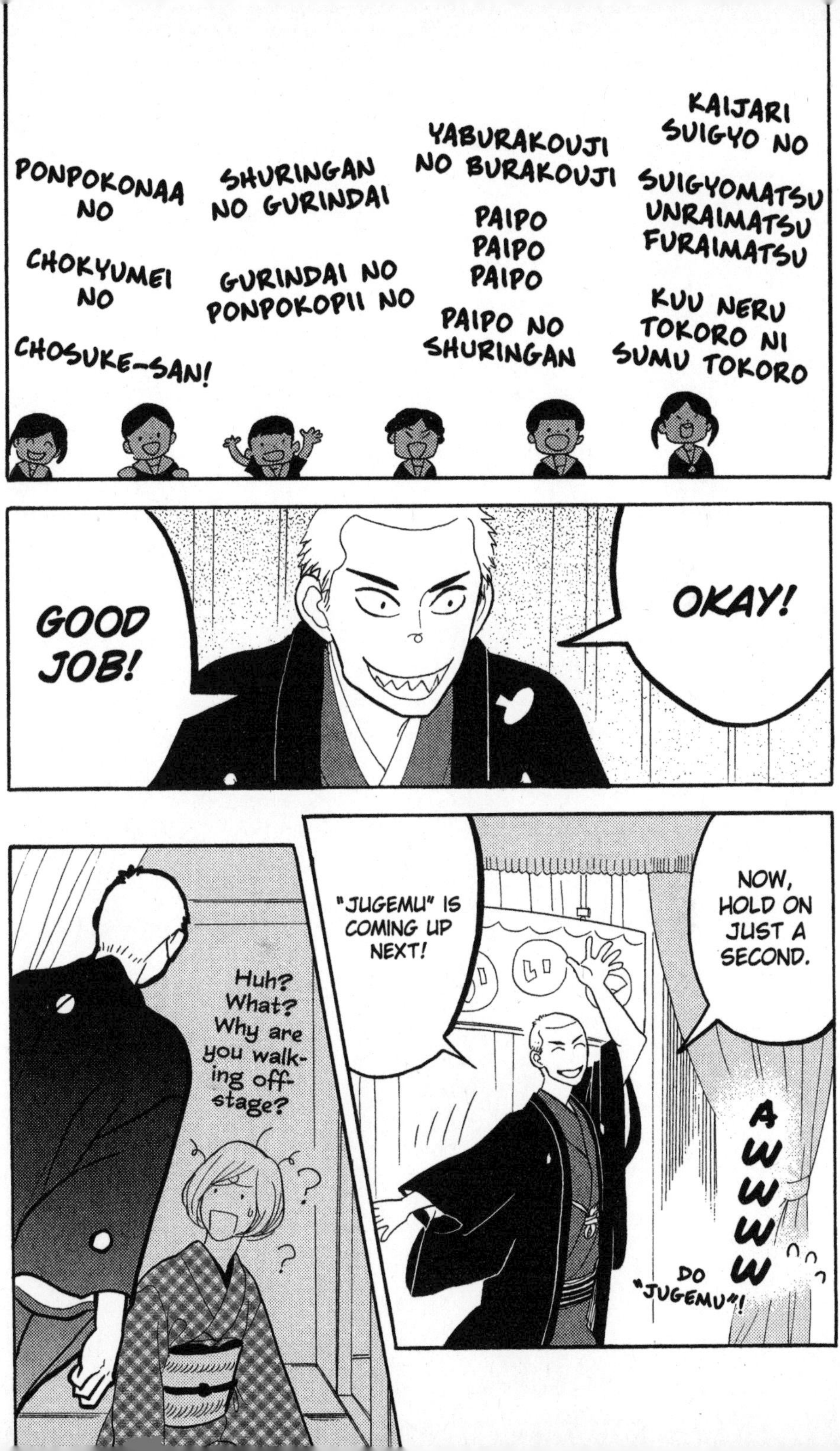
KAIJARI SUIGYO NO
SUIGYOMATSU UNRAIMATSU FURAIMATSU
KUU NERU TOKORO NI SUMU TOKORO
YABURAKOUJI NO BURAKOUJI
PAIPO PAIPO PAIPO
PAIPO NO SHURINGAN
SHURINGAN NO GURINDAI
GURINDAI NO PONPOKOPII NO
PONPOKONAA NO
CHOKYUMEI NO
CHOSUKE-SAN!
OKAY!
GOOD JOB!
NOW, HOLD ON JUST A SECOND.
"JUGEMU" IS COMING UP NEXT!
AWWWWW
DO "JUGEMU"!
Huh? What? Why are you walking off-stage?

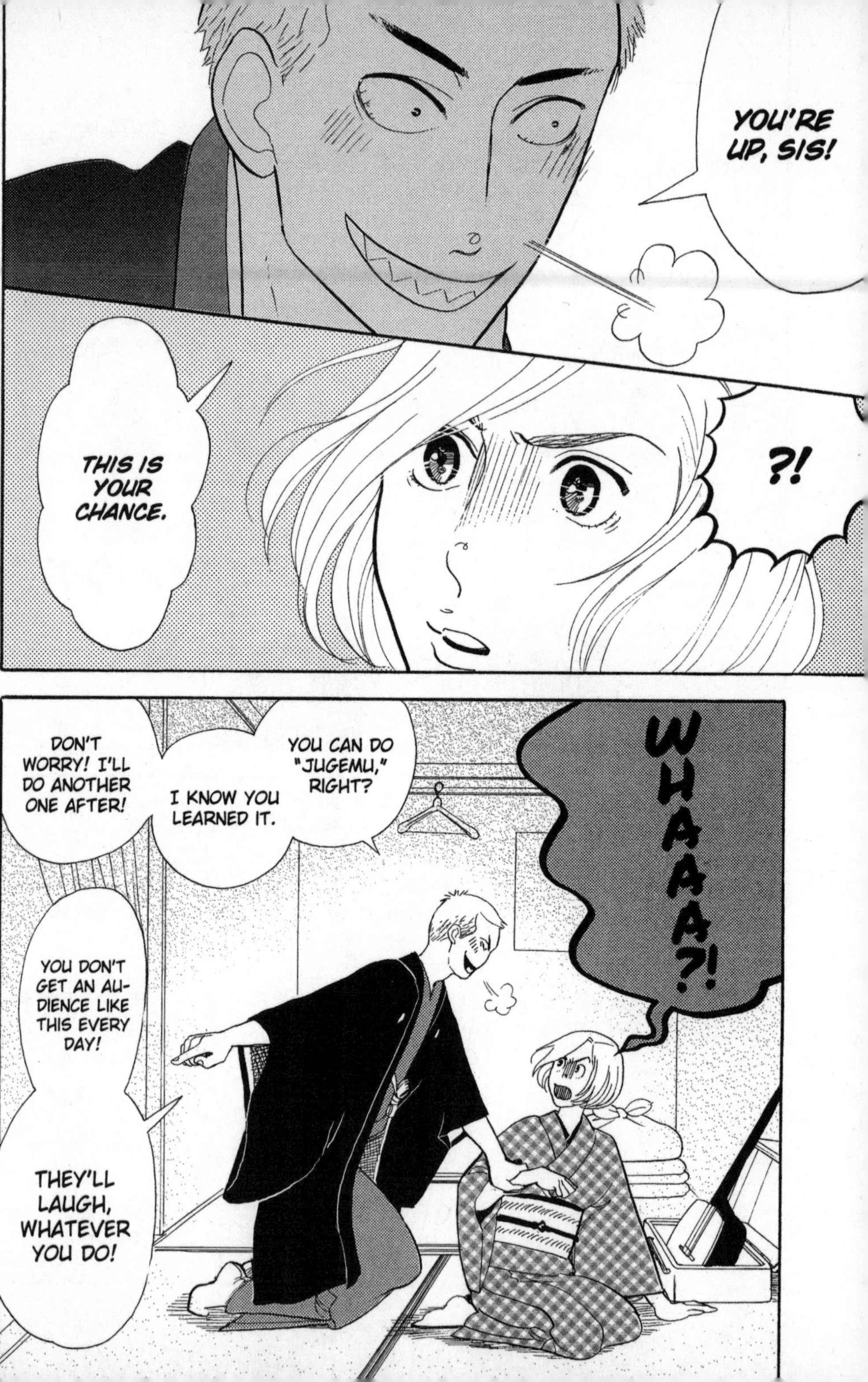
YOU'RE UP, SIS!
?!
THIS IS YOUR CHANCE.
WHAAAA?!
YOU CAN DO "JUGEMU," RIGHT?
I KNOW YOU LEARNED IT.
DON'T WORRY! I'LL DO ANOTHER ONE AFTER!
YOU DON'T GET AN AUDIENCE LIKE THIS EVERY DAY!
THEY'LL LAUGH, WHATEVER YOU DO!

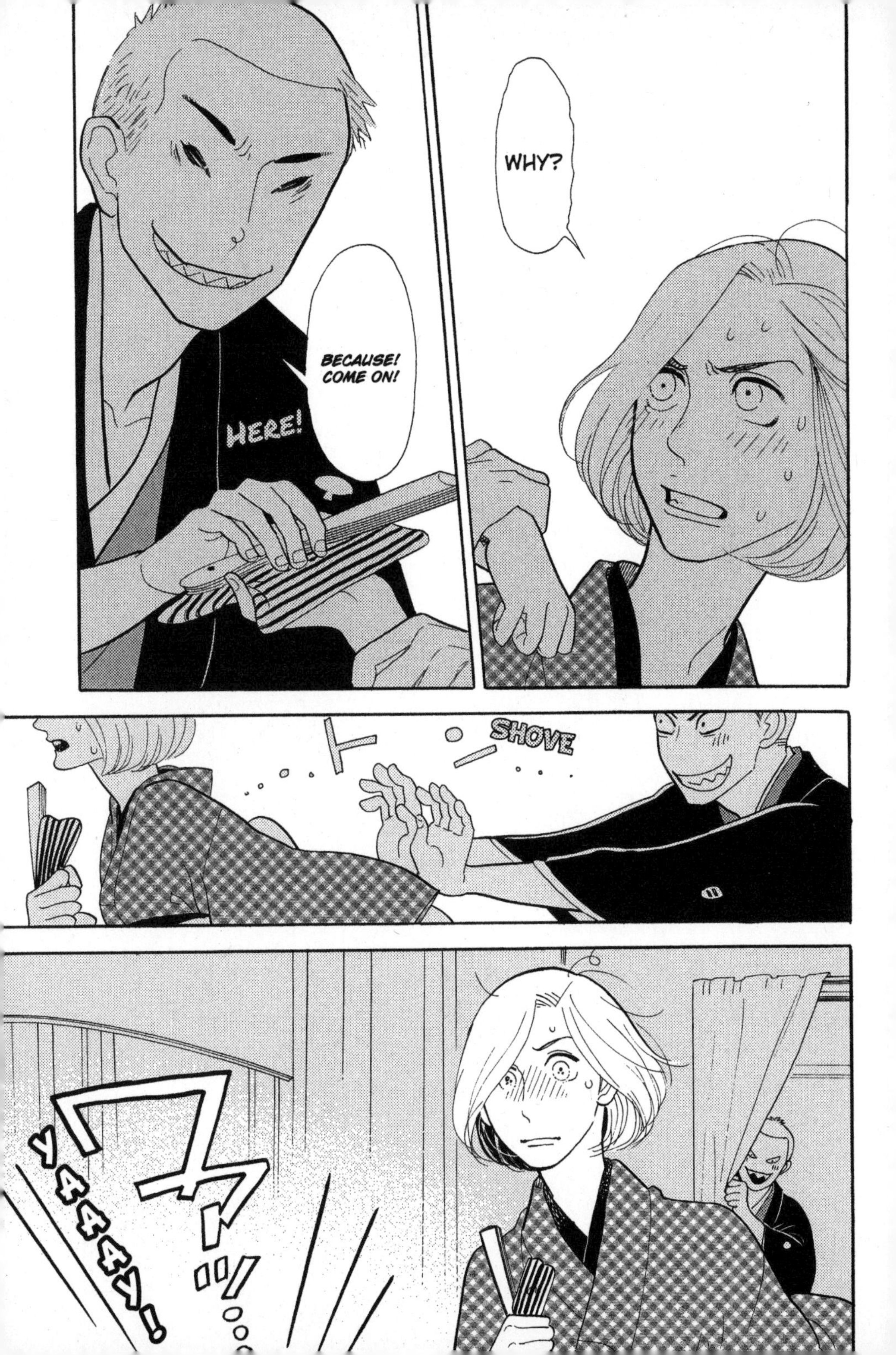
WHY?
BECAUSE! COME ON!
HERE!
SHOVE
YAAAY!

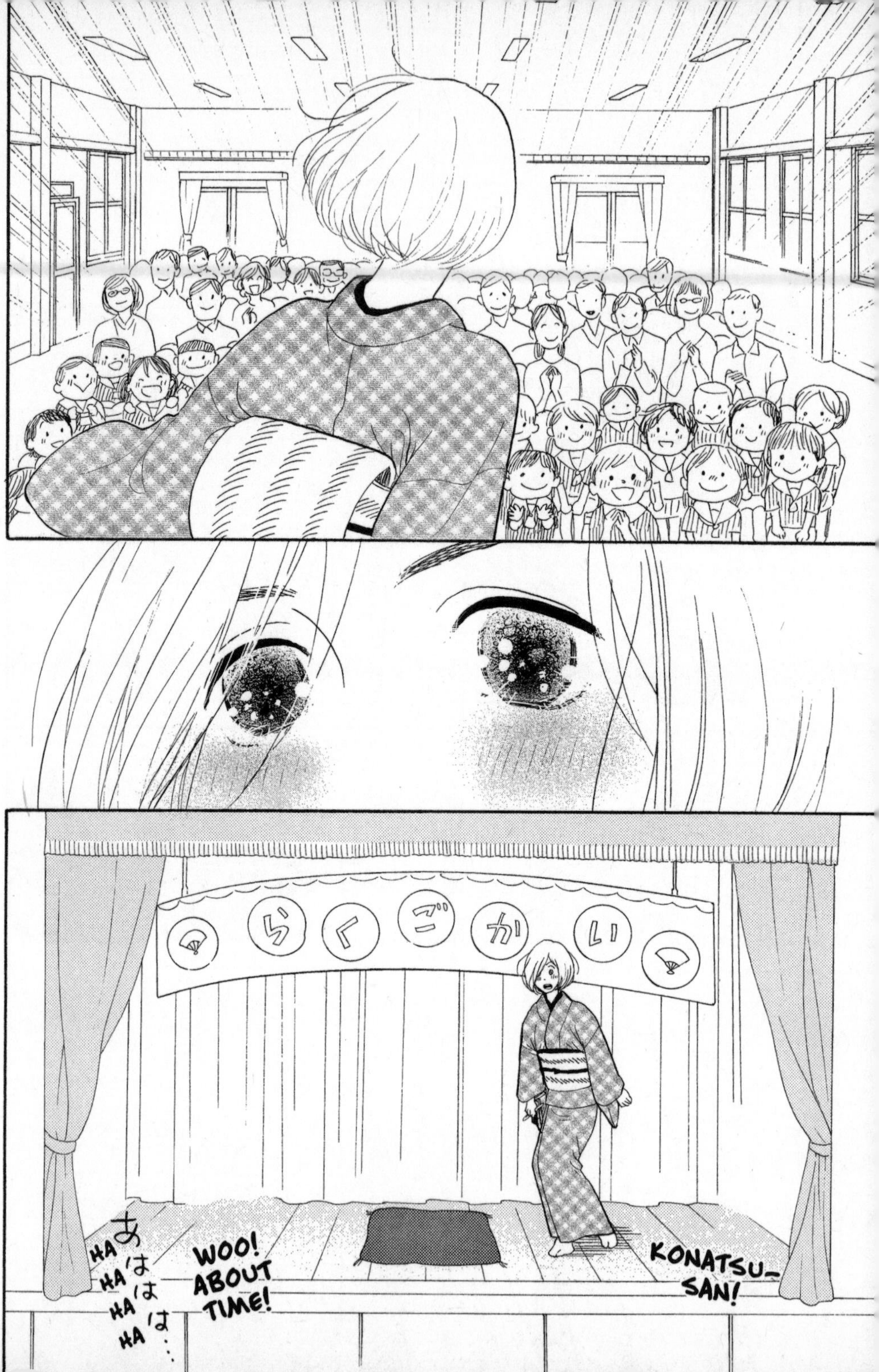
らくごかい
KONATSU-SAN!
WOO! ABOUT TIME!
あははは…
HA HA HA HA

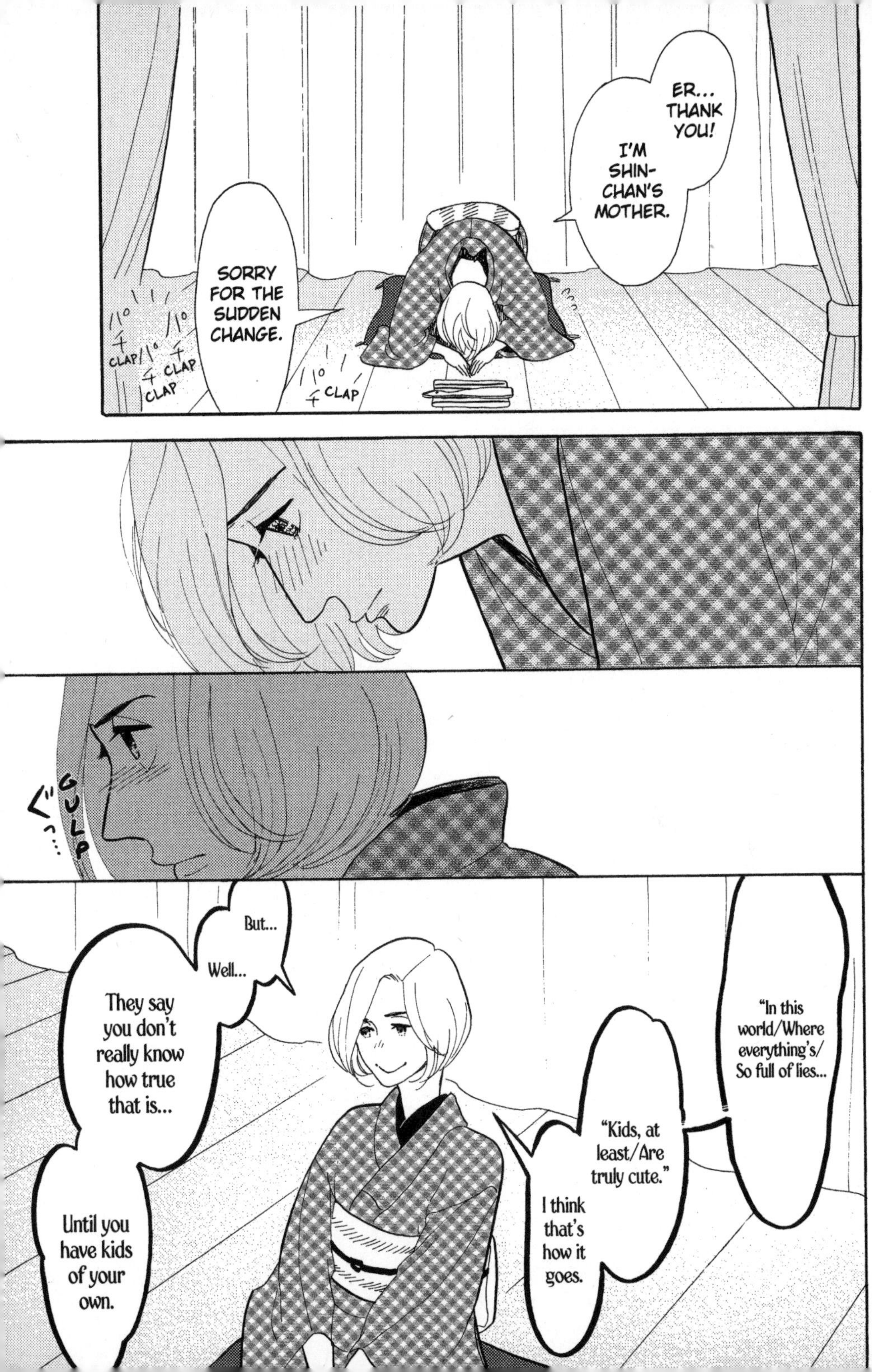
ER... THANK YOU!
I'M SHIN-CHAN'S MOTHER.
SORRY FOR THE SUDDEN CHANGE.
CLAP
CLAP
CLAP
CLAP
GULP
"In this world/Where everything's/ So full of lies...
"Kids, at least/Are truly cute."
I think that's how it goes.
But...
Well...
They say you don't really know how true that is...
Until you have kids of your own.

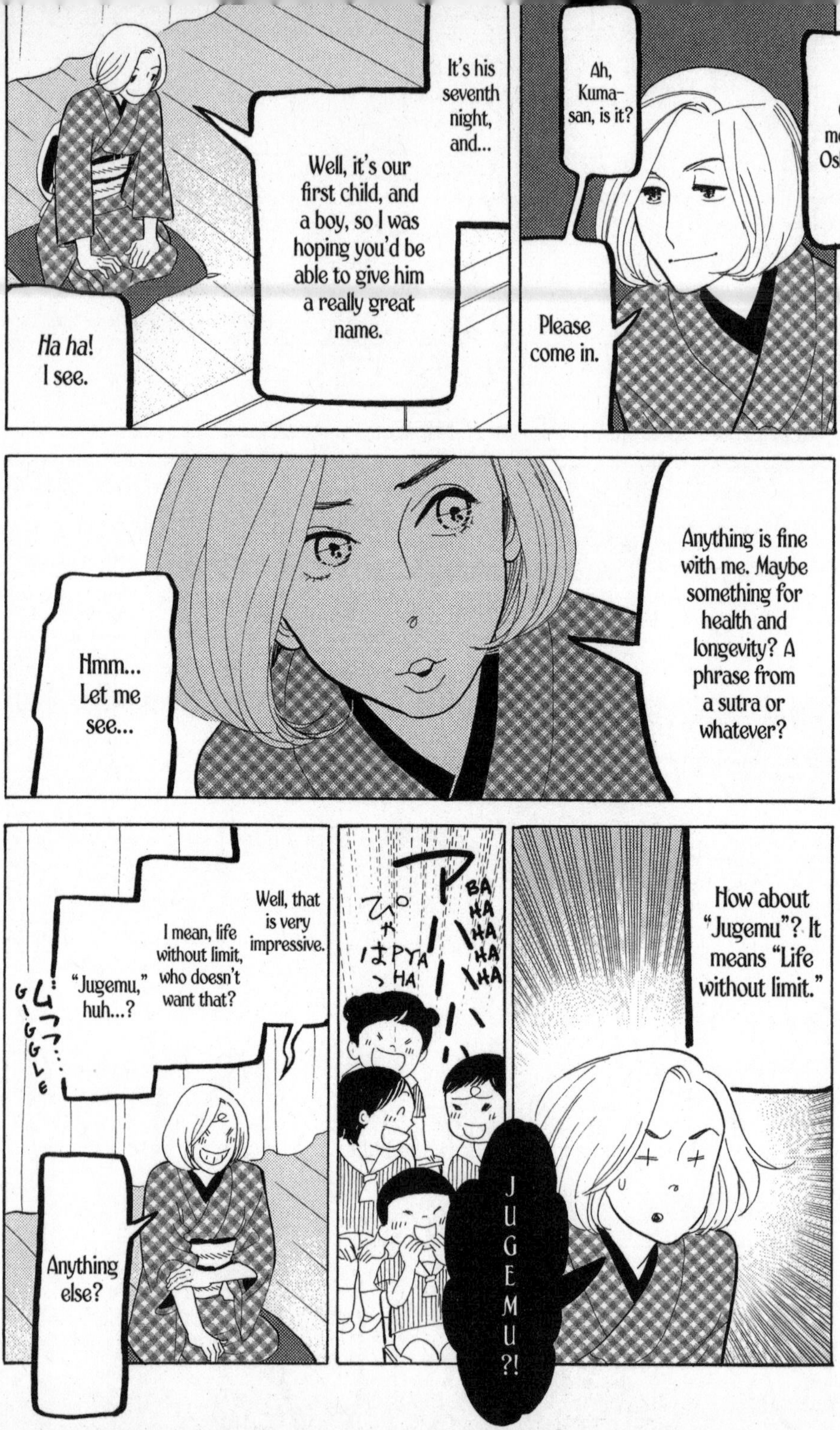

Good morning, Osho-san.
Ah, Kuma-san, is it?
Please come in.
It's his seventh night, and...
Well, it's our first child, and a boy, so I was hoping you'd be able to give him a really great name.
Ha ha! I see.
Anything is fine with me. Maybe something for health and longevity? A phrase from a sutra or whatever?
Hmm... Let me see...
How about "Jugemu"? It means "Life without limit."
JUGEMU?!
ア
BA HA HA HA HA
ぴゃはっ PYA HA
Well, that is very impressive.
I mean, life without limit, who doesn't want that?
"Jugemu," huh...?
ムフフ… GIGGLE
Anything else?

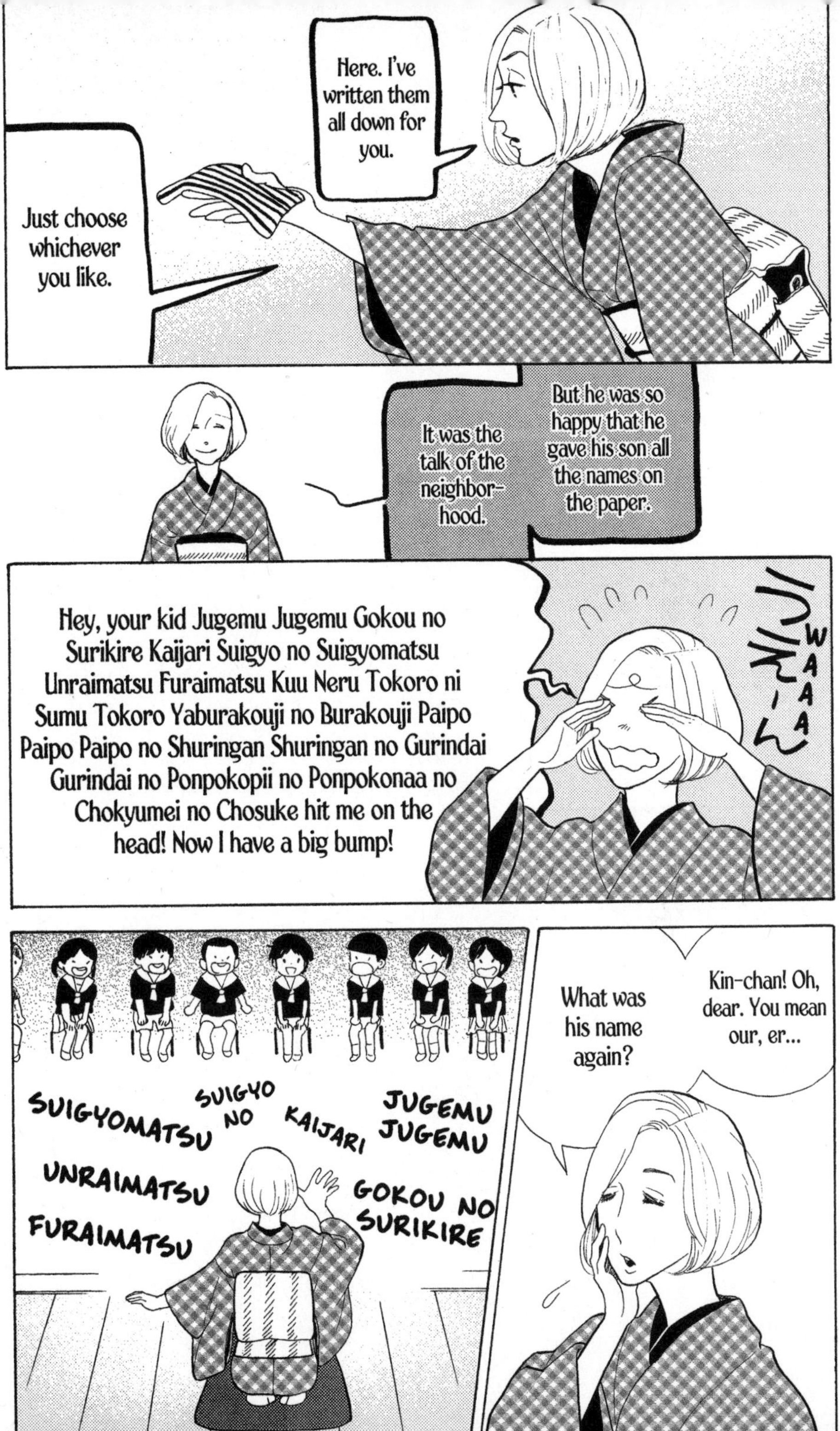
Here. I've written them all down for you.
Just choose whichever you like.
But he was so happy that he gave his son all the names on the paper.
It was the talk of the neighbor-hood.
WAAAA
Hey, your kid Jugemu Jugemu Gokou no Surikire Kaijari Suigyo no Suigyomatsu Unraimatsu Furaimatsu Kuu Neru Tokoro ni Sumu Tokoro Yaburakouji no Burakouji Paipo Paipo Paipo no Shuringan Shuringan no Gurindai Gurindai no Ponpokopii no Ponpokonaa no Chokyumei no Chosuke hit me on the head! Now I have a big bump!
Kin-chan! Oh, dear. You mean our, er...
What was his name again?
JUGEMU JUGEMU
KAIJARI
SUIGYO NO
SUIGYOMATSU
GOKOU NO SURIKIRE
UNRAIMATSU
FURAIMATSU

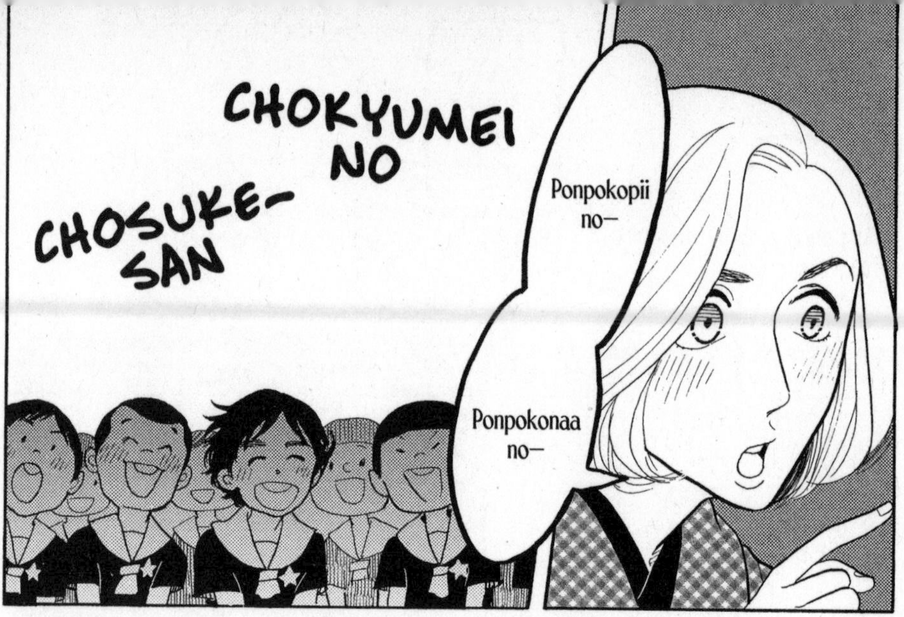
Ponpokopii no—
Ponpokonaa no—
CHOKYUMEI NO
CHOSUKE-SAN
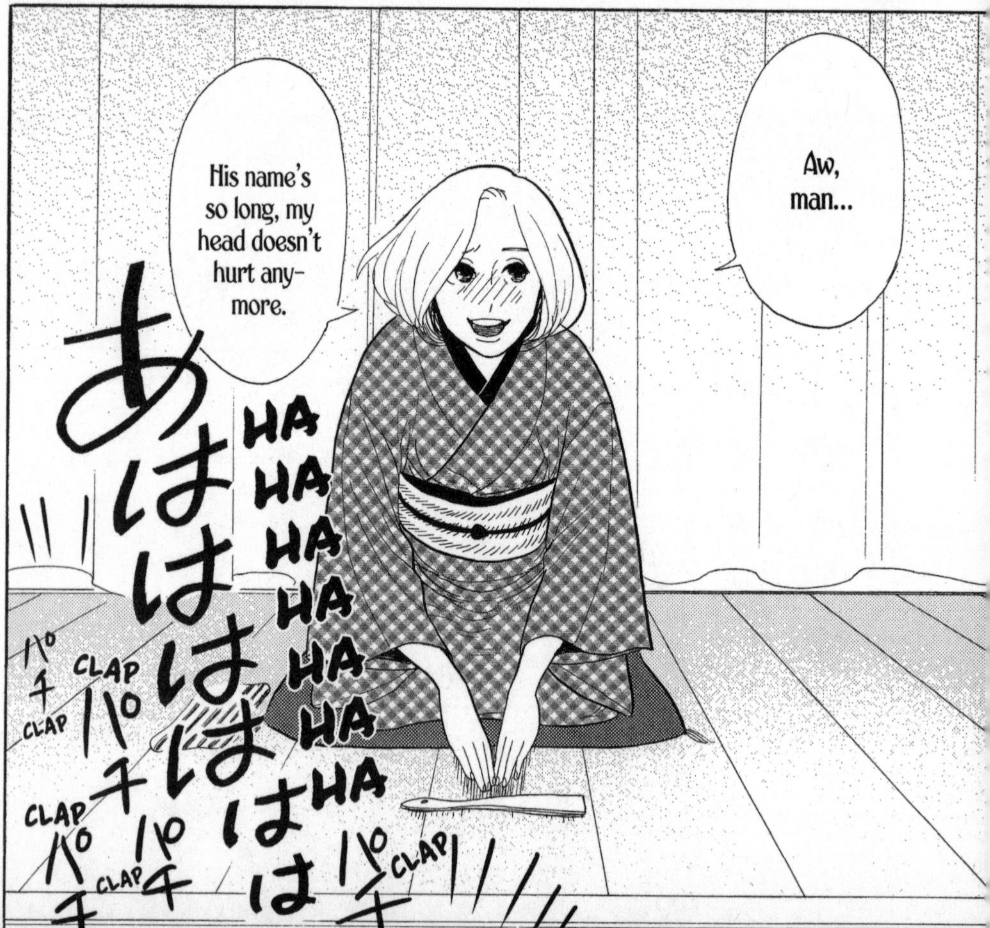
Aw, man...
His name's so long, my head doesn't hurt any-more.
HA HA HA HA HA HA HA
あははははは
CLAP CLAP CLAP CLAP CLAP CLAP
パチパチパチパチパチ

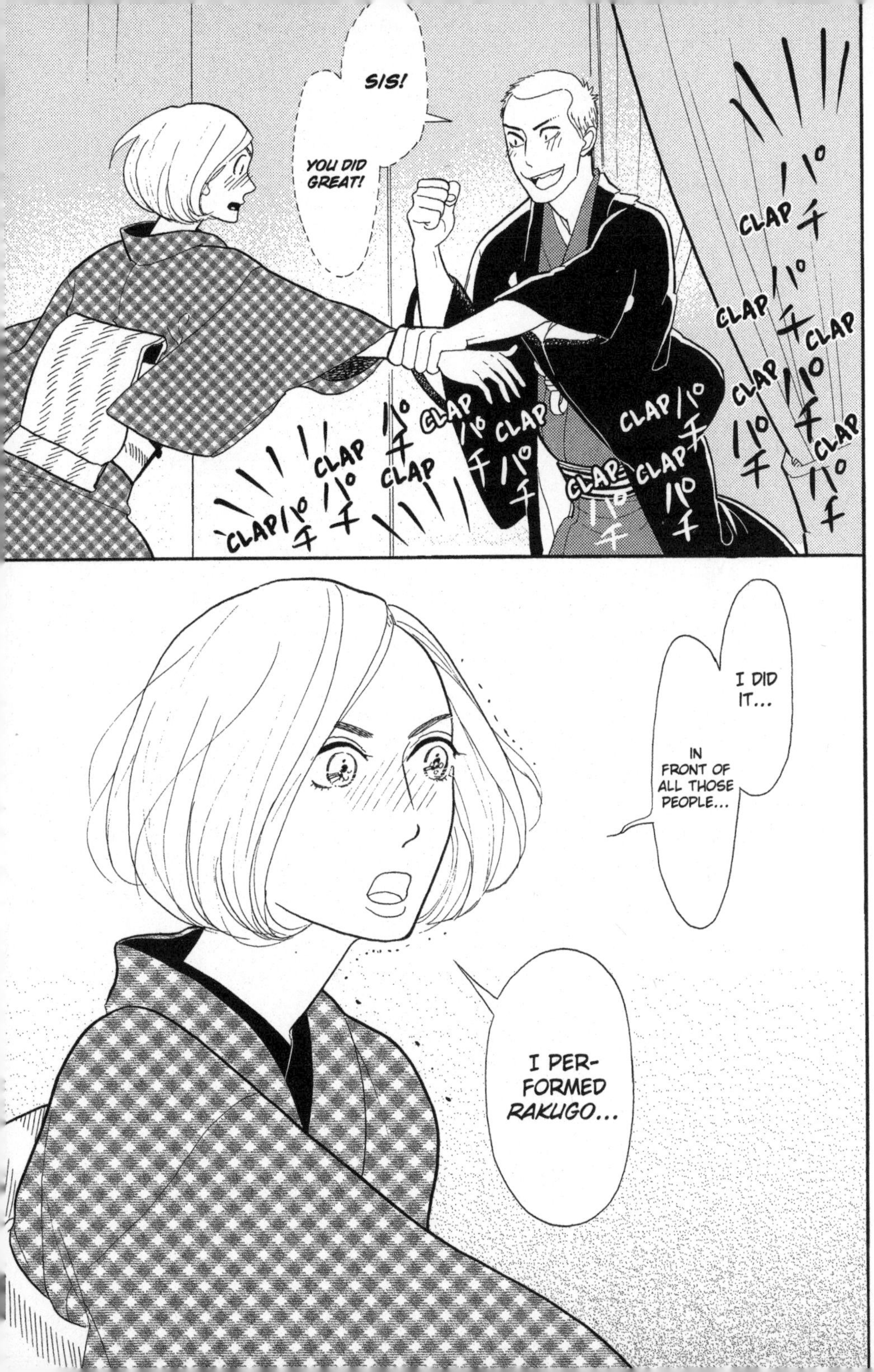
SIS!
YOU DID GREAT!
CLAP パチ
CLAP パチ
CLAP パチ
CLAP パチ
CLAP パチ
CLAP パチ
CLAP パチ
CLAP パチ
CLAP パチ
CLAP パチ
CLAP パチ
CLAP パチ
CLAP パチ
CLAP パチ
I DID IT...
IN FRONT OF ALL THOSE PEOPLE...
I PERFORMED RAKUGO...

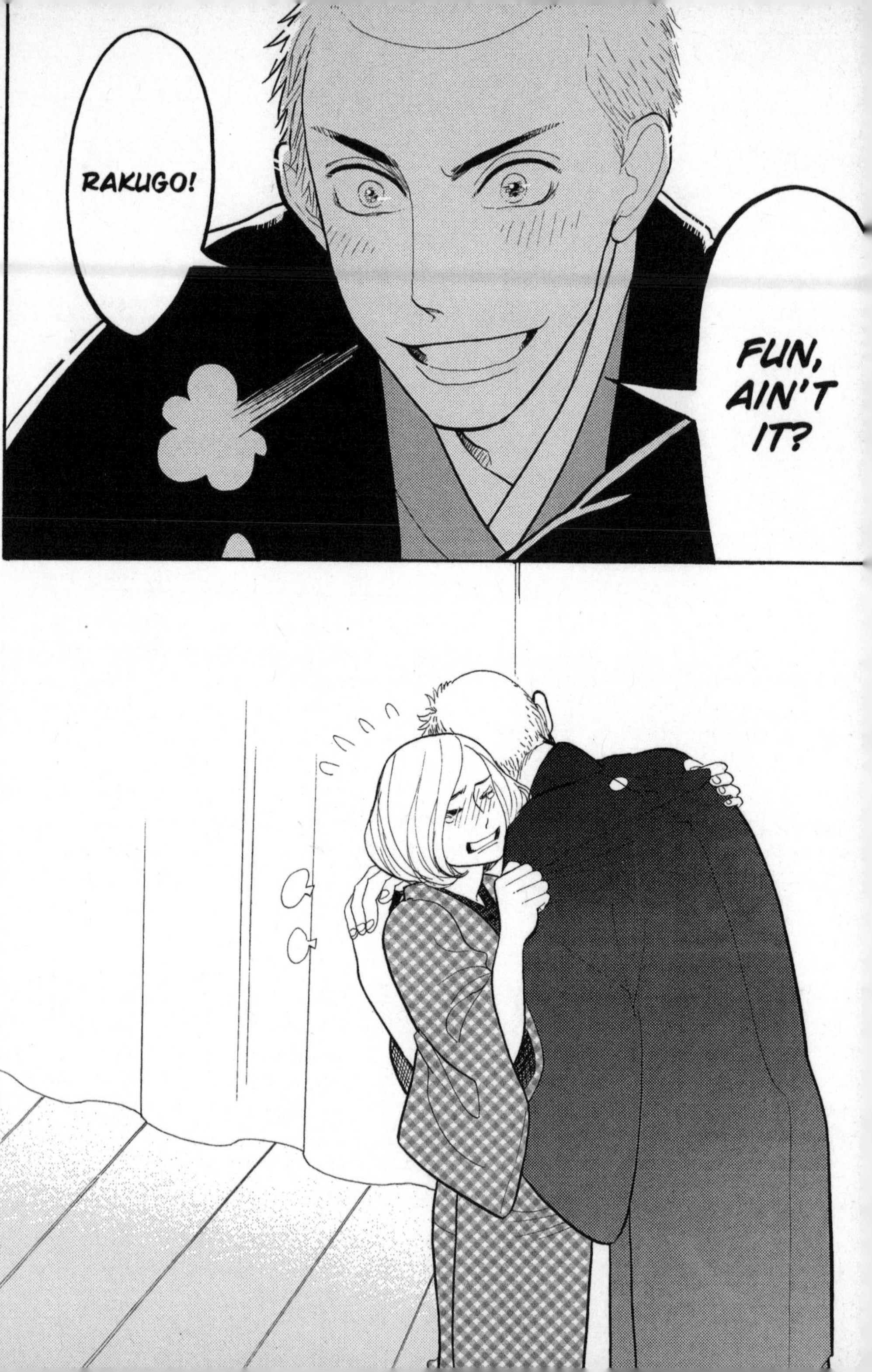
FUN, AIN'T IT?
RAKUGO!

DESCENDING
STORIES
SHOWA
GENROKU
RAKUGO
SHINJU

HARUKO KUMOTA

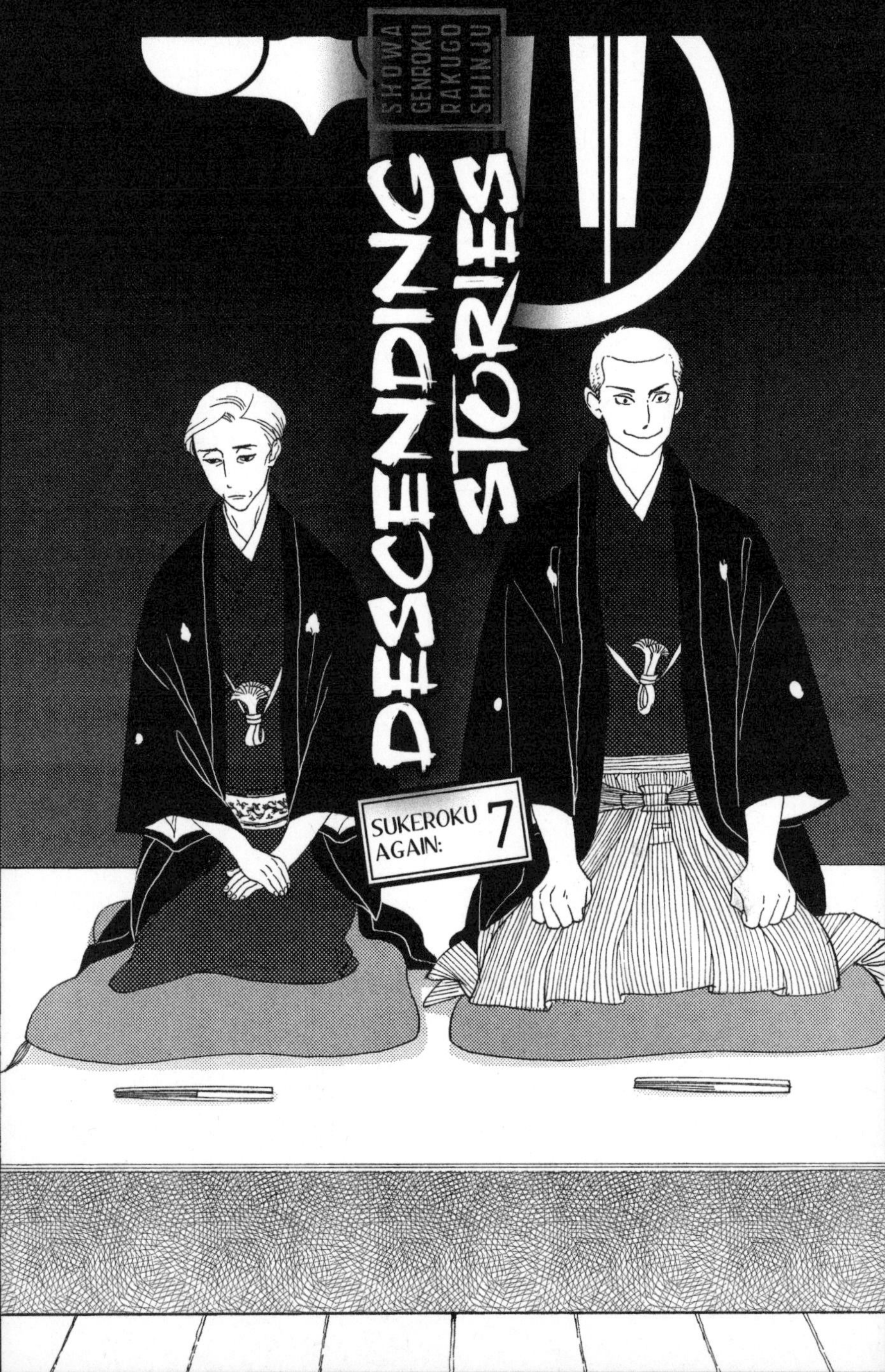
SHOWA GENROKU RAKUGO SHINJU
DESCENDING STORIES
SUKEROKU AGAIN: 7

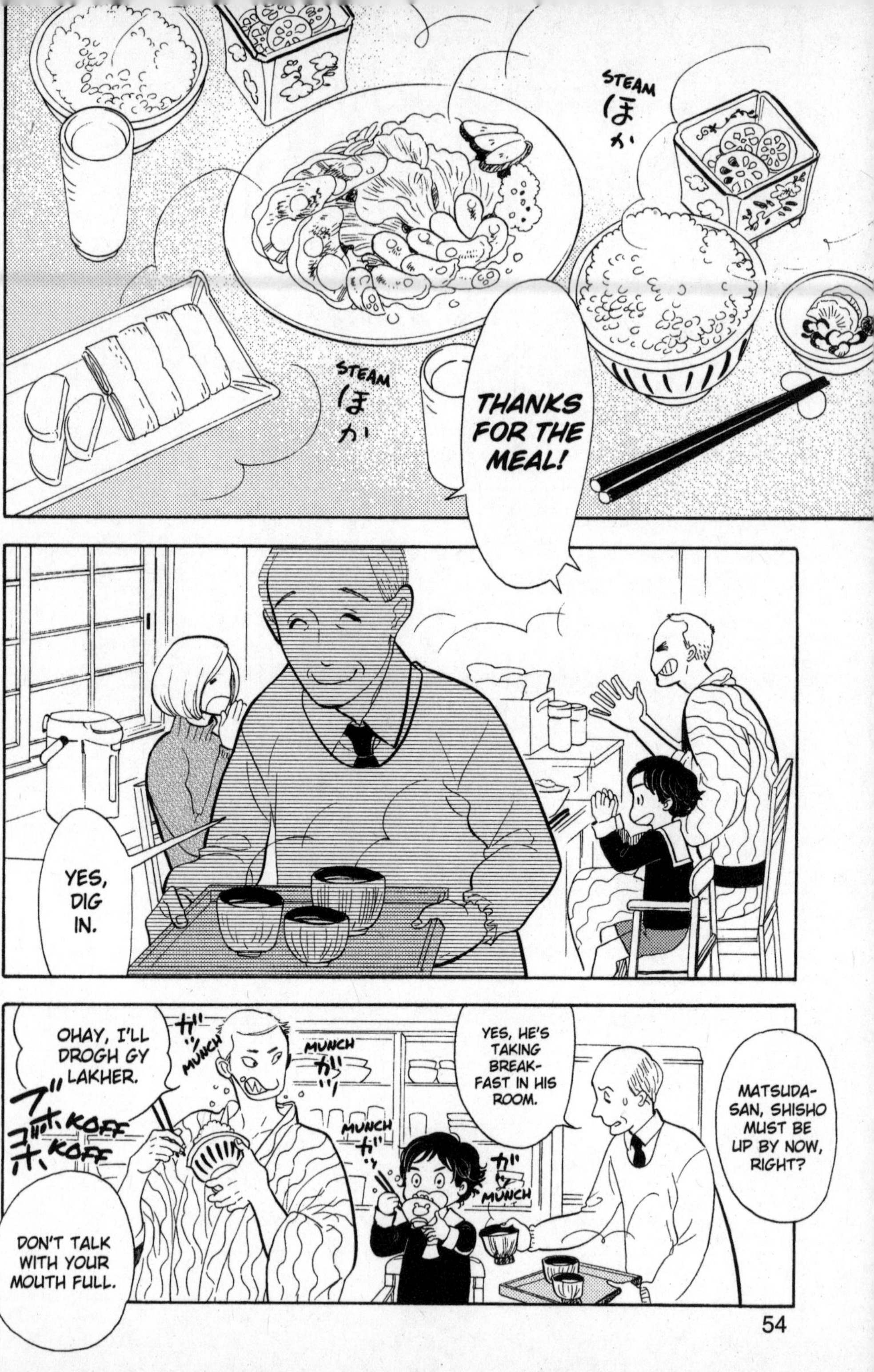
STEAM
ほか
STEAM
ほか
THANKS FOR THE MEAL!
YES, DIG IN.
MATSUDA-SAN, SHISHO MUST BE UP BY NOW, RIGHT?
ガッ
MUNCH
YES, HE'S TAKING BREAK-FAST IN HIS ROOM.
MUNCH
ガッ
MUNCH
ガッ
MUNCH
ガッ
MUNCH
OHAY, I'LL DROGH GY LAKHER.
ブホ
KOFF
コホ
KOFF
DON'T TALK WITH YOUR MOUTH FULL.

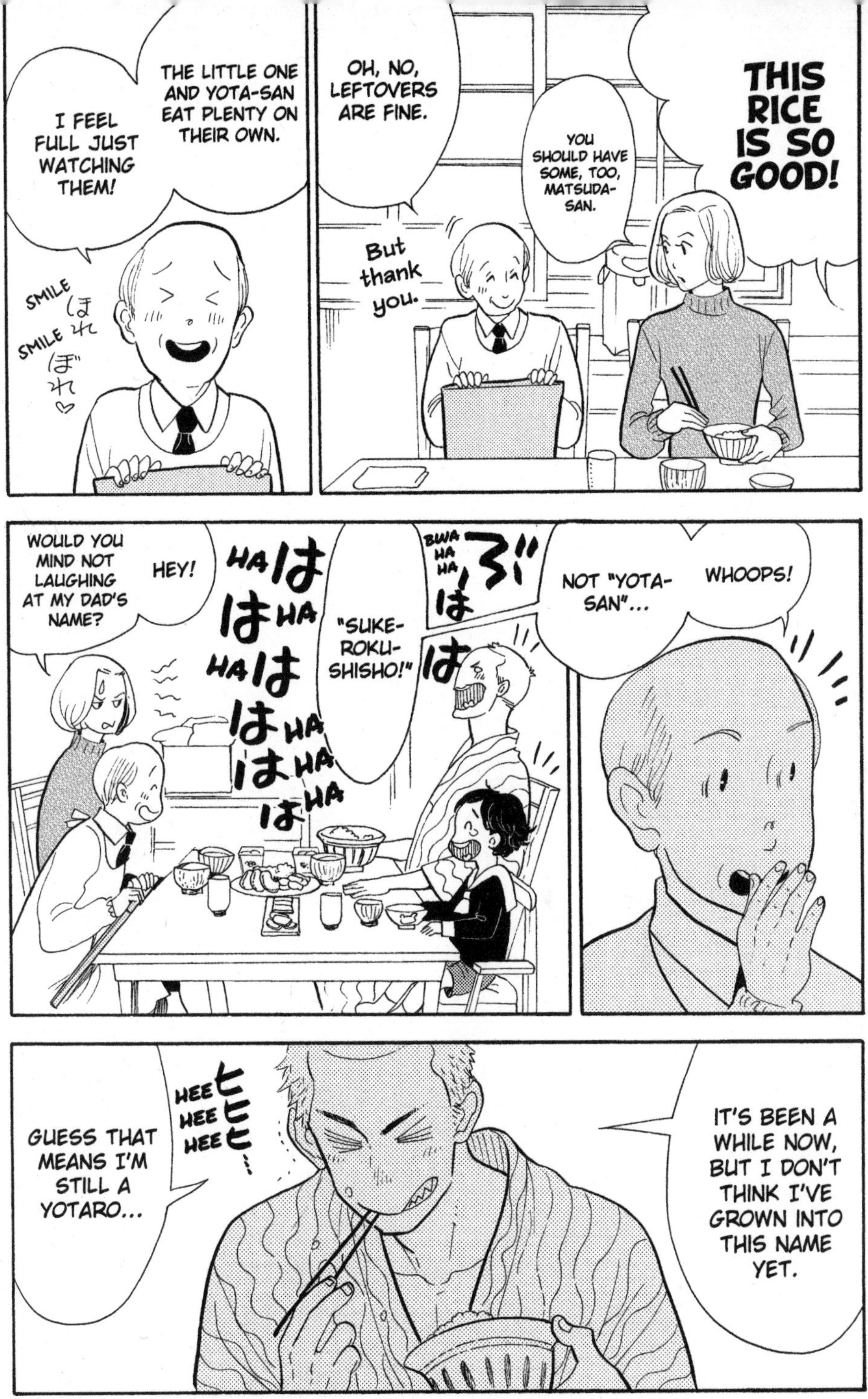
THIS RICE IS SO GOOD!
YOU SHOULD HAVE SOME, TOO, MATSUDA-SAN.
OH, NO, LEFTOVERS ARE FINE.
But thank you.
THE LITTLE ONE AND YOTA-SAN EAT PLENTY ON THEIR OWN.
I FEEL FULL JUST WATCHING THEM!
SMILE SMILE ほれぼれ♡
WHOOPS!
NOT "YOTA-SAN"...
BWA HA HA ぶはは
"SUKE-ROKU-SHISHO!"
HA HA HA HA HA HA ははははははは
HEY!
WOULD YOU MIND NOT LAUGHING AT MY DAD'S NAME?
IT'S BEEN A WHILE NOW, BUT I DON'T THINK I'VE GROWN INTO THIS NAME YET.
HEE HEE HEE ヒヒヒ...
GUESS THAT MEANS I'M STILL A YOTARO...

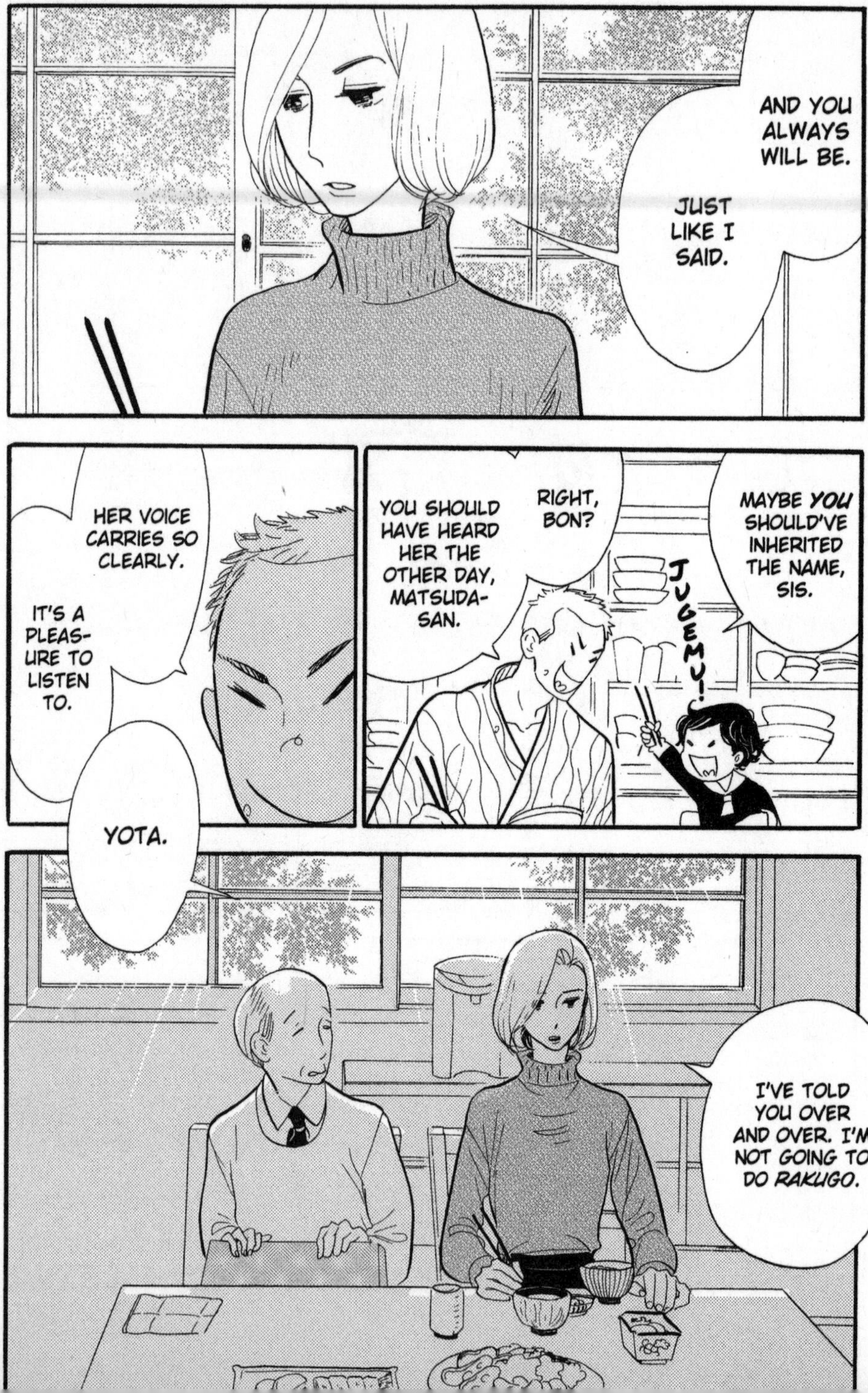
AND YOU ALWAYS WILL BE.
JUST LIKE I SAID.
MAYBE *YOU* SHOULD'VE INHERITED THE NAME, SIS.
JUGEMU!
RIGHT, BON?
YOU SHOULD HAVE HEARD HER THE OTHER DAY, MATSUDA-SAN.
HER VOICE CARRIES SO CLEARLY.
IT'S A PLEASURE TO LISTEN TO.
YOTA.
I'VE TOLD YOU OVER AND OVER. I'M NOT GOING TO DO *RAKUGO*.

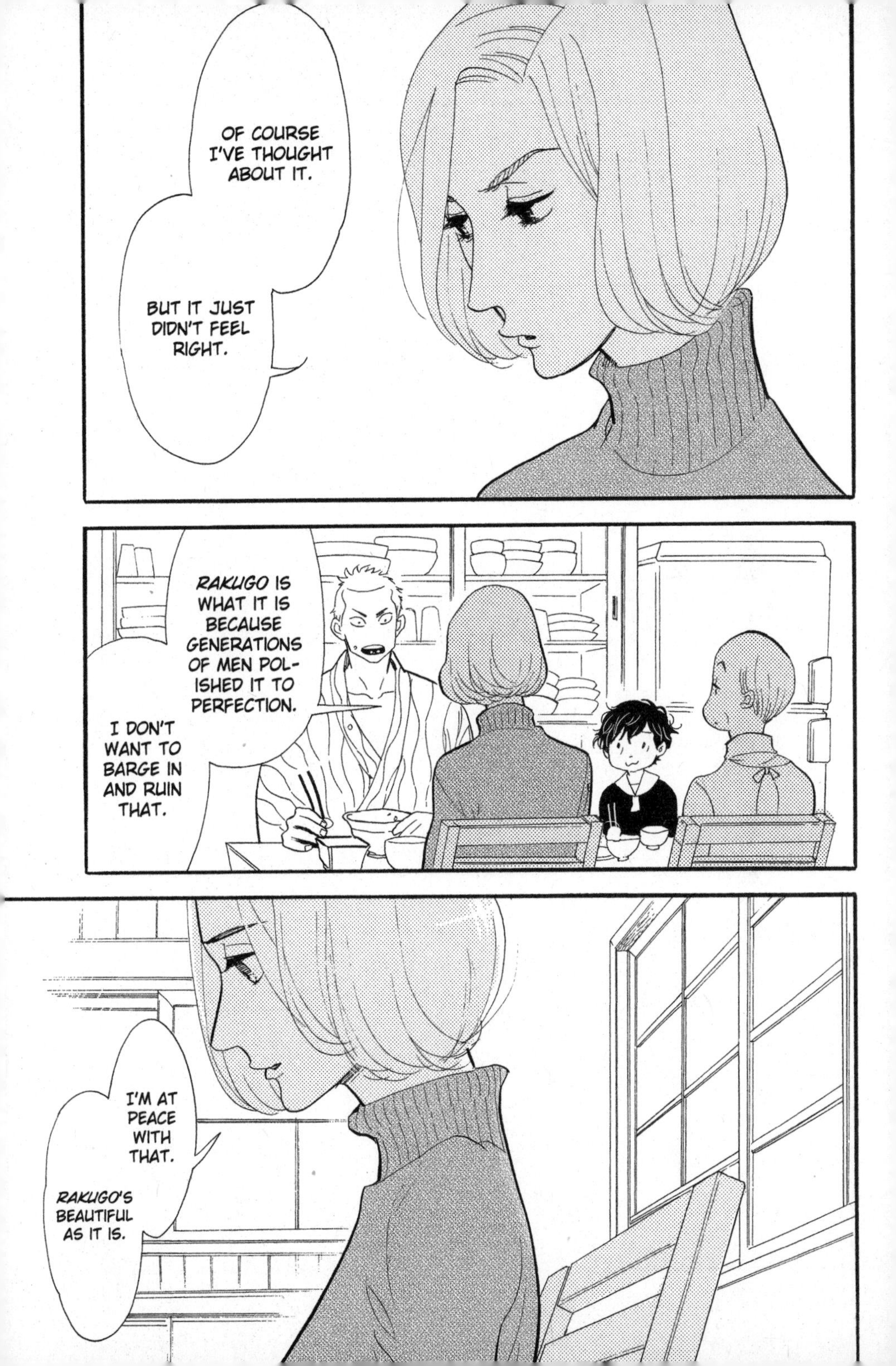
OF COURSE I'VE THOUGHT ABOUT IT.
BUT IT JUST DIDN'T FEEL RIGHT.
RAKUGO IS WHAT IT IS BECAUSE GENERATIONS OF MEN POL-ISHED IT TO PERFECTION.
I DON'T WANT TO BARGE IN AND RUIN THAT.
I'M AT PEACE WITH THAT.
RAKUGO'S BEAUTIFUL AS IT IS.

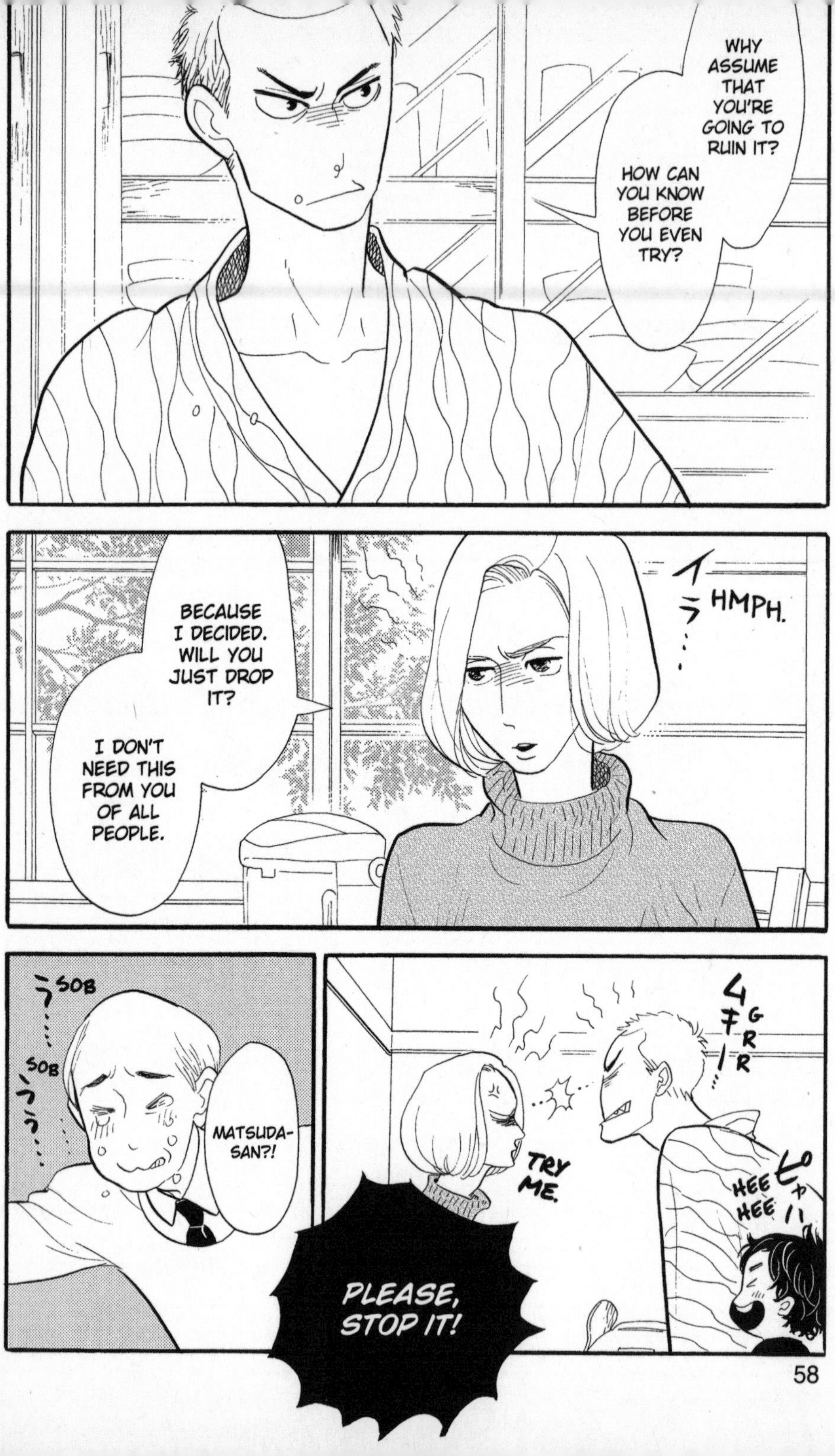
WHY ASSUME THAT YOU'RE GOING TO RUIN IT?
HOW CAN YOU KNOW BEFORE YOU EVEN TRY?
イラ…
HMPH.
BECAUSE I DECIDED. WILL YOU JUST DROP IT?
I DON'T NEED THIS FROM YOU OF ALL PEOPLE.
ムキー…
GRR
TRY ME.
ピャハ
HEE HEE
PLEASE, STOP IT!
う…
SOB
うう…
SOB
MATSUDA-SAN?!

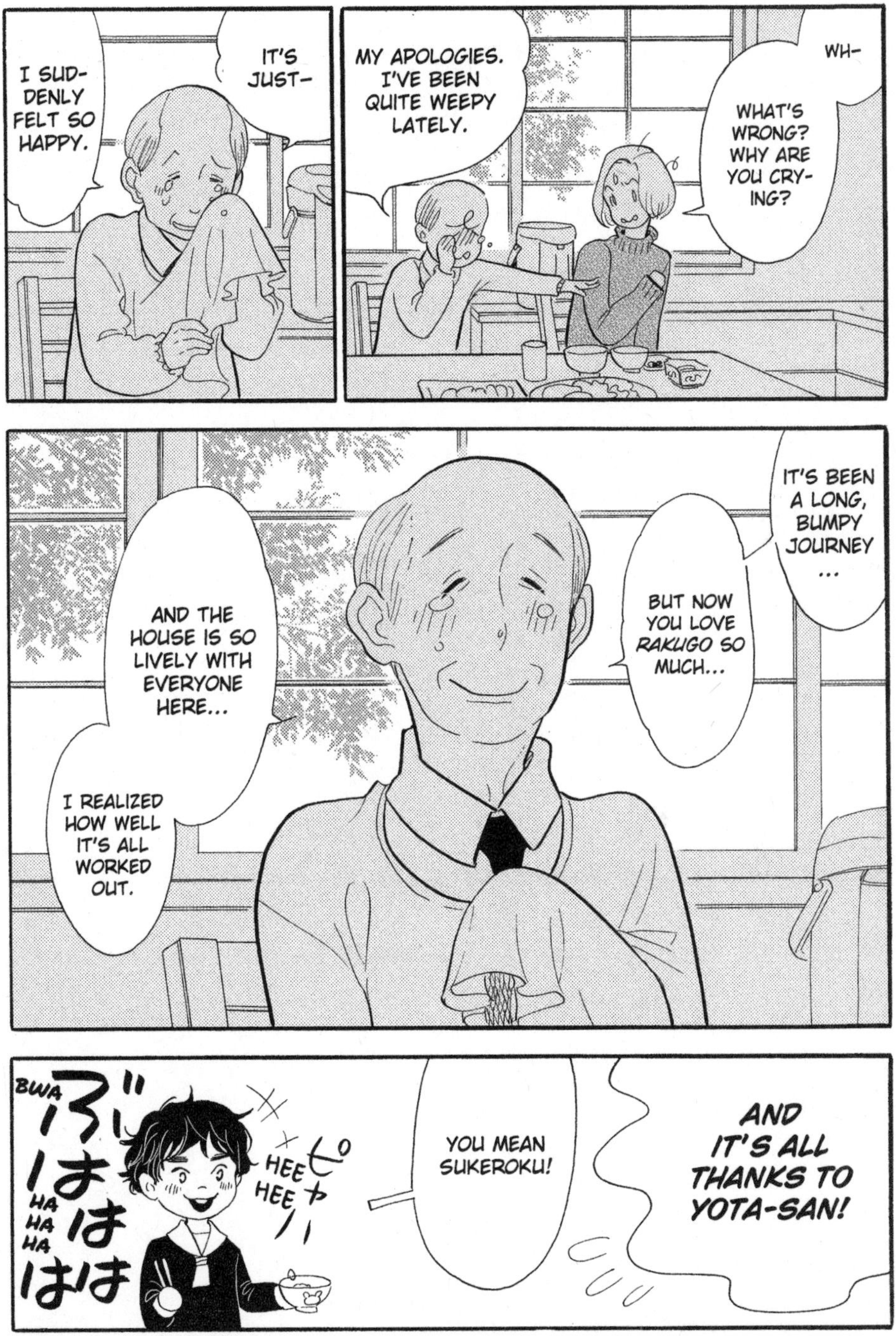
WH-
WHAT'S WRONG? WHY ARE YOU CRYING?
MY APOLOGIES. I'VE BEEN QUITE WEEPY LATELY.
IT'S JUST-
I SUDDENLY FELT SO HAPPY.
IT'S BEEN A LONG, BUMPY JOURNEY...
BUT NOW YOU LOVE RAKUGO SO MUCH...
AND THE HOUSE IS SO LIVELY WITH EVERYONE HERE...
I REALIZED HOW WELL IT'S ALL WORKED OUT.
AND IT'S ALL THANKS TO YOTA-SAN!
YOU MEAN SUKEROKU!
ピャハ HEE HEE
ぶははは BWA HA HA HA

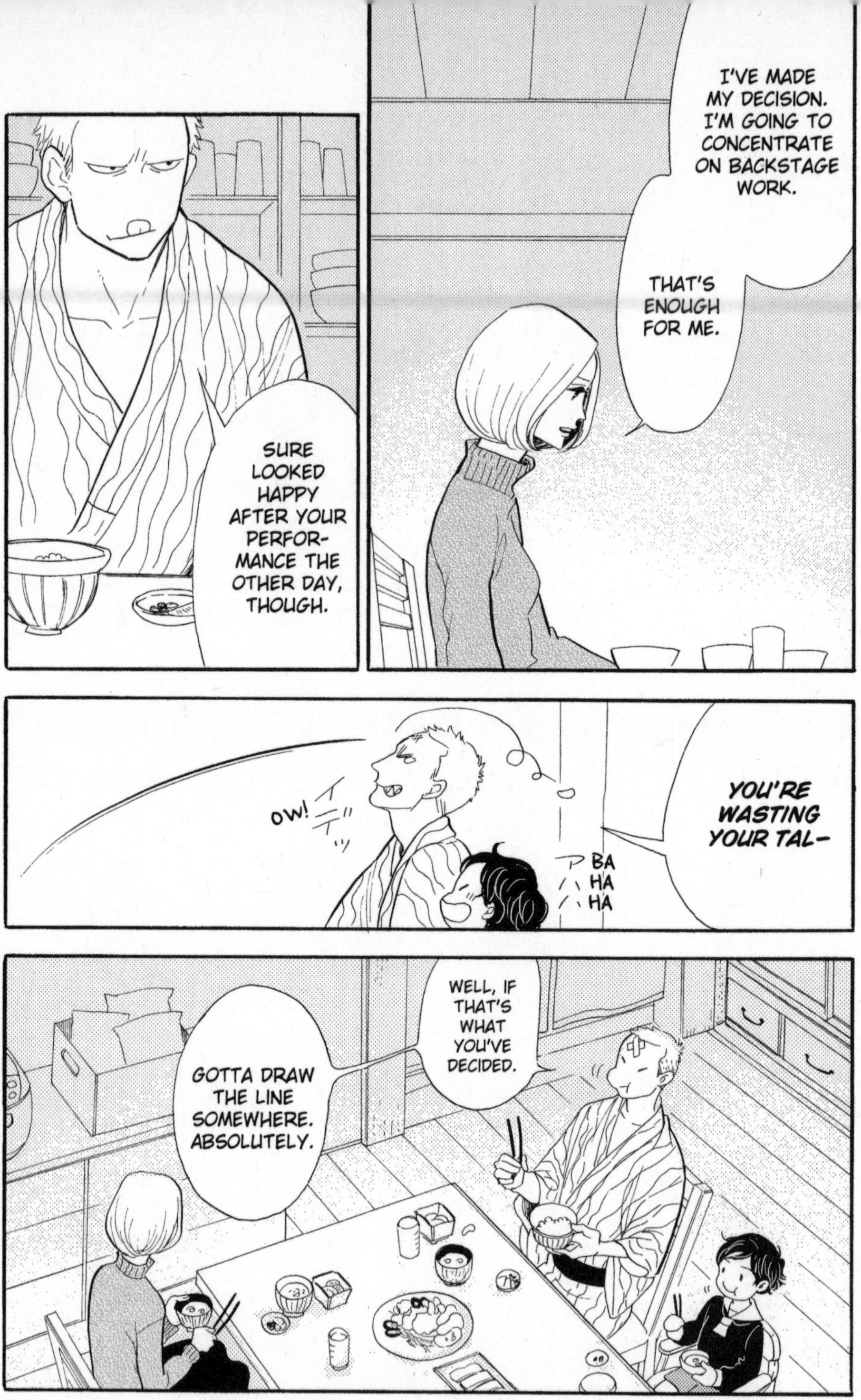
I'VE MADE MY DECISION. I'M GOING TO CONCENTRATE ON BACKSTAGE WORK.
THAT'S ENOUGH FOR ME.
SURE LOOKED HAPPY AFTER YOUR PERFORMANCE THE OTHER DAY, THOUGH.
YOU'RE WASTING YOUR TAL-
BA HA HA
OW!
WELL, IF THAT'S WHAT YOU'VE DECIDED.
GOTTA DRAW THE LINE SOMEWHERE. ABSOLUTELY.

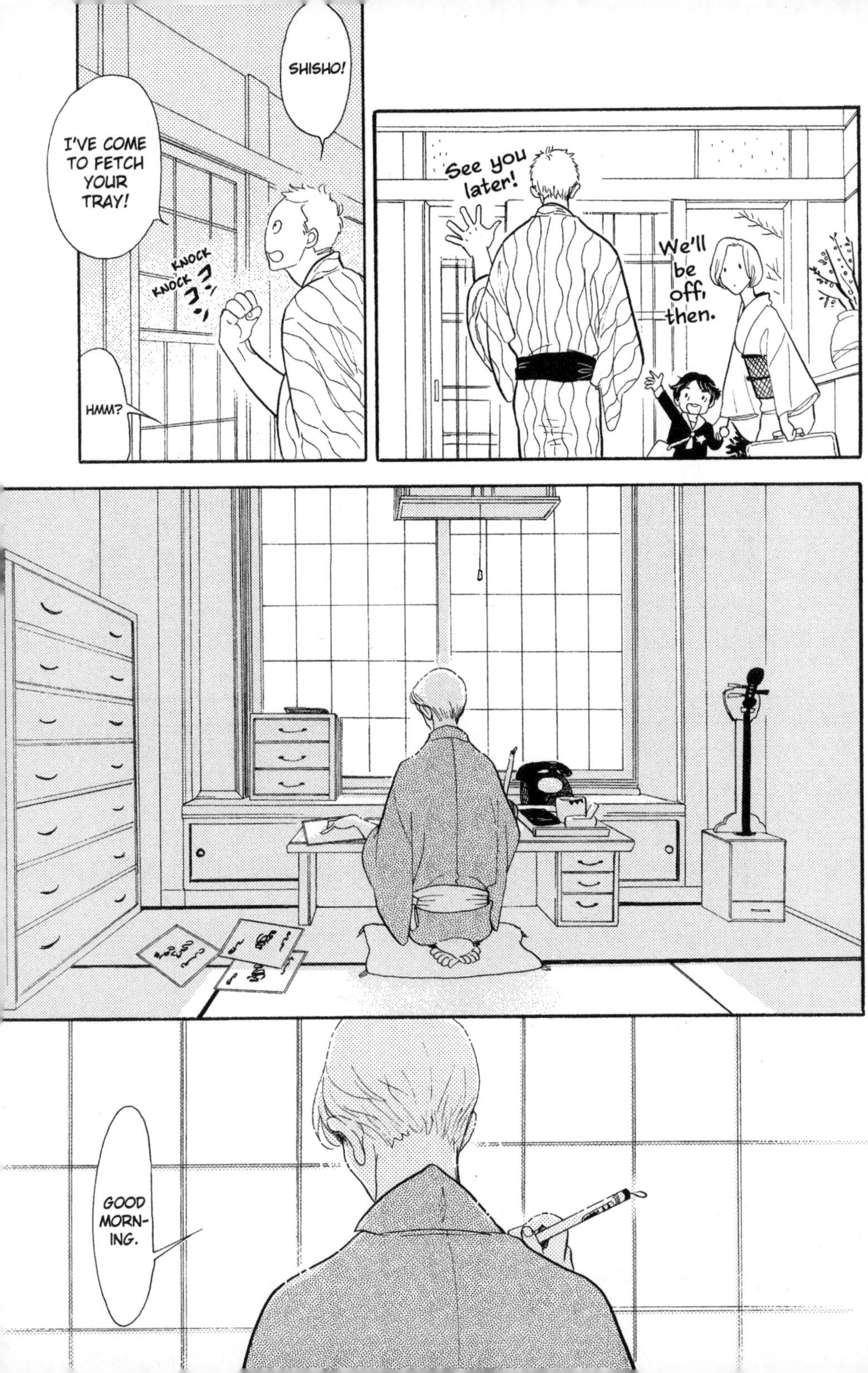
See you later!
We'll be off, then.
SHISHO!
I'VE COME TO FETCH YOUR TRAY!
KNOCK KNOCK
HMM?
GOOD MORNING.

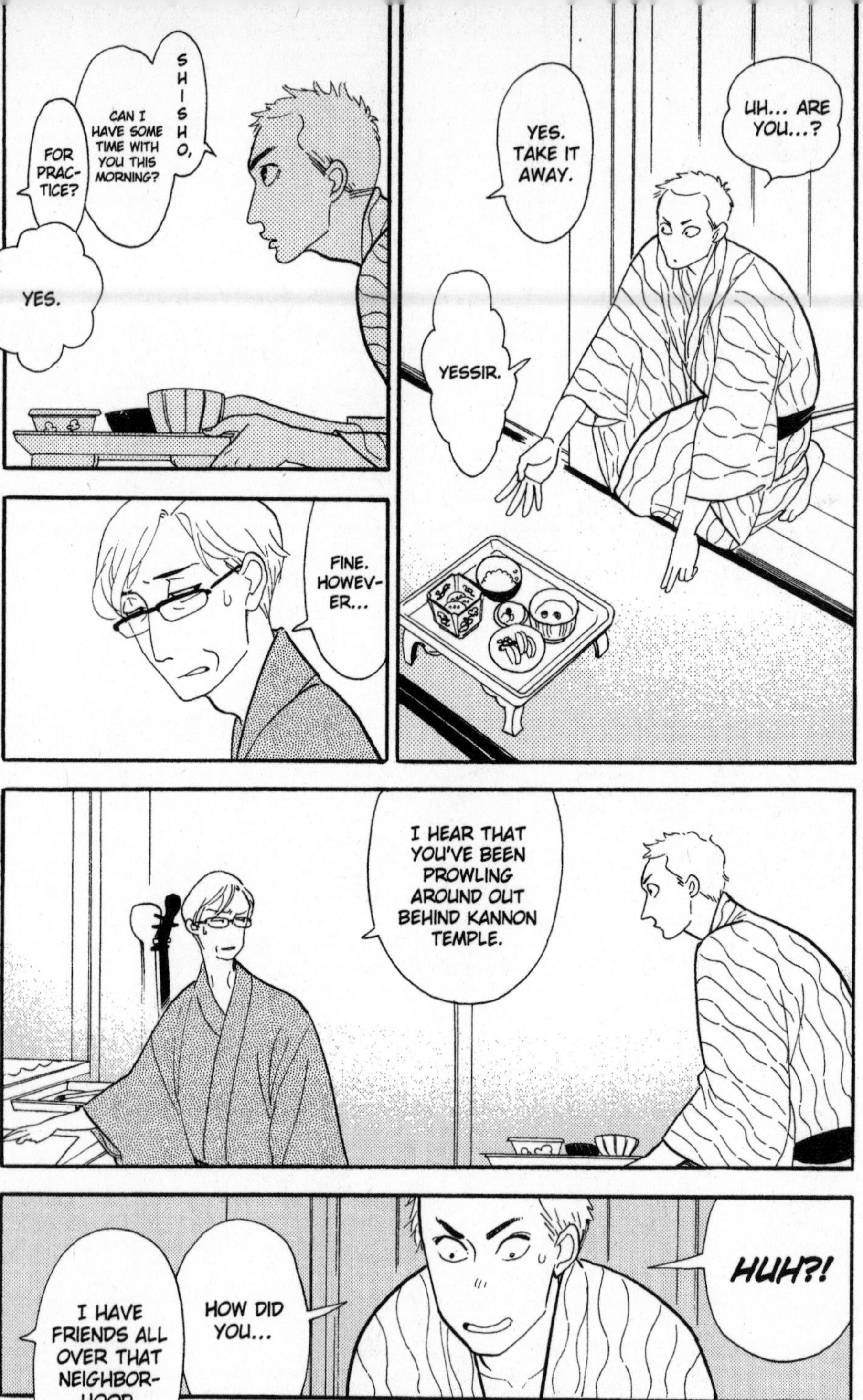

UH... ARE YOU...?
YES. TAKE IT AWAY.
YESSIR.
SHISHO, CAN I HAVE SOME TIME WITH YOU THIS MORNING?
FOR PRAC-TICE?
YES.
FINE. HOWEV-ER...
I HEAR THAT YOU'VE BEEN PROWLING AROUND OUT BEHIND KANNON TEMPLE.
HUH?!
HOW DID YOU...
I HAVE FRIENDS ALL OVER THAT NEIGHBOR-HOOD.

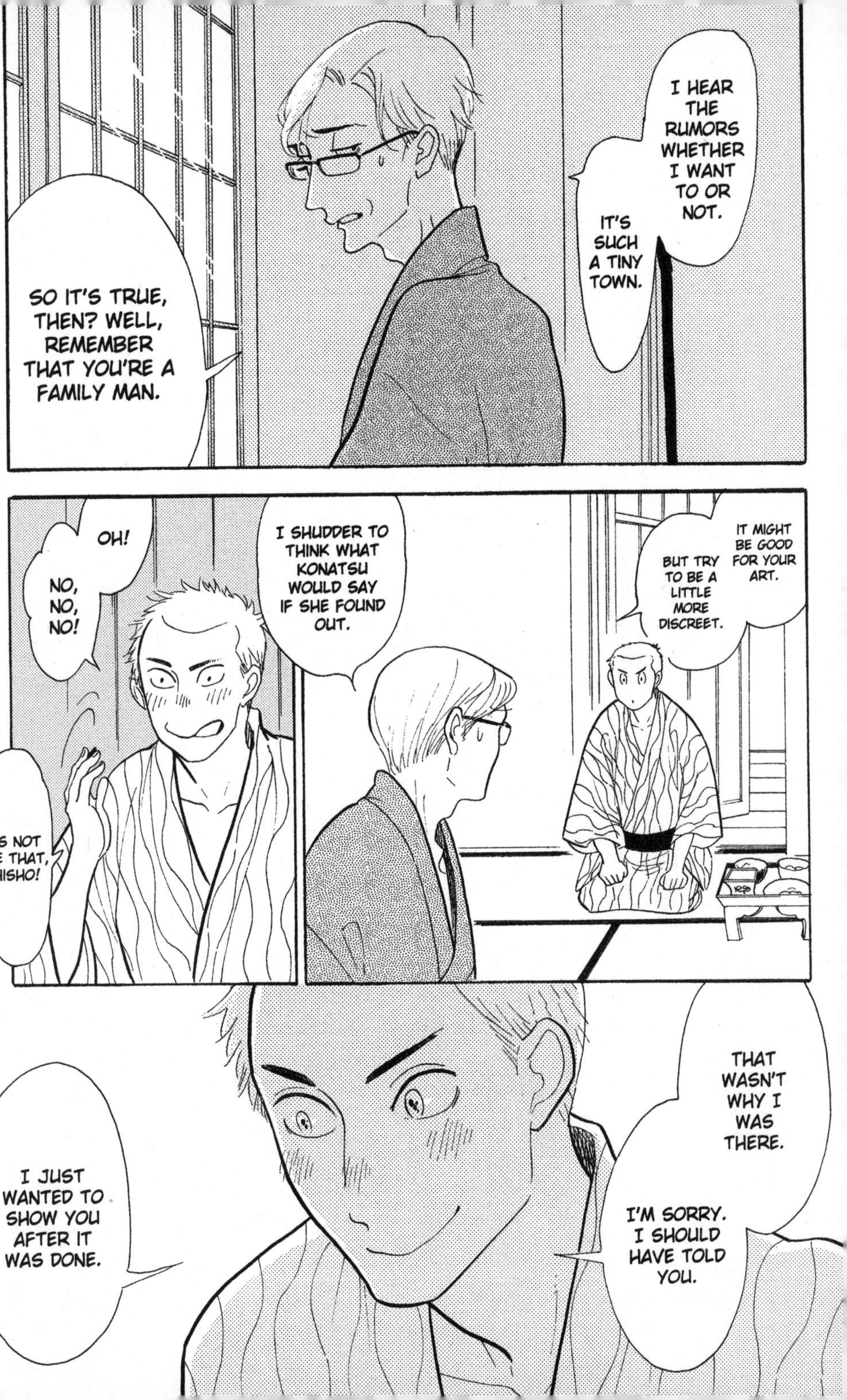
I HEAR THE RUMORS WHETHER I WANT TO OR NOT.
IT'S SUCH A TINY TOWN.
SO IT'S TRUE, THEN? WELL, REMEMBER THAT YOU'RE A FAMILY MAN.
IT MIGHT BE GOOD FOR YOUR ART.
BUT TRY TO BE A LITTLE MORE DISCREET.
I SHUDDER TO THINK WHAT KONATSU WOULD SAY IF SHE FOUND OUT.
OH!
NO, NO, NO!
IT'S NOT LIKE THAT, SHISHO!
THAT WASN'T WHY I WAS THERE.
I'M SORRY. I SHOULD HAVE TOLD YOU.
I JUST WANTED TO SHOW YOU AFTER IT WAS DONE.

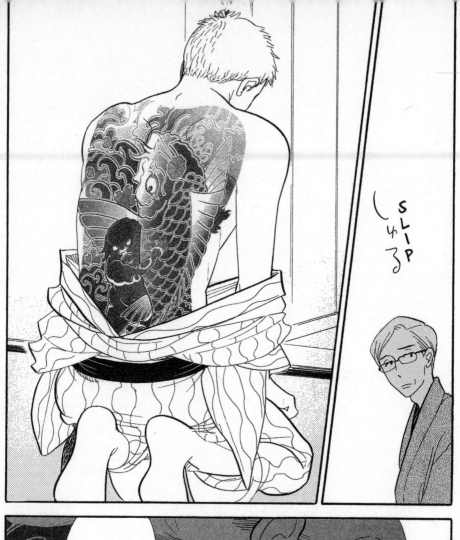

SLIP

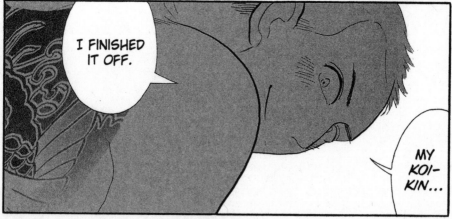

I FINISHED IT OFF.

MY KOI-KIN...

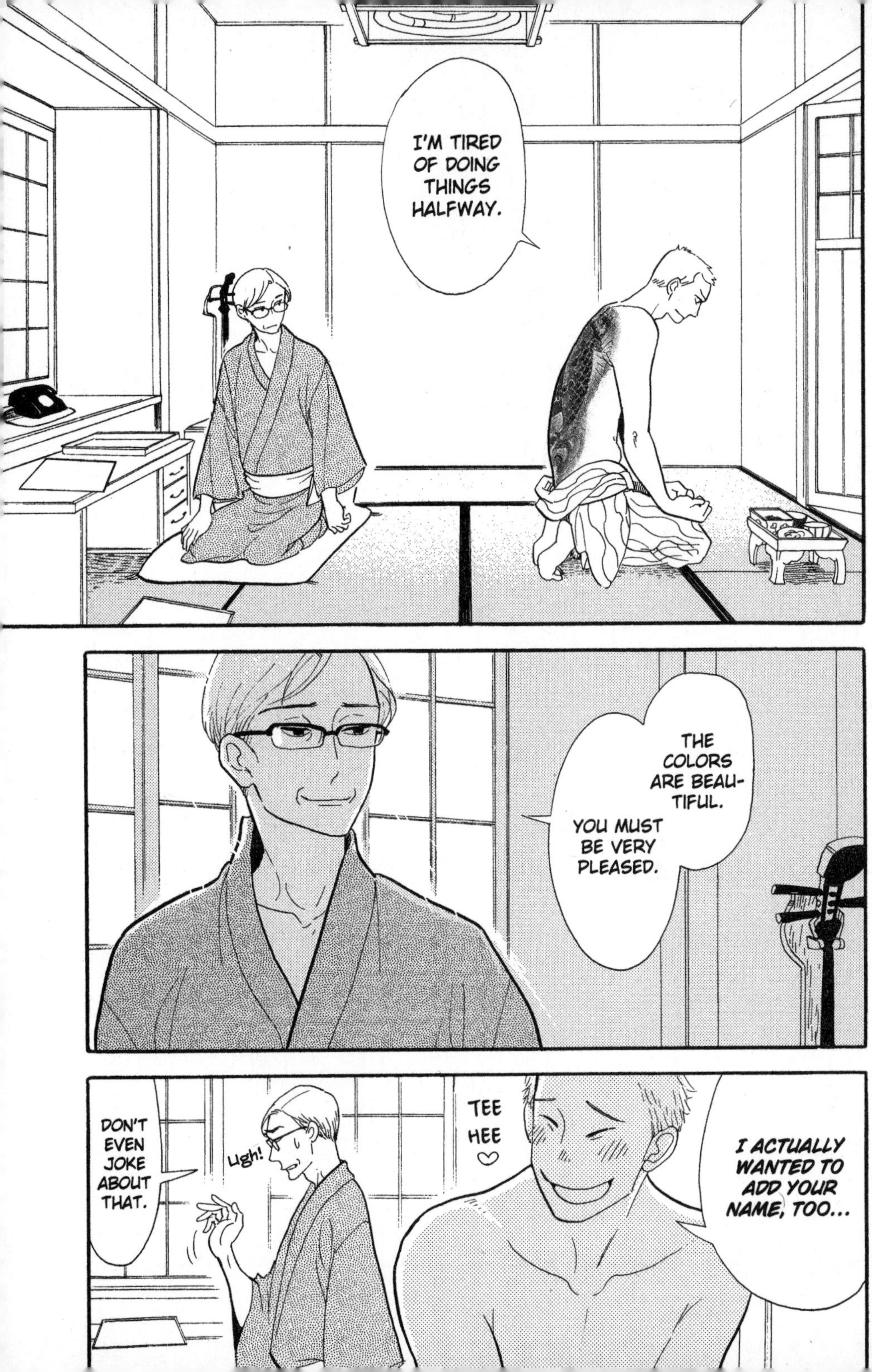
I'M TIRED OF DOING THINGS HALFWAY.
THE COLORS ARE BEAU-TIFUL.
YOU MUST BE VERY PLEASED.
I ACTUALLY WANTED TO ADD YOUR NAME, TOO...
TEE HEE ♡
Ugh!
DON'T EVEN JOKE ABOUT THAT.

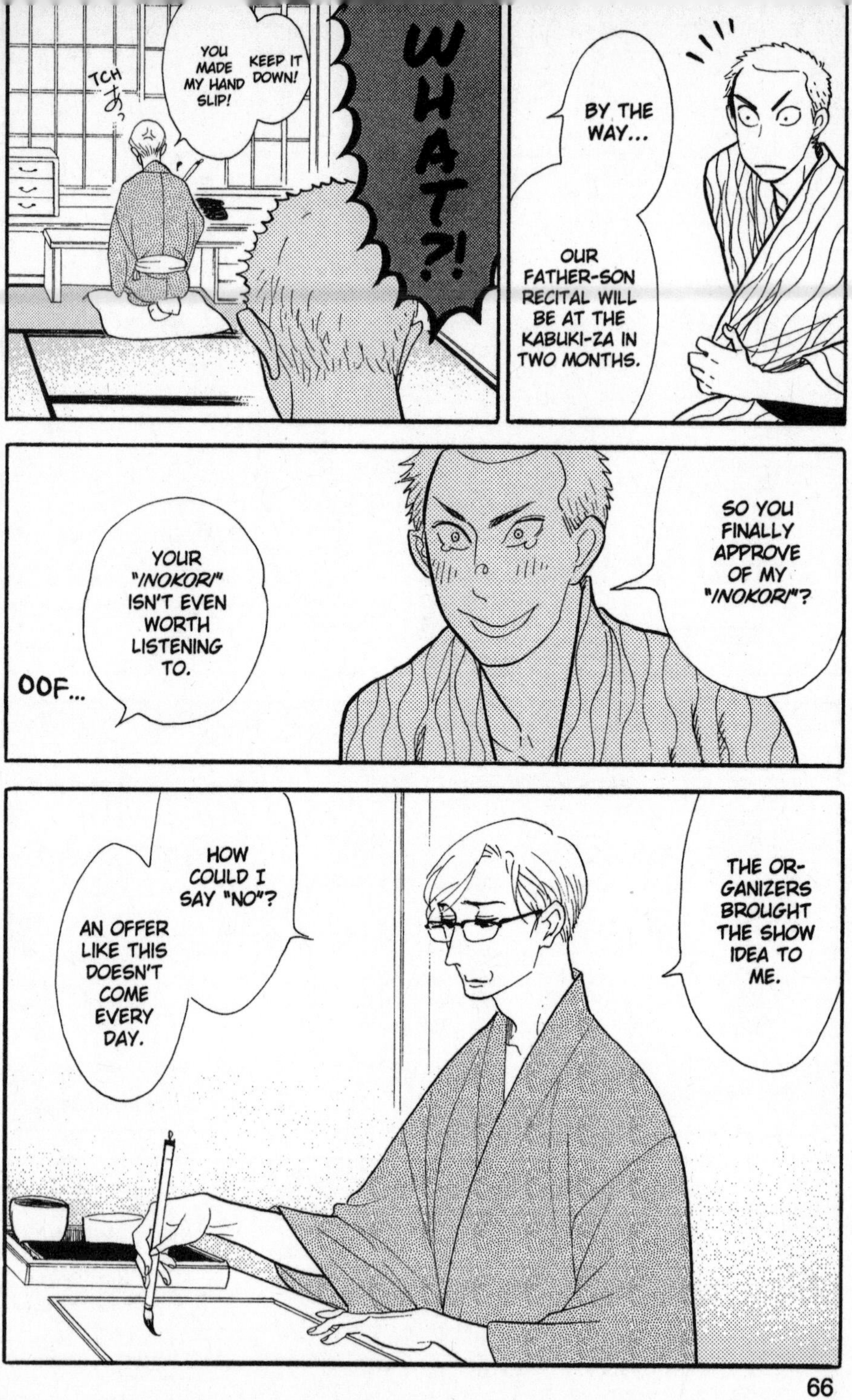
BY THE WAY...
OUR FATHER-SON RECITAL WILL BE AT THE KABUKI-ZA IN TWO MONTHS.
WHAT?!
KEEP IT DOWN!
YOU MADE MY HAND SLIP!
TCH あっ
SO YOU FINALLY APPROVE OF MY "*INOKORI*"?
YOUR "*INOKORI*" ISN'T EVEN WORTH LISTENING TO.
OOF...
THE OR-GANIZERS BROUGHT THE SHOW IDEA TO ME.
HOW COULD I SAY "NO"?
AN OFFER LIKE THIS DOESN'T COME EVERY DAY.

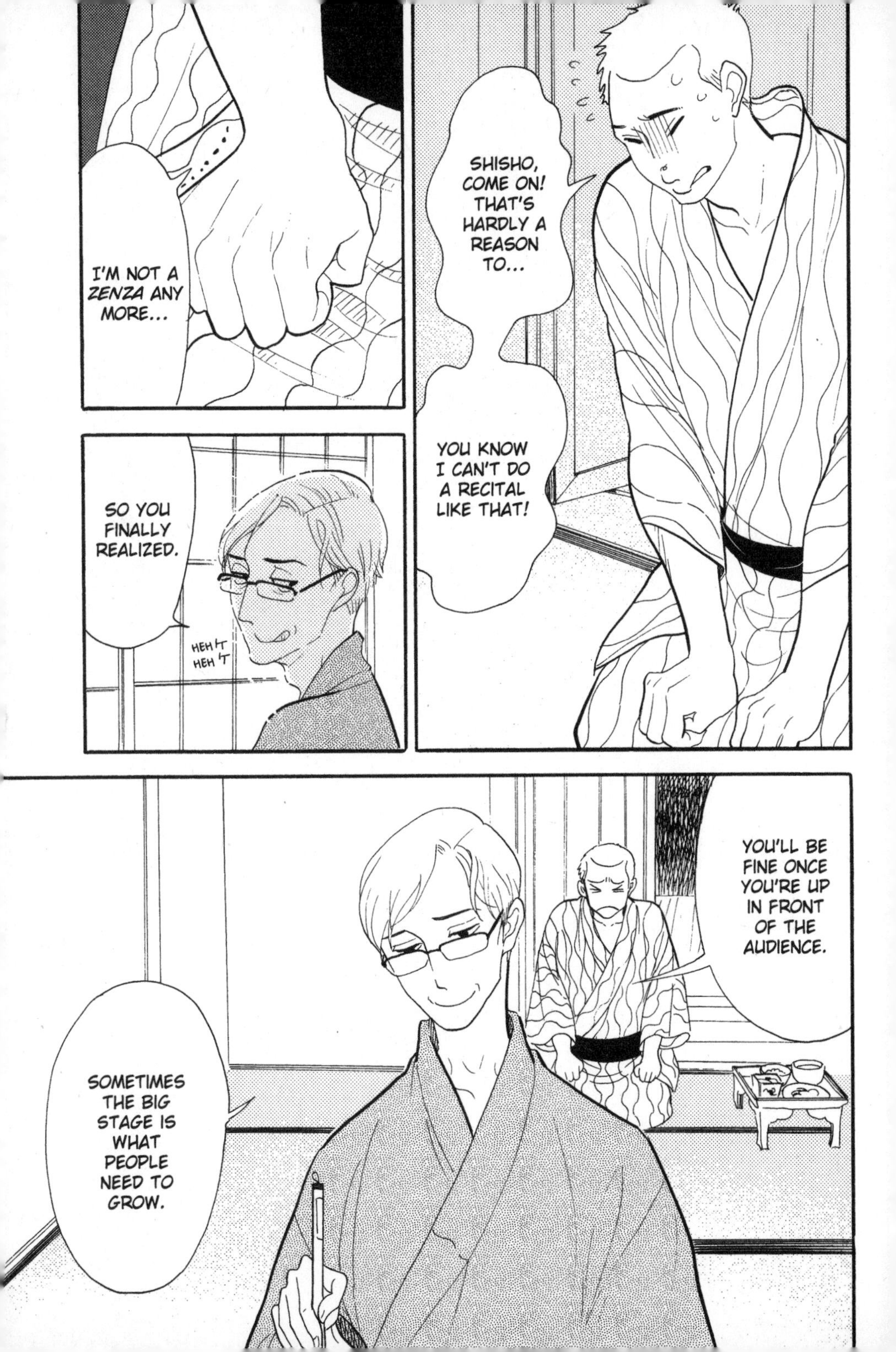
SHISHO, COME ON! THAT'S HARDLY A REASON TO...
YOU KNOW I CAN'T DO A RECITAL LIKE THAT!
I'M NOT A ZENZA ANY MORE...
SO YOU FINALLY REALIZED.
HEH HEH
YOU'LL BE FINE ONCE YOU'RE UP IN FRONT OF THE AUDIENCE.
SOMETIMES THE BIG STAGE IS WHAT PEOPLE NEED TO GROW.

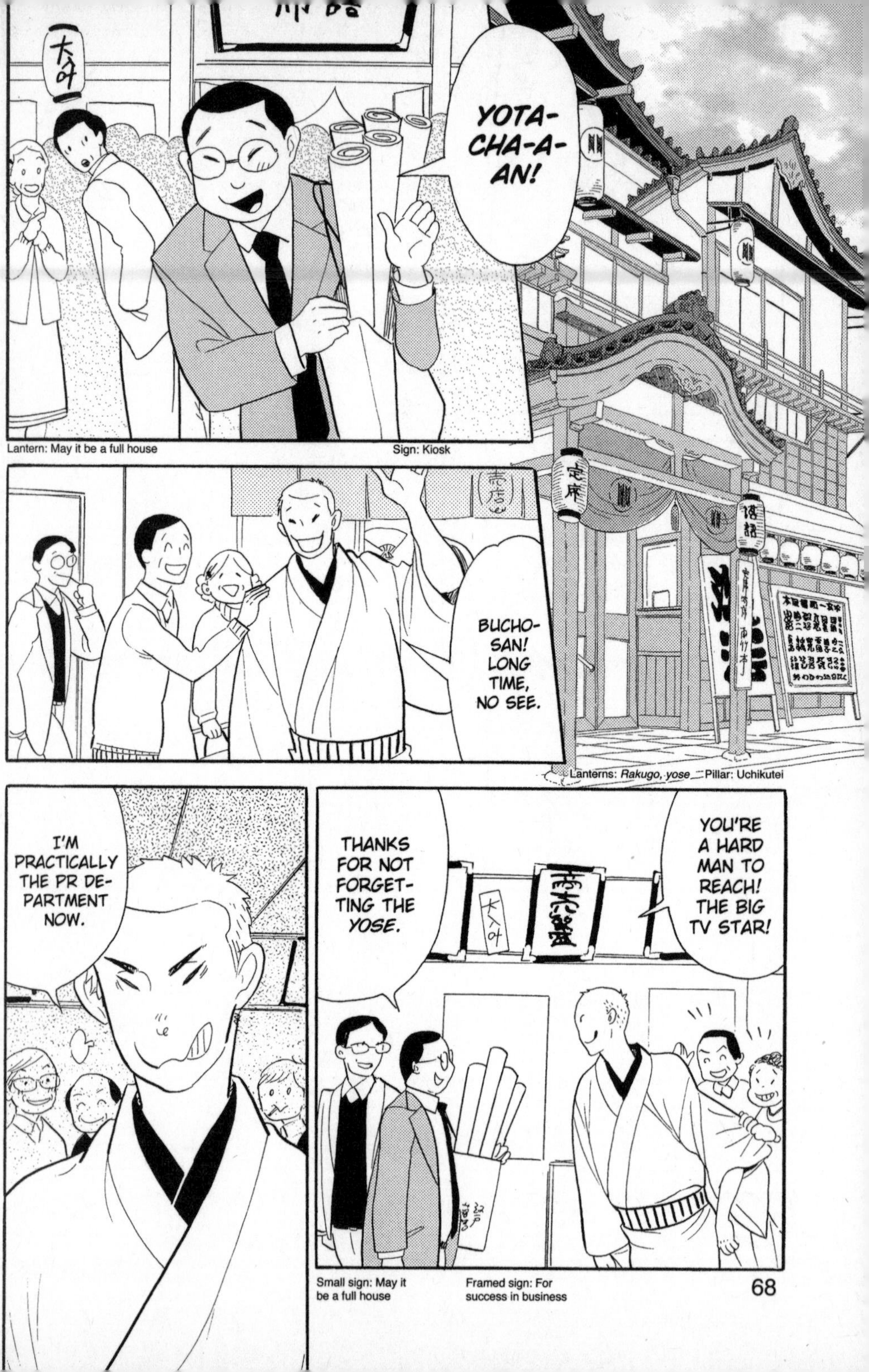
YOTA-CHA-A-AN!
BUCHO-SAN! LONG TIME, NO SEE.
YOU'RE A HARD MAN TO REACH! THE BIG TV STAR!
THANKS FOR NOT FORGETTING THE *YOSE*.
I'M PRACTICALLY THE PR DEPARTMENT NOW.

Lanterns: *Rakugo*, *yose* Pillar: Uchikutei

Lantern: May it be a full house Sign: Kiosk

Small sign: May it be a full house Framed sign: For success in business

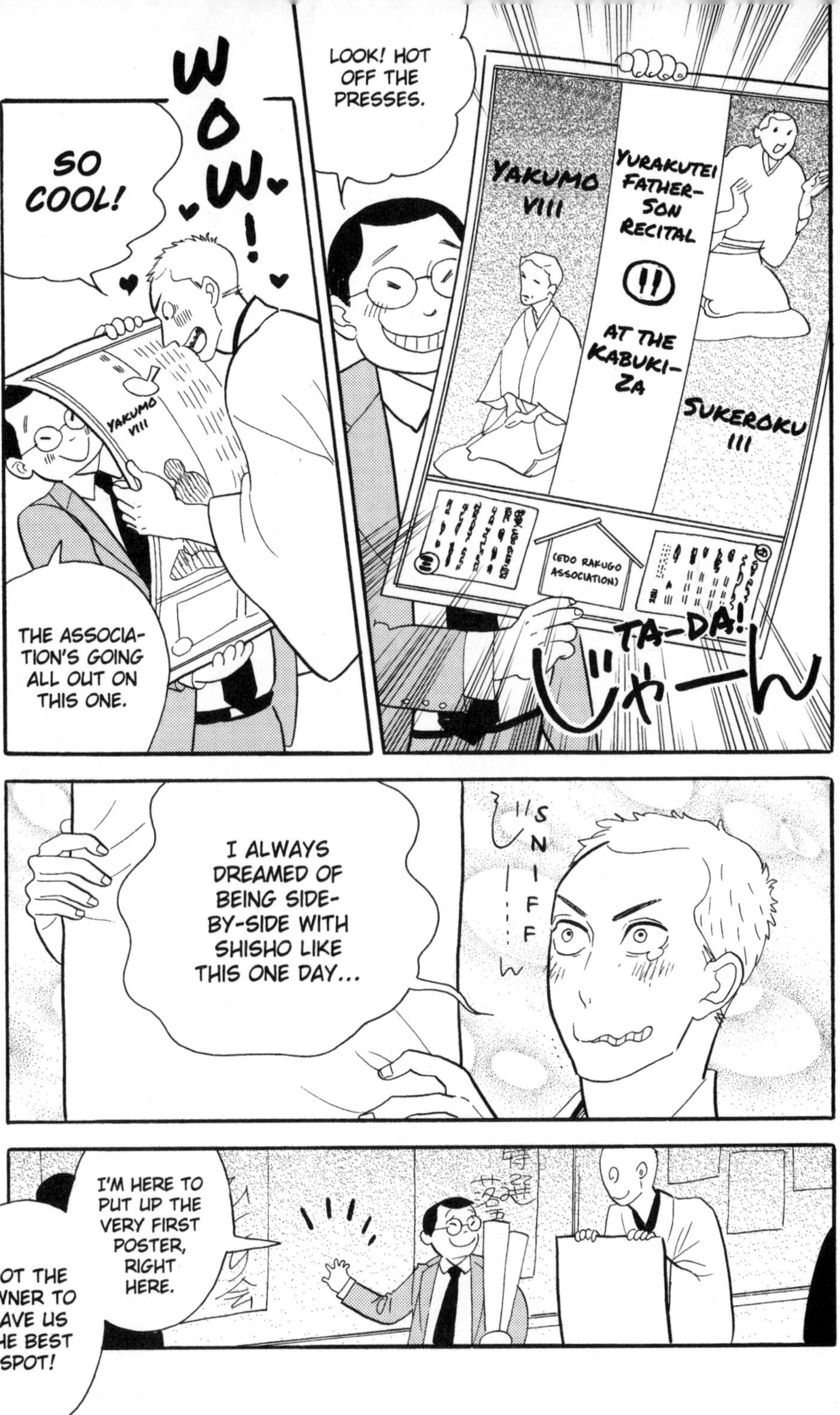
LOOK! HOT OFF THE PRESSES.
YAKUMO VIII
YURAKUTEI FATHER-SON RECITAL
!!
AT THE KABUKI-ZA
SUKEROKU III
(EDO RAKUGO ASSOCIATION)
TA-DA!
じゃーん
WOW!
SO COOL!
YAKUMO VIII
THE ASSOCIATION'S GOING ALL OUT ON THIS ONE.
SNIFF
I ALWAYS DREAMED OF BEING SIDE-BY-SIDE WITH SHISHO LIKE THIS ONE DAY...
I'M HERE TO PUT UP THE VERY FIRST POSTER, RIGHT HERE.
GOT THE OWNER TO SAVE US THE BEST SPOT!

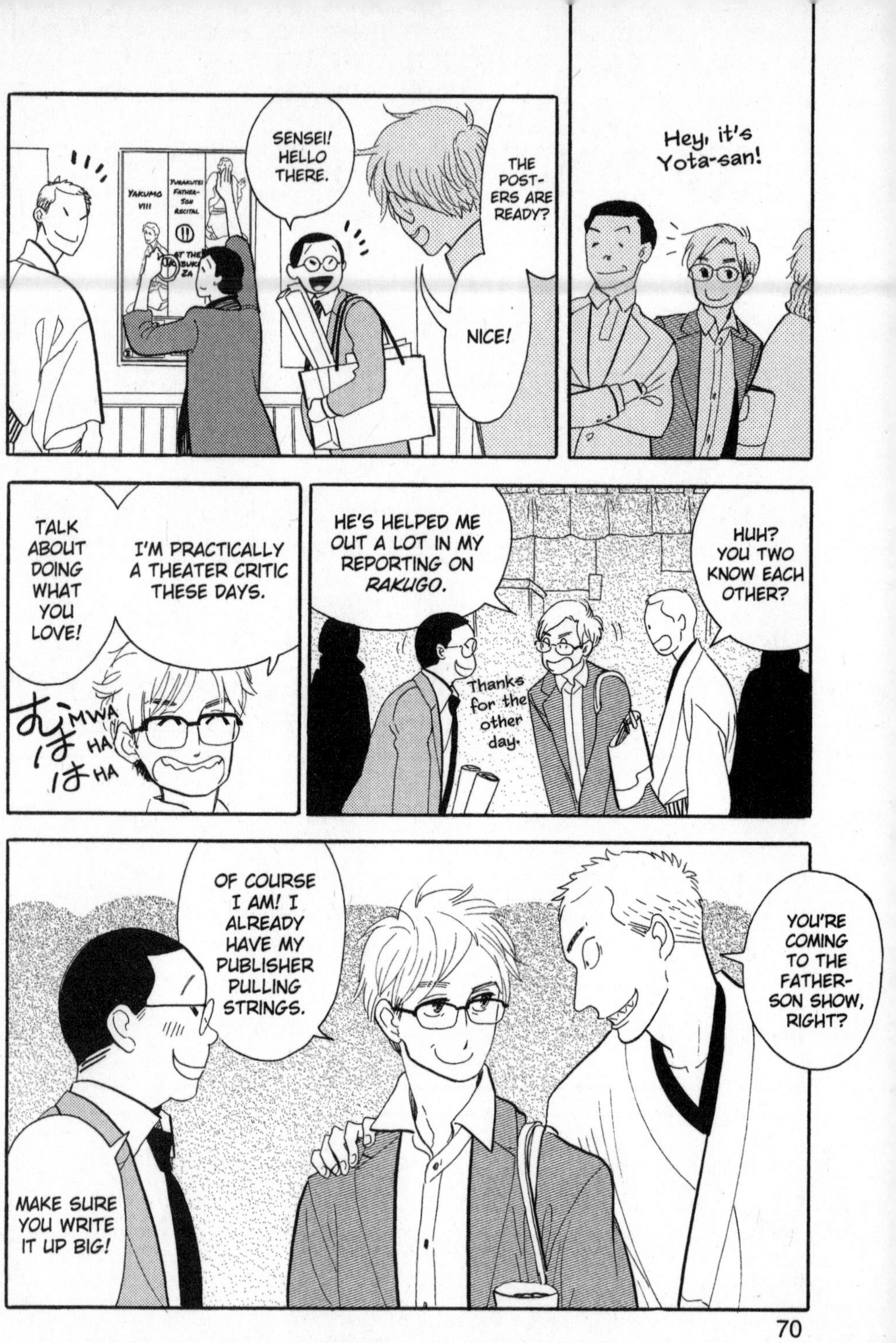
Hey, it's Yota-san!
THE POST-ERS ARE READY?
SENSEI! HELLO THERE.
YAKUMO VIII
YURAKUTEI FATHER-SON RECITAL
NICE!
HUH? YOU TWO KNOW EACH OTHER?
HE'S HELPED ME OUT A LOT IN MY REPORTING ON *RAKUGO*.
Thanks for the other day.
I'M PRACTICALLY A THEATER CRITIC THESE DAYS.
TALK ABOUT DOING WHAT YOU LOVE!
むははは MWA HA HA
YOU'RE COMING TO THE FATHER-SON SHOW, RIGHT?
OF COURSE I AM! I ALREADY HAVE MY PUBLISHER PULLING STRINGS.
MAKE SURE YOU WRITE IT UP BIG!

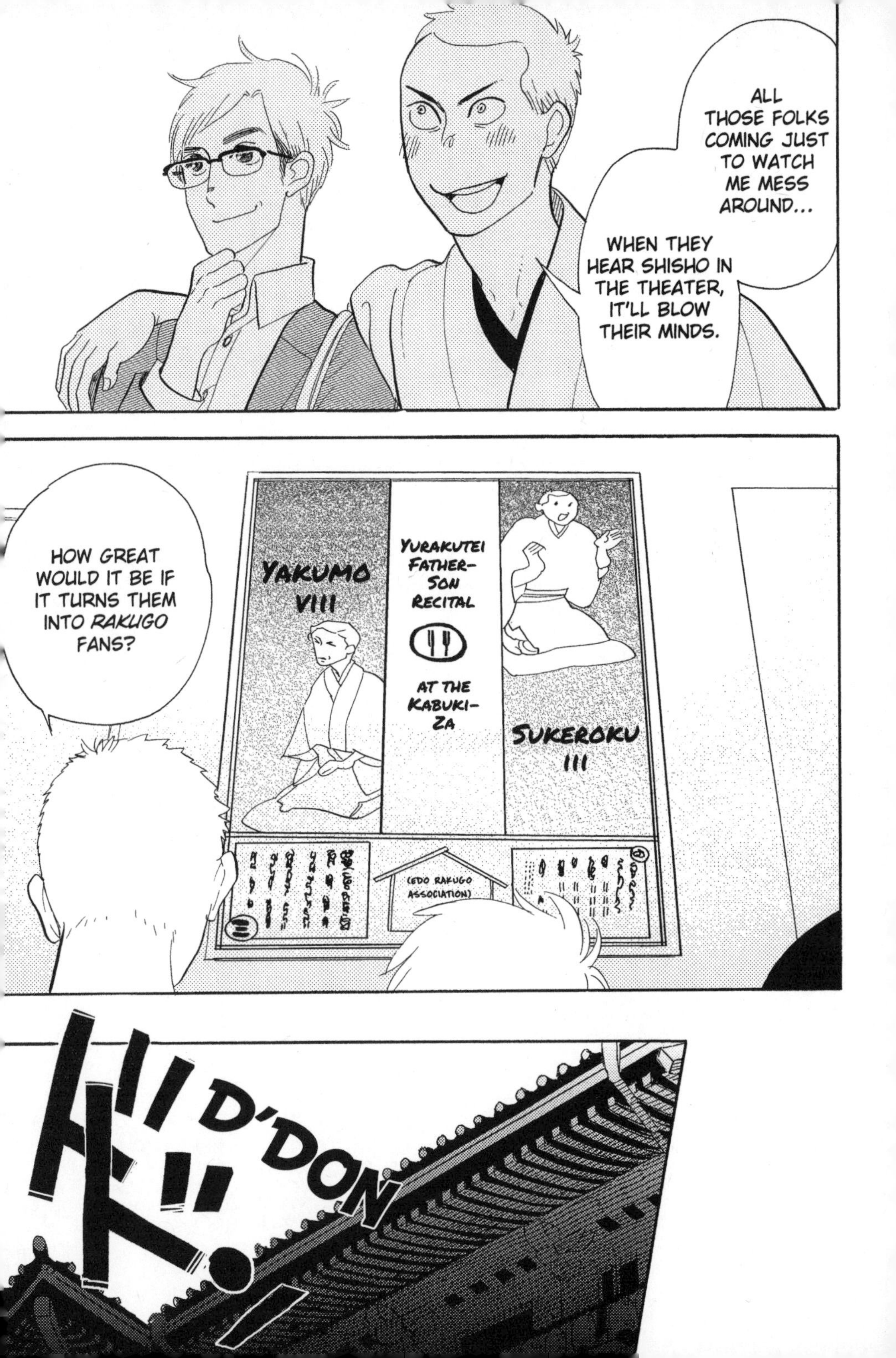
ALL THOSE FOLKS COMING JUST TO WATCH ME MESS AROUND...
WHEN THEY HEAR SHISHO IN THE THEATER, IT'LL BLOW THEIR MINDS.
Yurakutei Father-Son Recital
at the Kabuki-Za
Yakumo VIII
Sukeroku III
(EDO RAKUGO ASSOCIATION)
HOW GREAT WOULD IT BE IF IT TURNS THEM INTO RAKUGO FANS?
D'DON

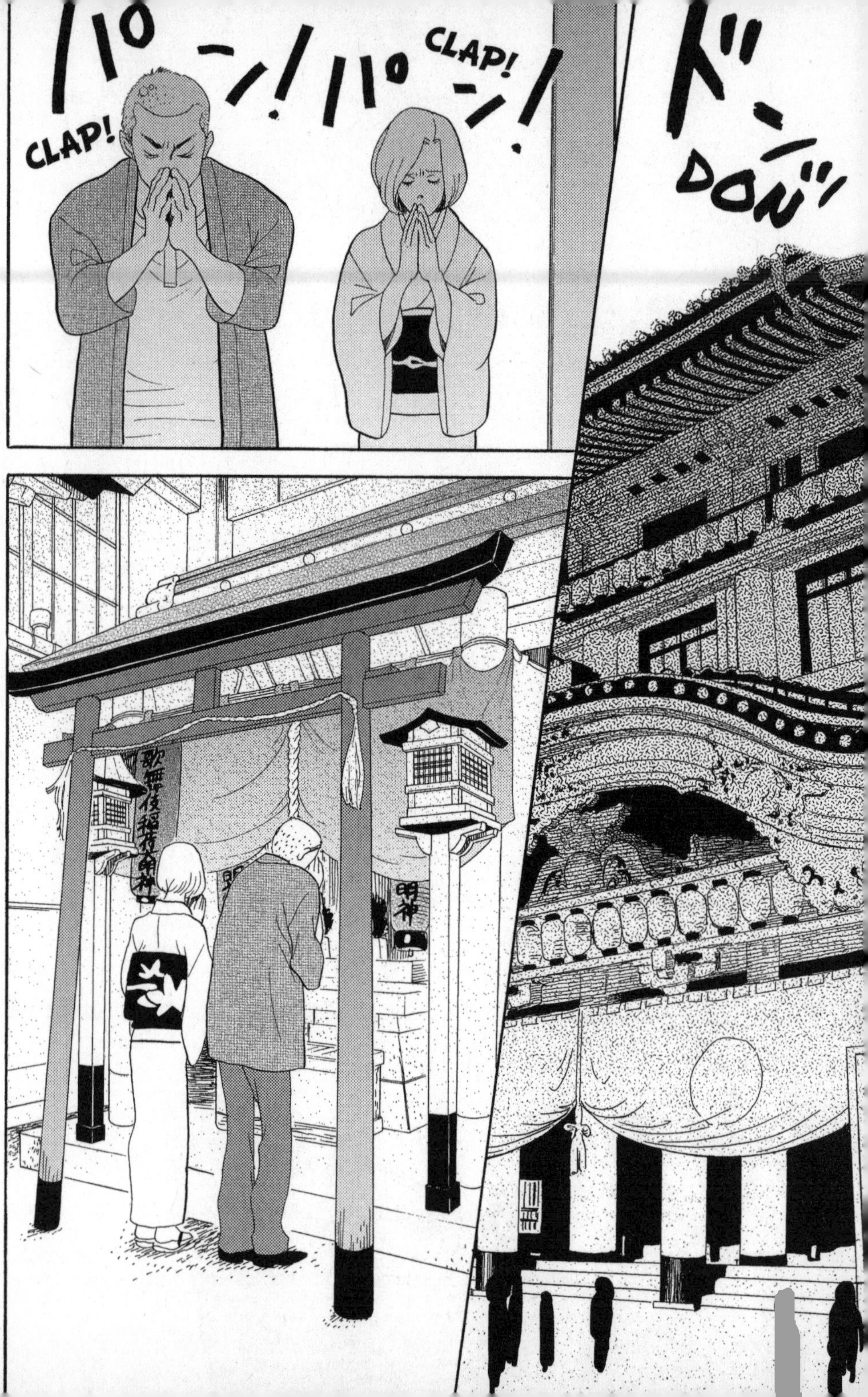
ドーン
DON
パーン!
CLAP!
パーン!
CLAP!

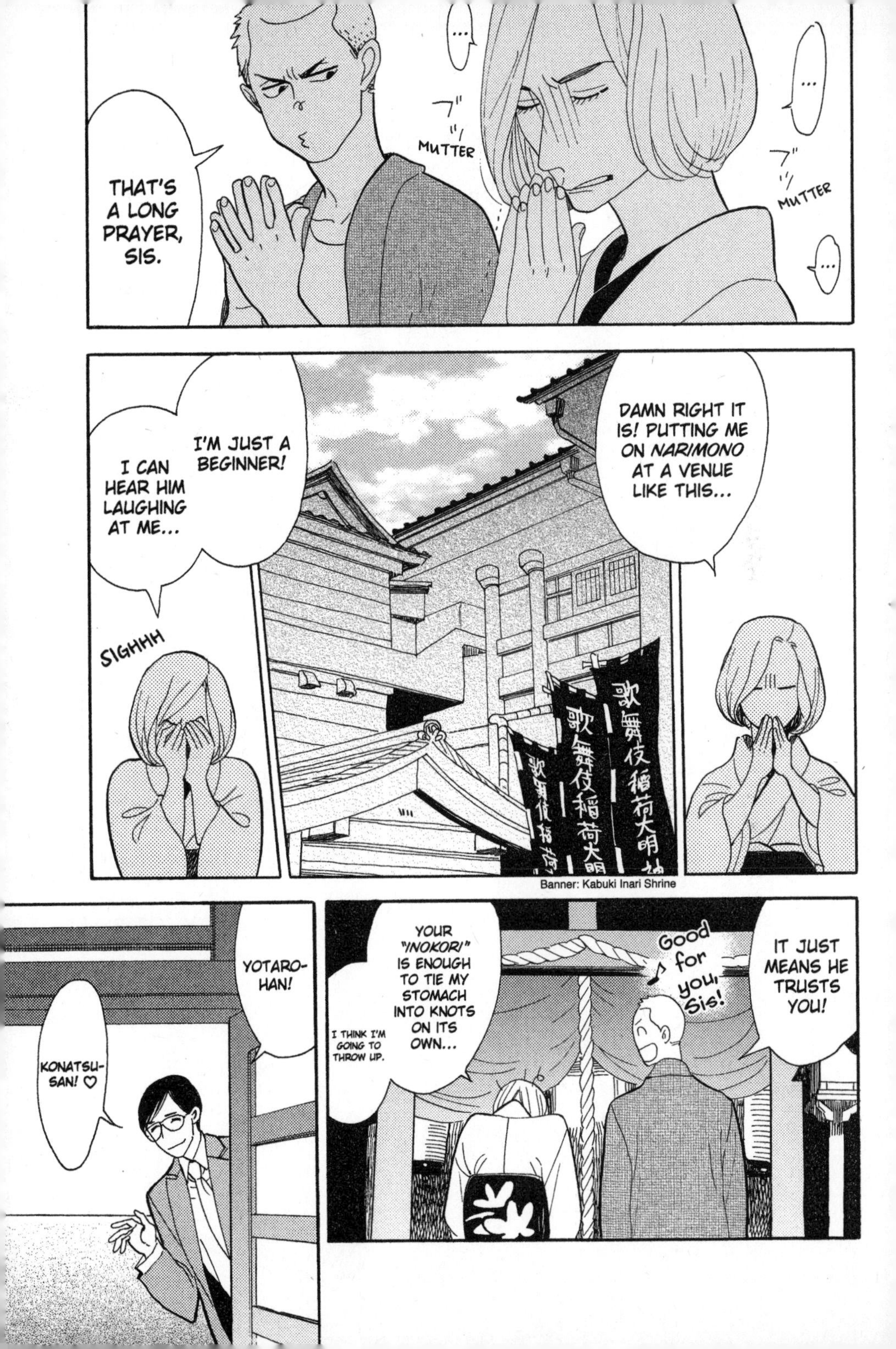
...
MUTTER
...
...
MUTTER
THAT'S A LONG PRAYER, SIS.
DAMN RIGHT IT IS! PUTTING ME ON *NARIMONO* AT A VENUE LIKE THIS...
歌舞伎稲荷大明神
Banner: Kabuki Inari Shrine
I'M JUST A BEGINNER!
I CAN HEAR HIM LAUGHING AT ME...
SIGHHH
IT JUST MEANS HE TRUSTS YOU!
Good for you, Sis!
YOUR *"INOKORI"* IS ENOUGH TO TIE MY STOMACH INTO KNOTS ON ITS OWN...
I THINK I'M GOING TO THROW UP.
YOTARO-HAN!
KONATSU-SAN! ♡

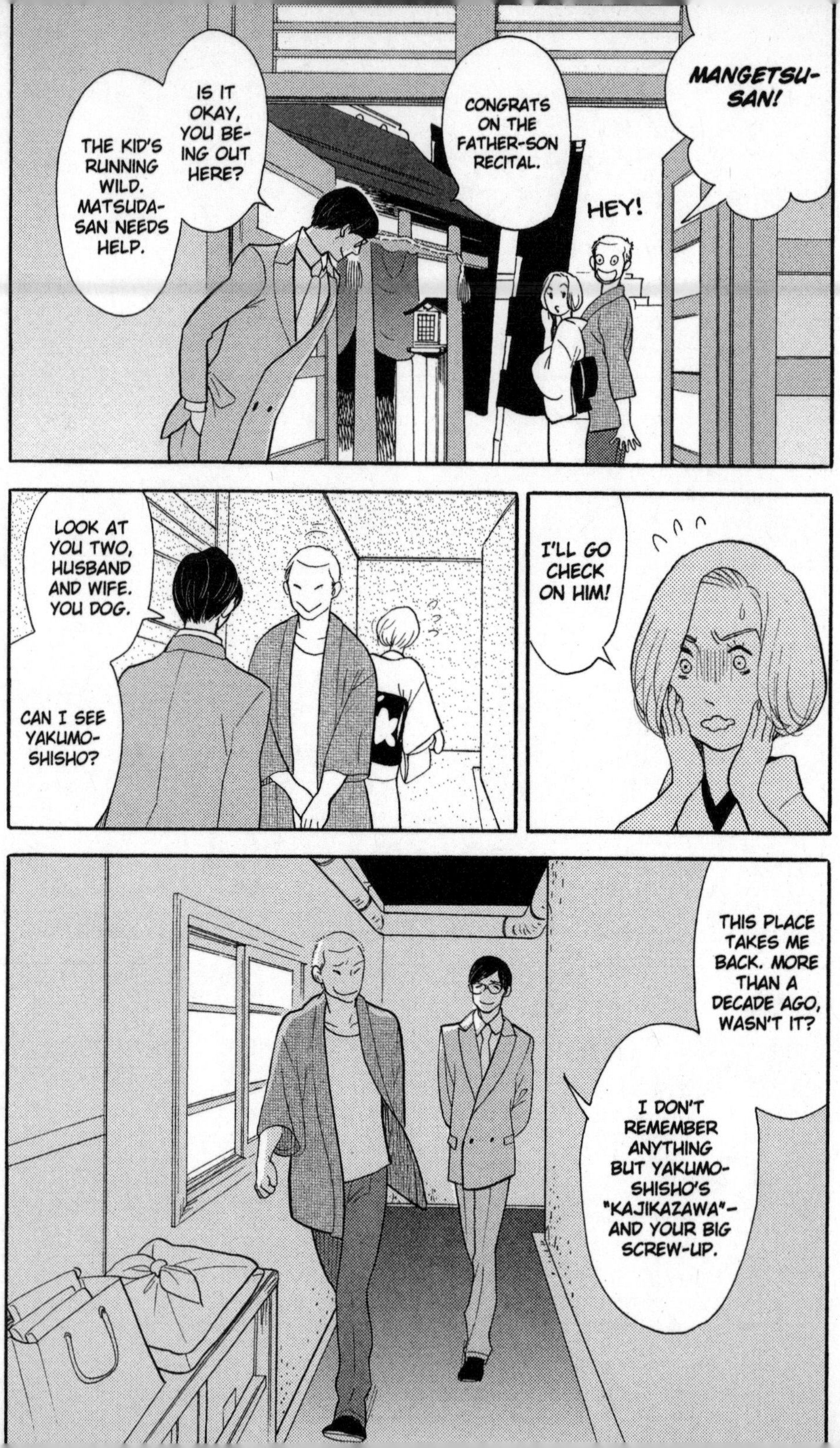
MANGETSU-SAN!
HEY!
CONGRATS ON THE FATHER-SON RECITAL.
IS IT OKAY, YOU BEING OUT HERE?
THE KID'S RUNNING WILD. MATSUDA-SAN NEEDS HELP.
I'LL GO CHECK ON HIM!
LOOK AT YOU TWO, HUSBAND AND WIFE. YOU DOG.
CAN I SEE YAKUMO-SHISHO?
THIS PLACE TAKES ME BACK. MORE THAN A DECADE AGO, WASN'T IT?
I DON'T REMEMBER ANYTHING BUT YAKUMO-SHISHO'S "KAJIKAZAWA"—AND YOUR BIG SCREW-UP.

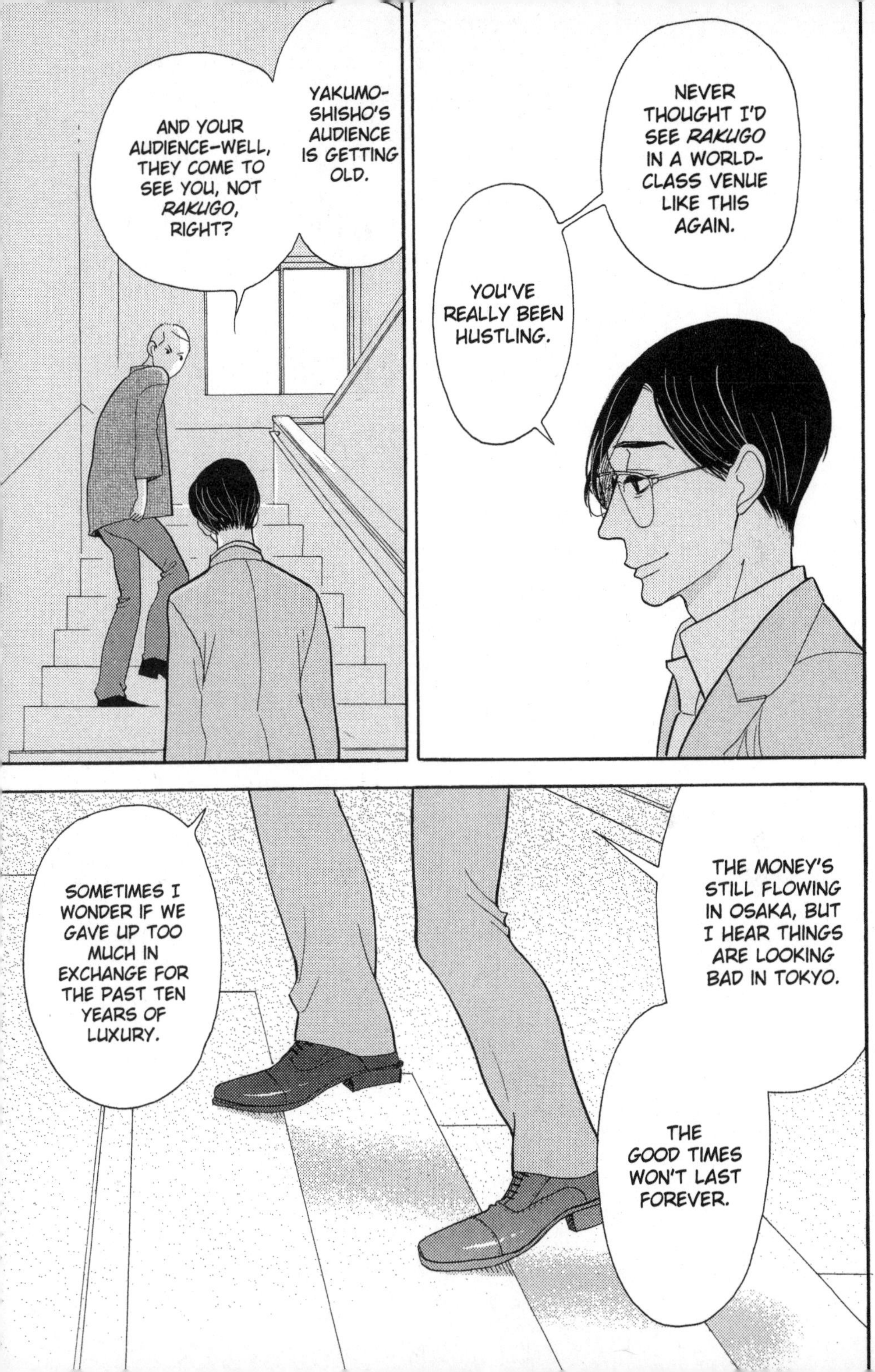
NEVER THOUGHT I'D SEE *RAKUGO* IN A WORLD-CLASS VENUE LIKE THIS AGAIN.
YOU'VE REALLY BEEN HUSTLING.
YAKUMO-SHISHO'S AUDIENCE IS GETTING OLD.
AND YOUR AUDIENCE—WELL, THEY COME TO SEE YOU, NOT *RAKUGO*, RIGHT?
THE MONEY'S STILL FLOWING IN OSAKA, BUT I HEAR THINGS ARE LOOKING BAD IN TOKYO.
THE GOOD TIMES WON'T LAST FOREVER.
SOMETIMES I WONDER IF WE GAVE UP TOO MUCH IN EXCHANGE FOR THE PAST TEN YEARS OF LUXURY.

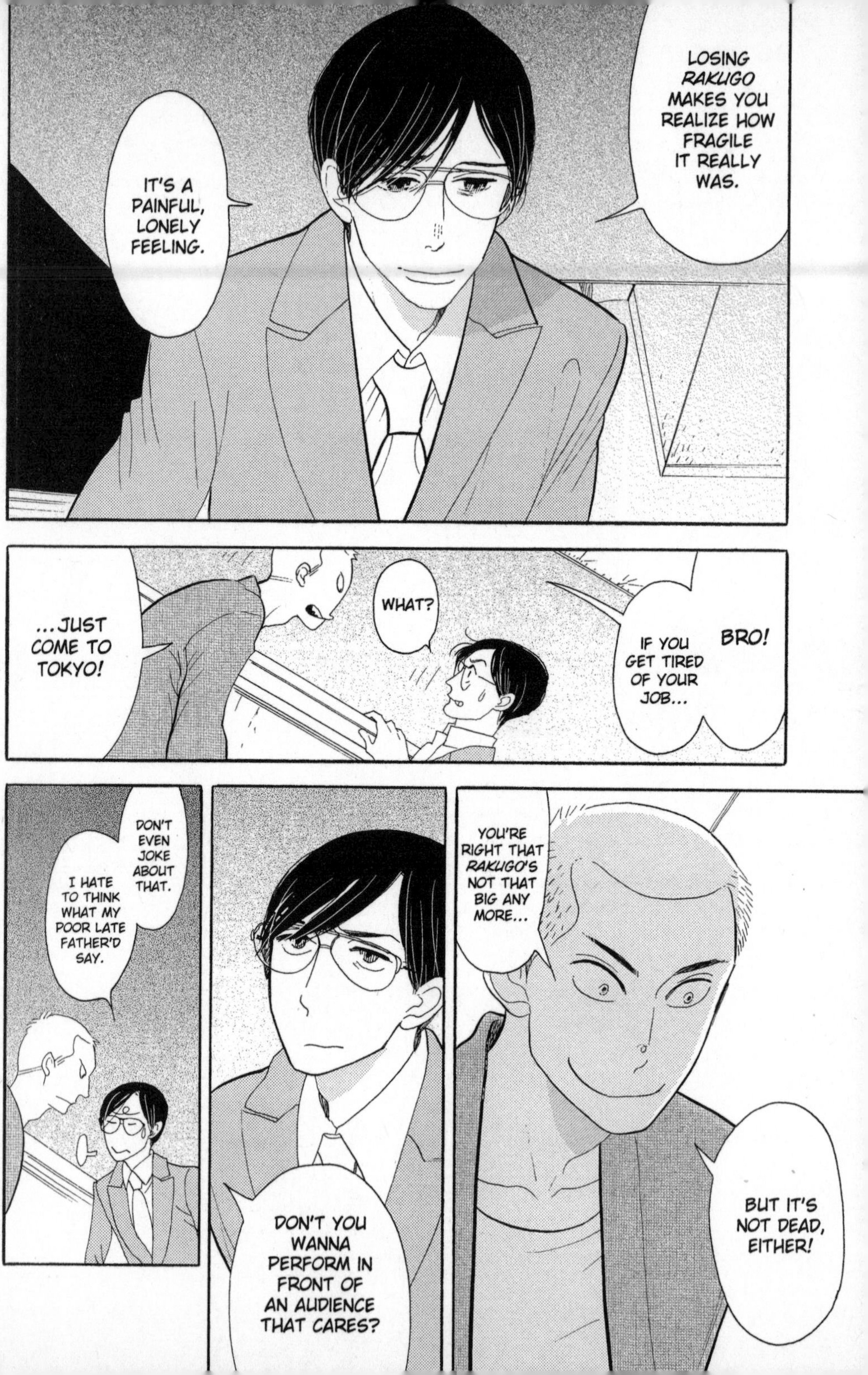
LOSING RAKUGO MAKES YOU REALIZE HOW FRAGILE IT REALLY WAS.
IT'S A PAINFUL, LONELY FEELING.
BRO!
IF YOU GET TIRED OF YOUR JOB...
WHAT?
...JUST COME TO TOKYO!
YOU'RE RIGHT THAT RAKUGO'S NOT THAT BIG ANY MORE...
BUT IT'S NOT DEAD, EITHER!
DON'T YOU WANNA PERFORM IN FRONT OF AN AUDIENCE THAT CARES?
DON'T EVEN JOKE ABOUT THAT.
I HATE TO THINK WHAT MY POOR LATE FATHER'D SAY.

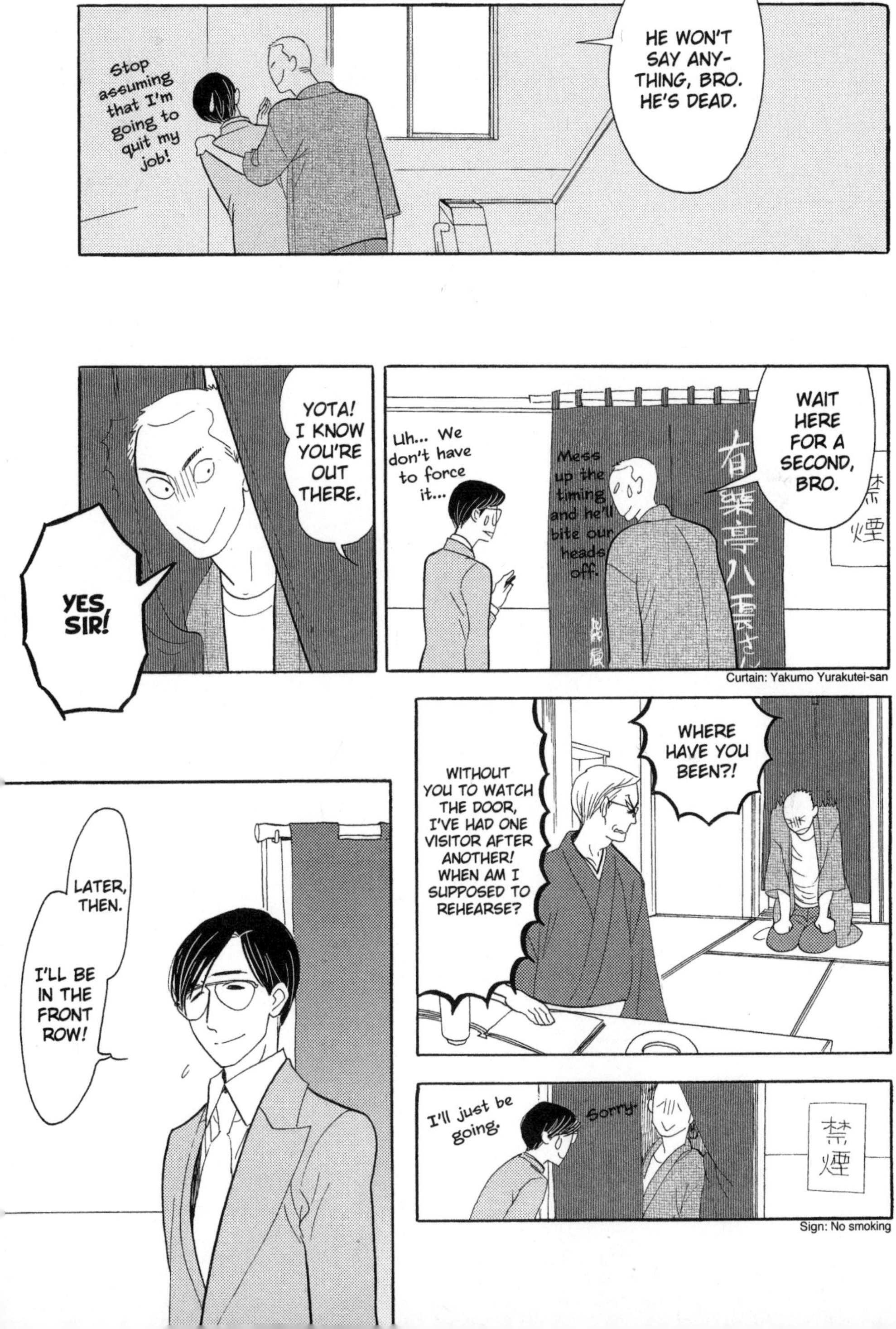
HE WON'T SAY ANY-THING, BRO. HE'S DEAD.
Stop assuming that I'm going to quit my job!
WAIT HERE FOR A SECOND, BRO.
Mess up the timing and he'll bite our heads off.
Uh... We don't have to force it...
Curtain: Yakumo Yurakutei-san
YOTA! I KNOW YOU'RE OUT THERE.
YES, SIR!
WHERE HAVE YOU BEEN?!
WITHOUT YOU TO WATCH THE DOOR, I'VE HAD ONE VISITOR AFTER ANOTHER! WHEN AM I SUPPOSED TO REHEARSE?
Sorry.
I'll just be going.
Sign: No smoking
LATER, THEN.
I'LL BE IN THE FRONT ROW!

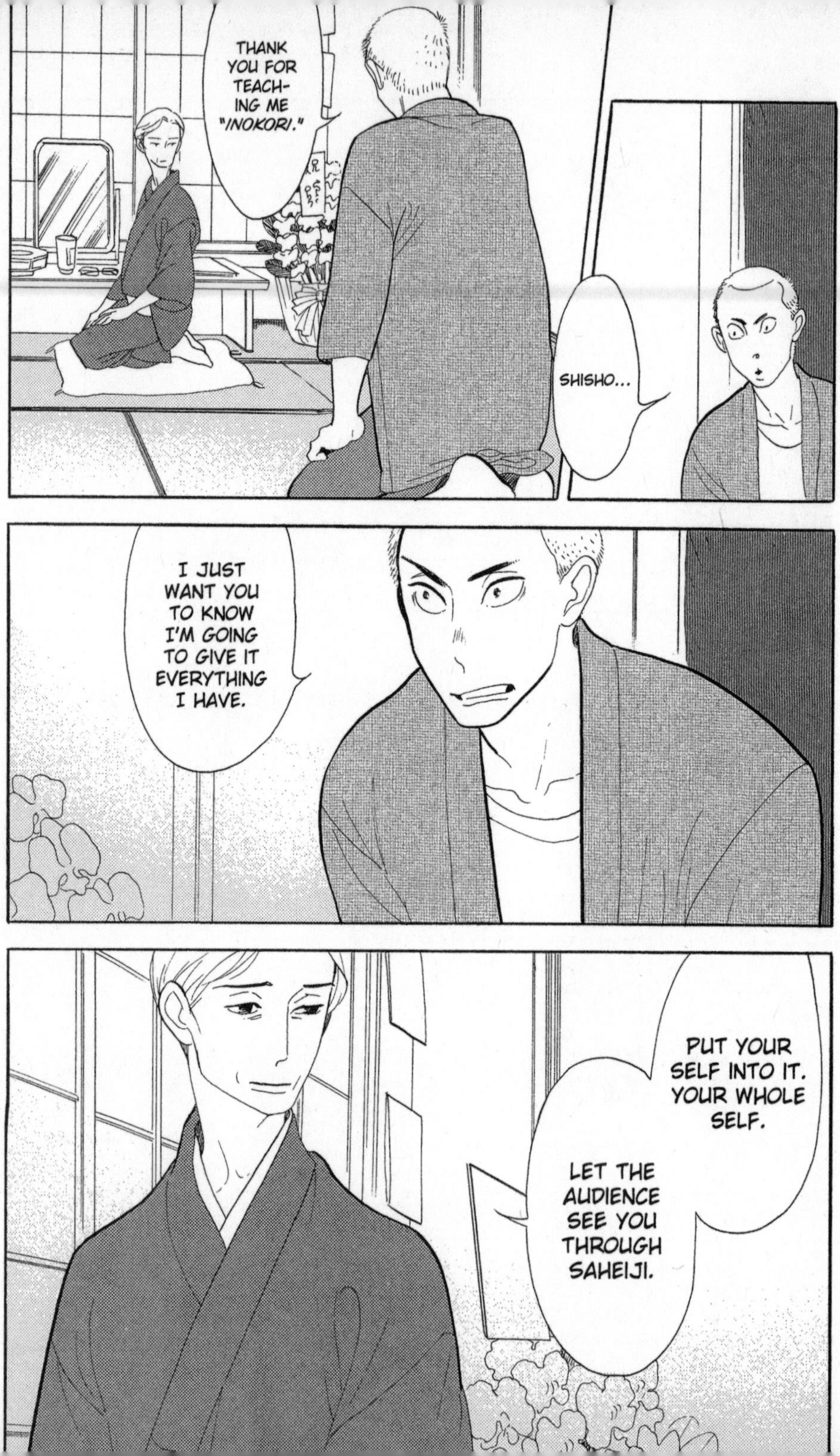
SHISHO...
THANK YOU FOR TEACHING ME "*INOKORI*."
I JUST WANT YOU TO KNOW I'M GOING TO GIVE IT EVERYTHING I HAVE.
PUT YOUR SELF INTO IT. YOUR WHOLE SELF.
LET THE AUDIENCE SEE YOU THROUGH SAHEIJI.

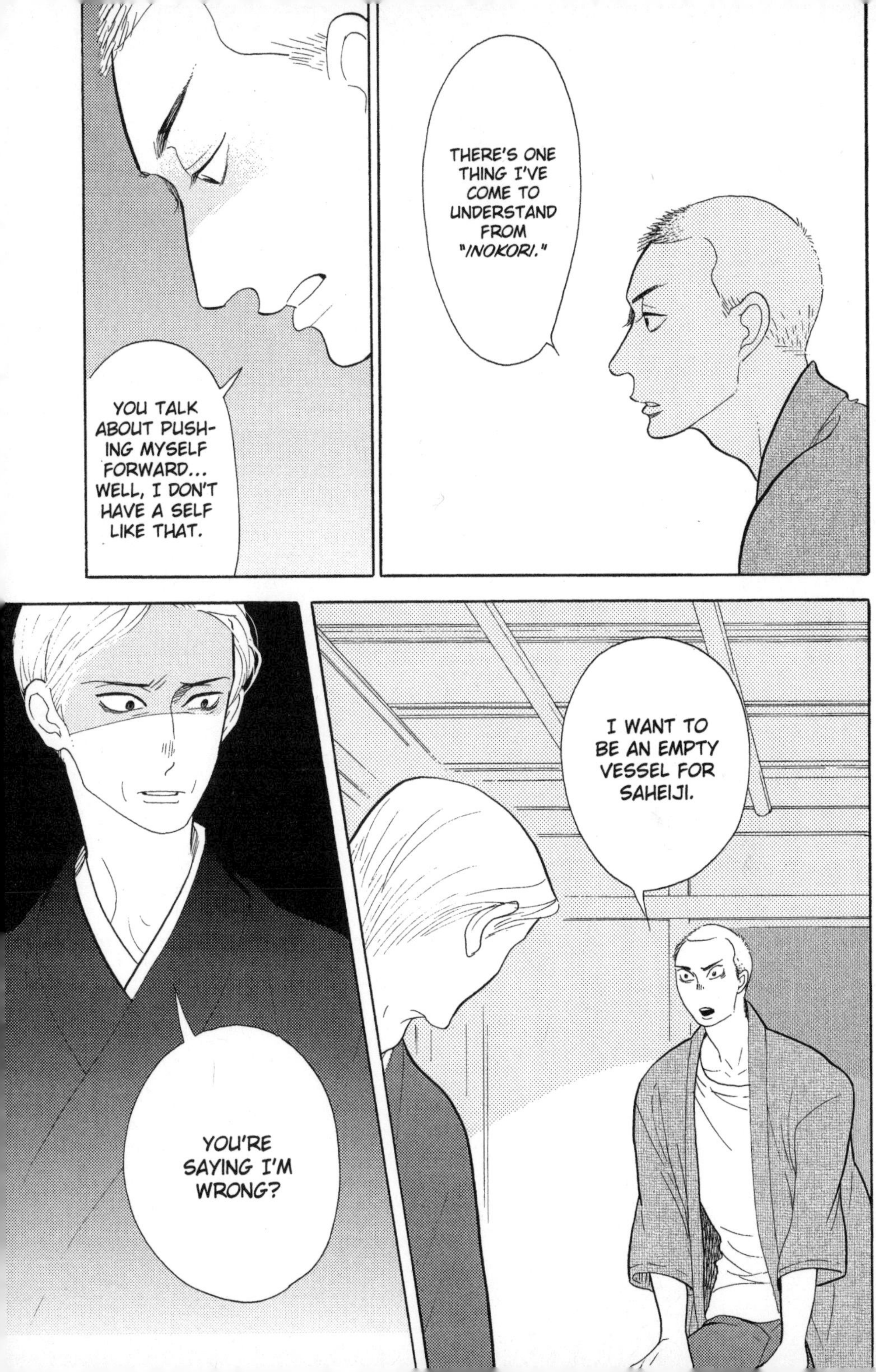
THERE'S ONE THING I'VE COME TO UNDERSTAND FROM "*INOKORI.*"
YOU TALK ABOUT PUSHING MYSELF FORWARD... WELL, I DON'T HAVE A SELF LIKE THAT.
I WANT TO BE AN EMPTY VESSEL FOR SAHEIJI.
YOU'RE SAYING I'M WRONG?

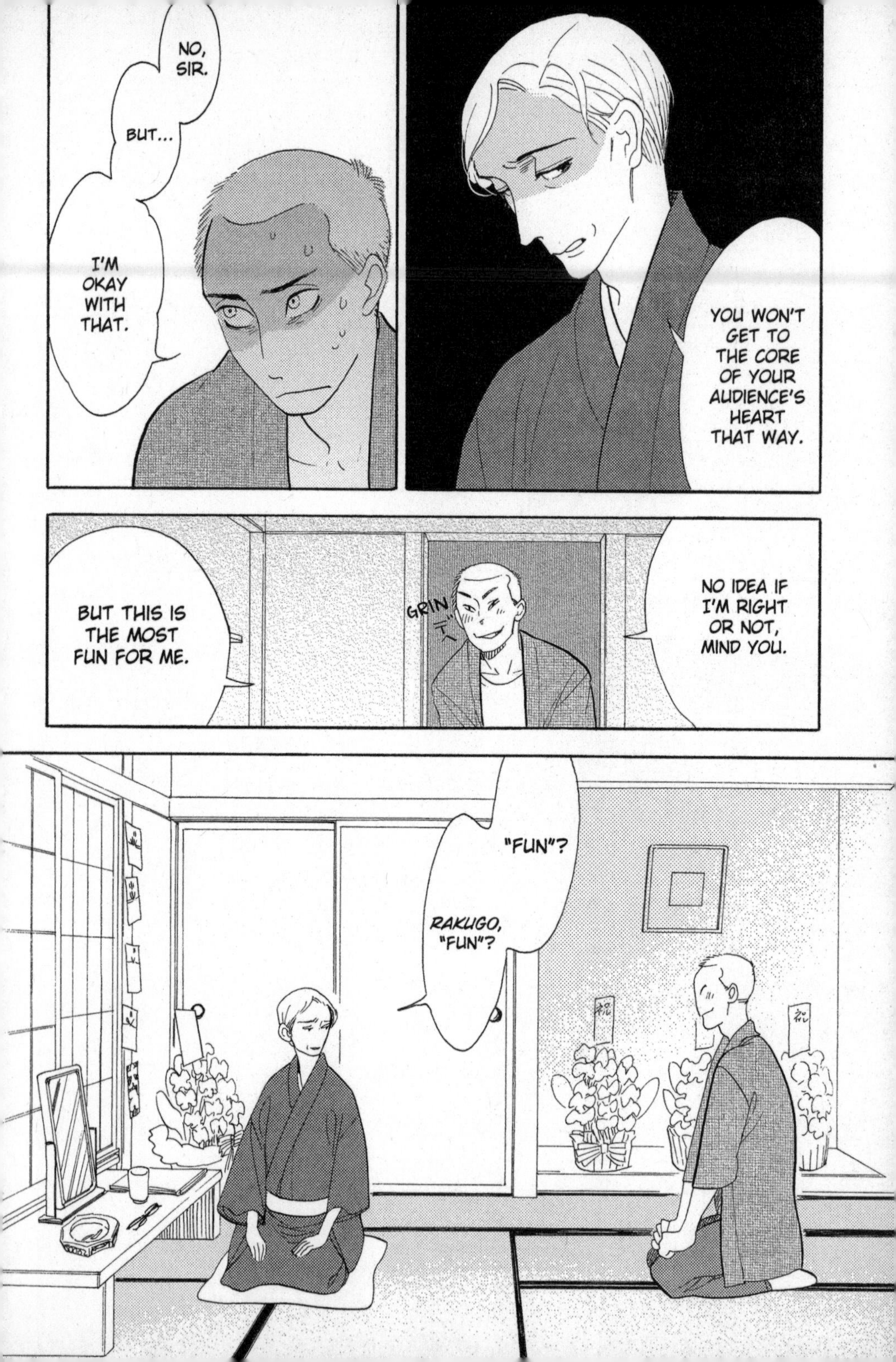
YOU WON'T GET TO THE CORE OF YOUR AUDIENCE'S HEART THAT WAY.
NO, SIR.
BUT...
I'M OKAY WITH THAT.
NO IDEA IF I'M RIGHT OR NOT, MIND YOU.
GRIN
BUT THIS IS THE MOST FUN FOR ME.
"FUN"?
RAKUGO, "FUN"?

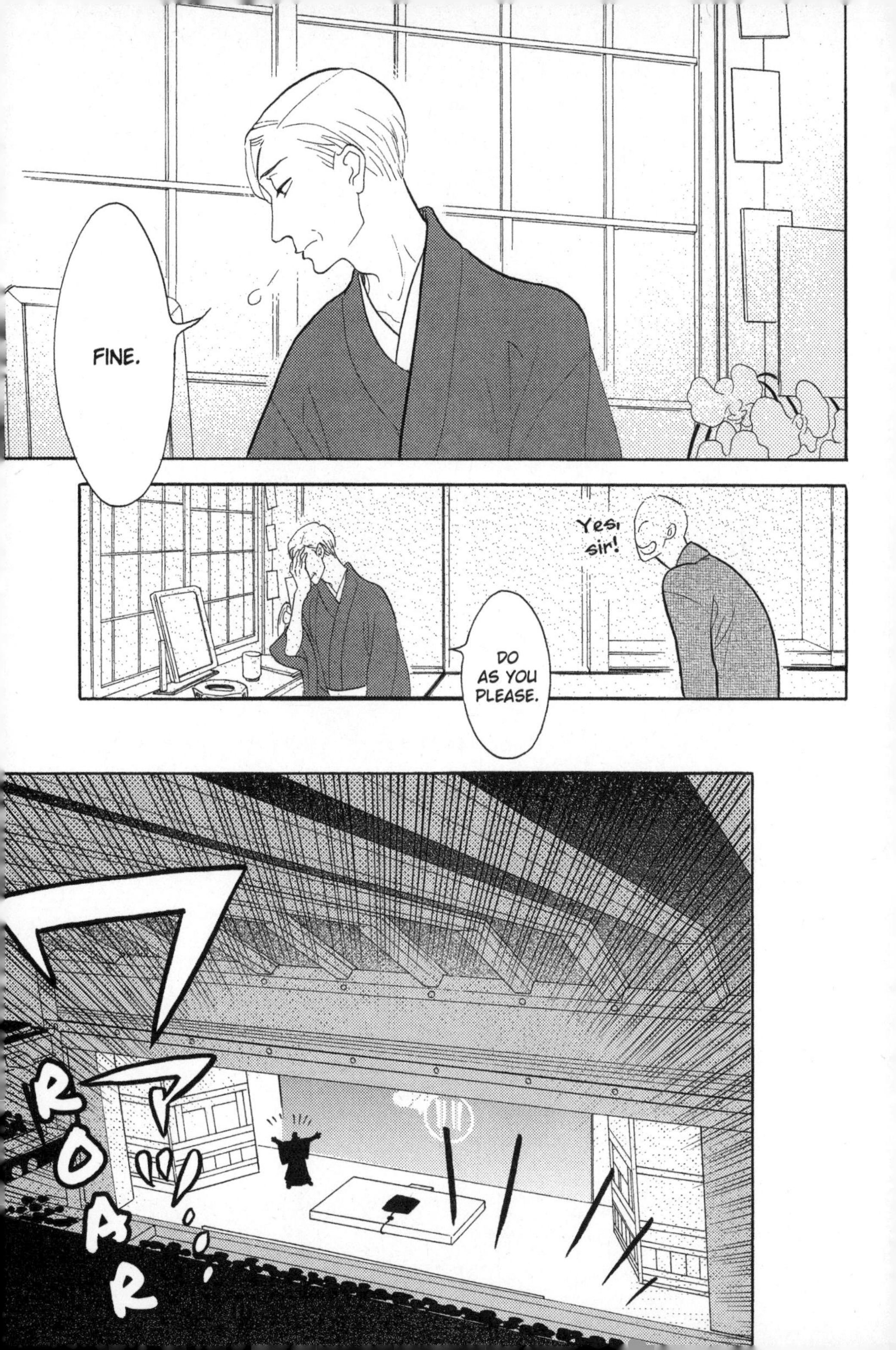
FINE.
Yes, sir!
DO AS YOU PLEASE.
ROAR

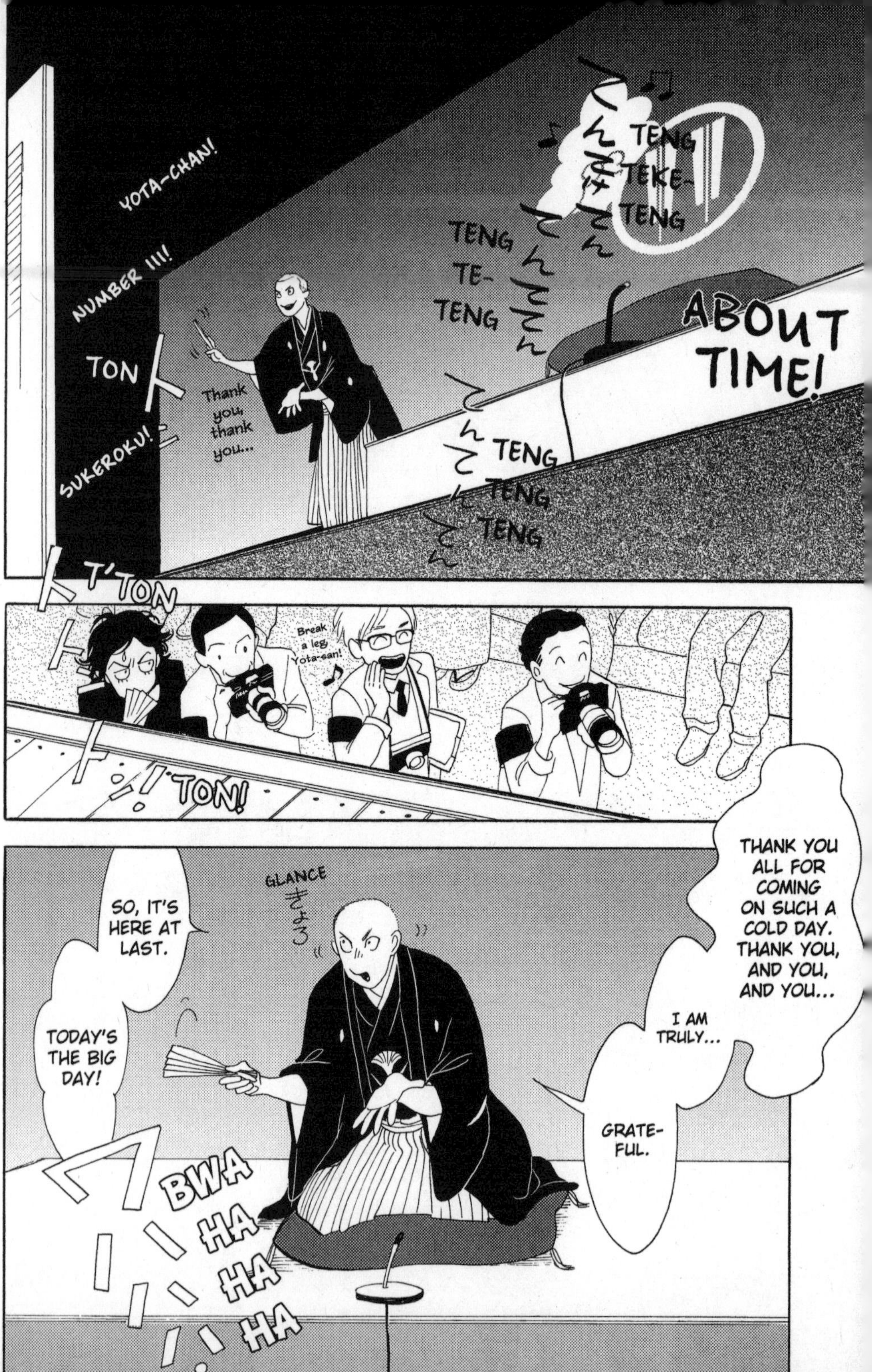
ABOUT TIME!
TENG TEKE-TENG
TENG TE-TENG
TENG TENG TENG
Thank you, thank you...
YOTA-CHAN!
NUMBER 111!
TON
SUKEROKU!
T'TON
TON!
Break a leg Yota-san!
THANK YOU ALL FOR COMING ON SUCH A COLD DAY. THANK YOU, AND YOU, AND YOU...
I AM TRULY...
GRATE-FUL.
GLANCE
きょろ
SO, IT'S HERE AT LAST.
TODAY'S THE BIG DAY!
BWA HA HA HA

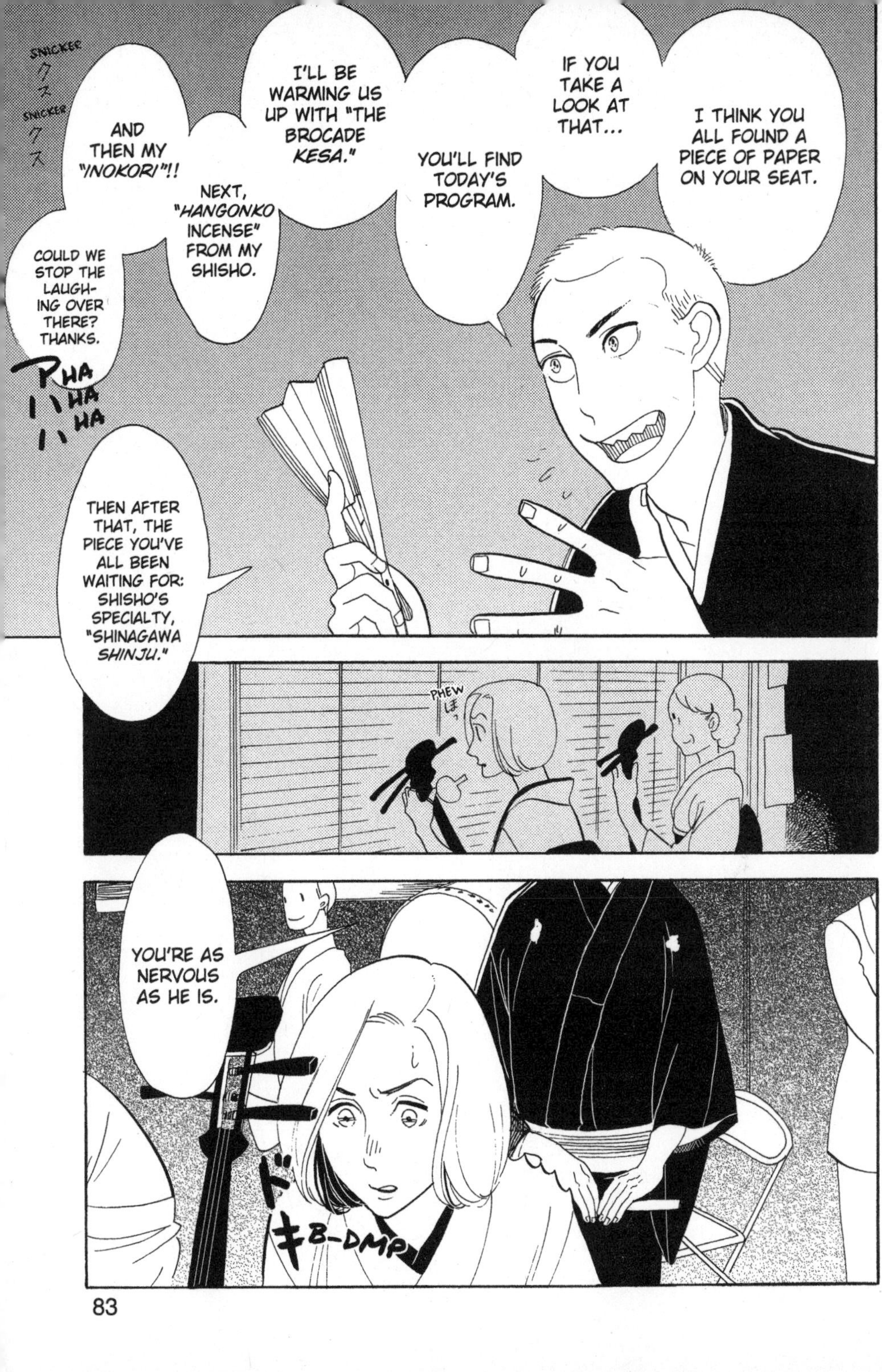
I THINK YOU ALL FOUND A PIECE OF PAPER ON YOUR SEAT.
IF YOU TAKE A LOOK AT THAT...
YOU'LL FIND TODAY'S PROGRAM.
I'LL BE WARMING US UP WITH "THE BROCADE *KESA*."
NEXT, "*HANGONKO* INCENSE" FROM MY SHISHO.
AND THEN MY "*INOKORI*"!!
SNICKER クス SNICKER クス
COULD WE STOP THE LAUGHING OVER THERE? THANKS.
PHA ハ HA ハ HA
THEN AFTER THAT, THE PIECE YOU'VE ALL BEEN WAITING FOR: SHISHO'S SPECIALTY, "SHINAGAWA *SHINJU*."
PHEW
YOU'RE AS NERVOUS AS HE IS.
ドキ B-DMP

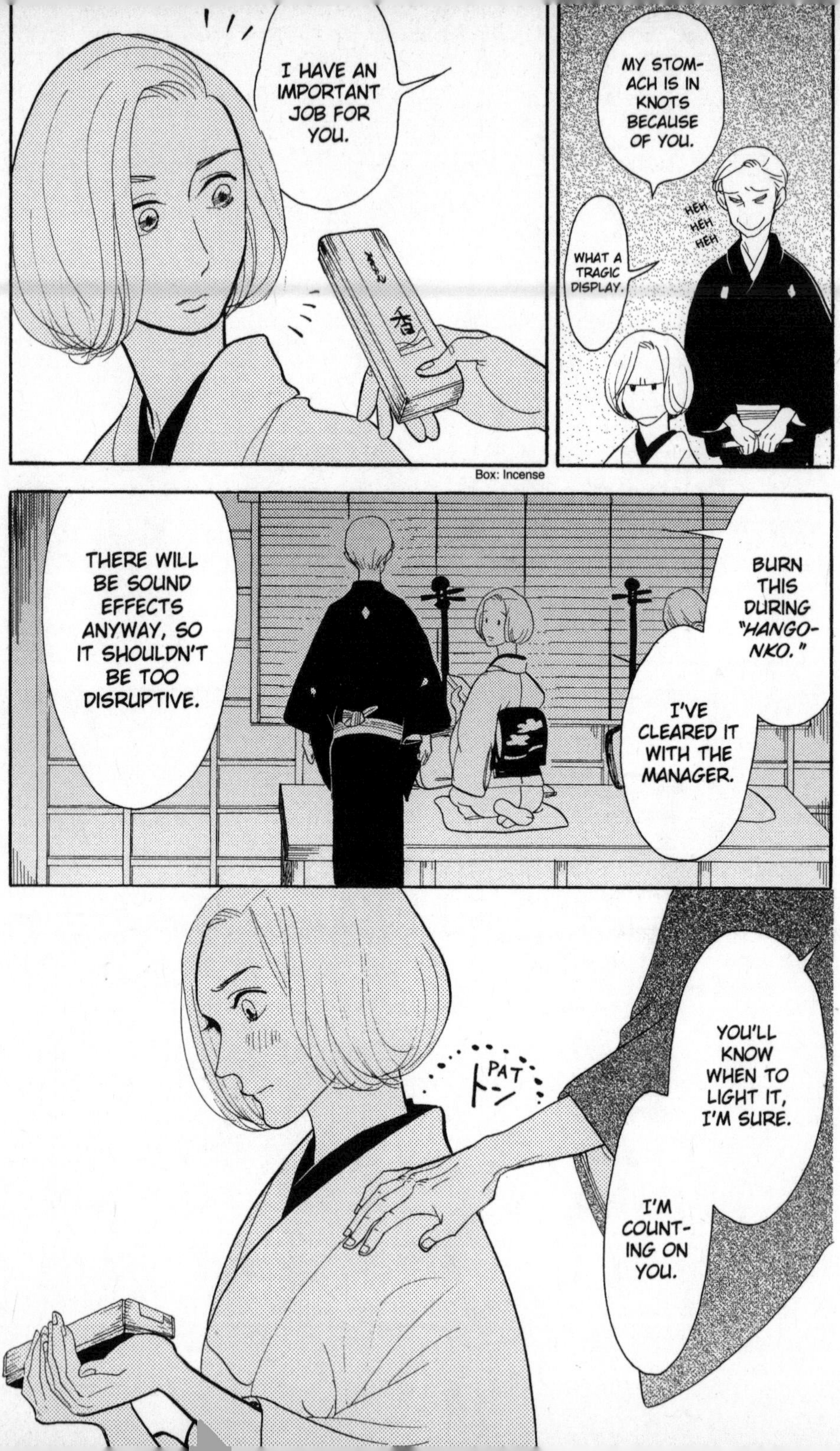
MY STOMACH IS IN KNOTS BECAUSE OF YOU.
HEH HEH HEH
WHAT A TRAGIC DISPLAY.
I HAVE AN IMPORTANT JOB FOR YOU.
Box: Incense
BURN THIS DURING "HANGONKO."
I'VE CLEARED IT WITH THE MANAGER.
THERE WILL BE SOUND EFFECTS ANYWAY, SO IT SHOULDN'T BE TOO DISRUPTIVE.
YOU'LL KNOW WHEN TO LIGHT IT, I'M SURE.
I'M COUNTING ON YOU.
PAT

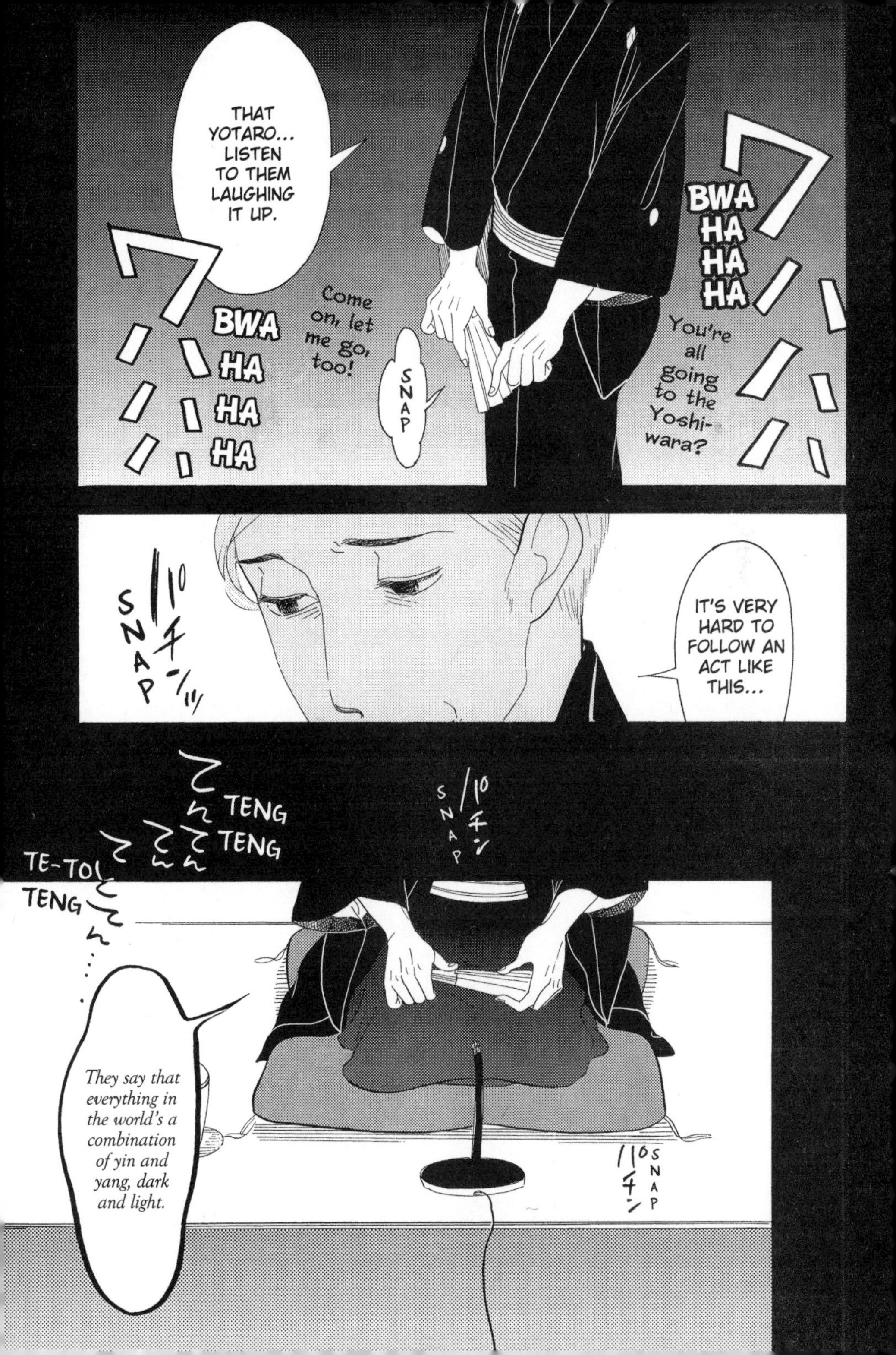
BWA HA HA HA
You're all going to the Yoshiwara?
THAT YOTARO... LISTEN TO THEM LAUGHING IT UP.
SNAP
Come on, let me go, too!
BWA HA HA HA
IT'S VERY HARD TO FOLLOW AN ACT LIKE THIS...
SNAP
SNAP
TENG TENG
TE-TO TENG...
SNAP
They say that everything in the world's a combination of yin and yang, dark and light.

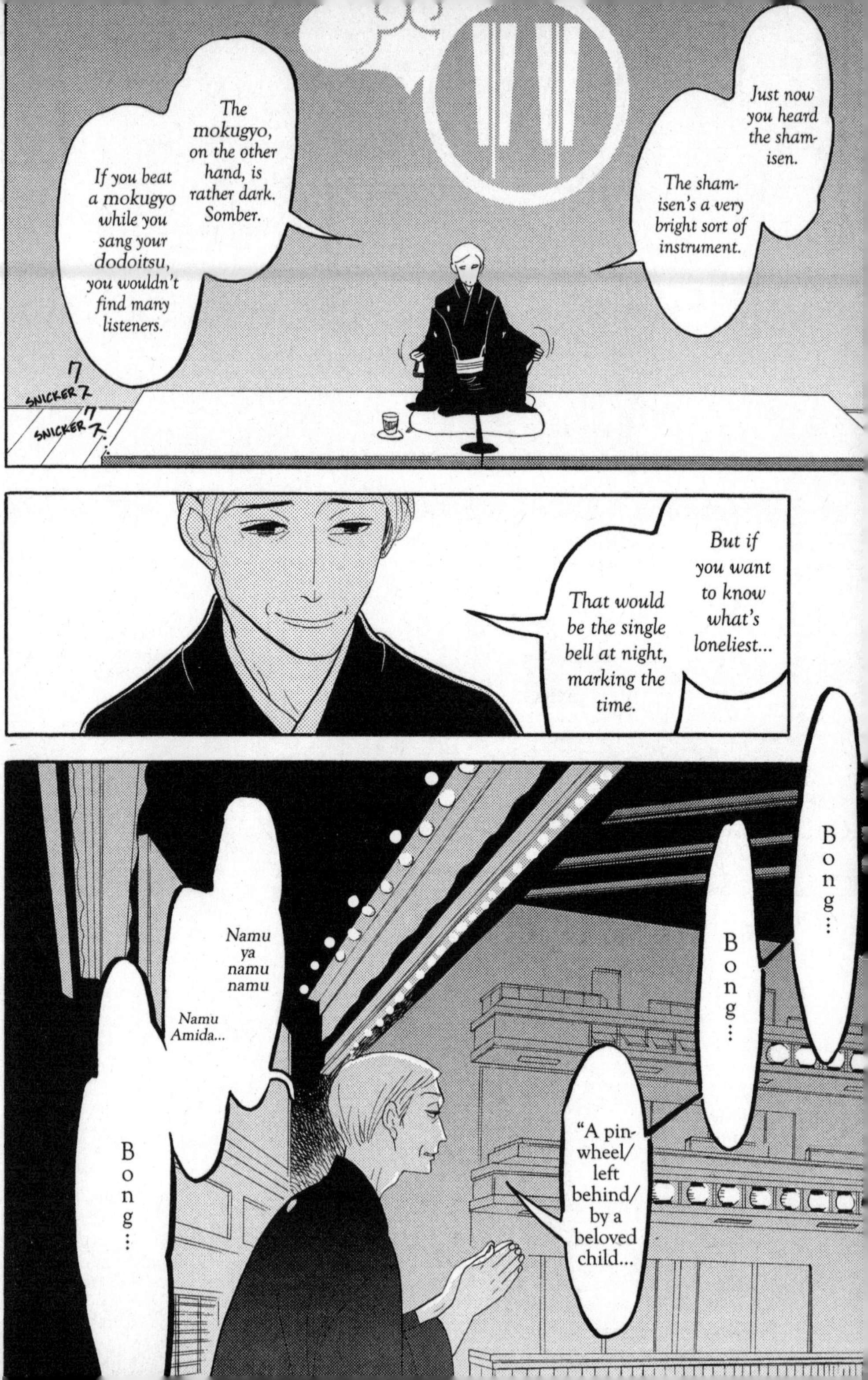
Just now you heard the shamisen.
The shamisen's a very bright sort of instrument.
The mokugyo, on the other hand, is rather dark. Somber.
If you beat a mokugyo while you sang your dodoitsu, you wouldn't find many listeners.
SNICKER
SNICKER
But if you want to know what's loneliest...
That would be the single bell at night, marking the time.
Bong...
Bong...
"A pinwheel/ left behind/ by a beloved child...
Namu ya namu namu
Namu Amida...
Bong...

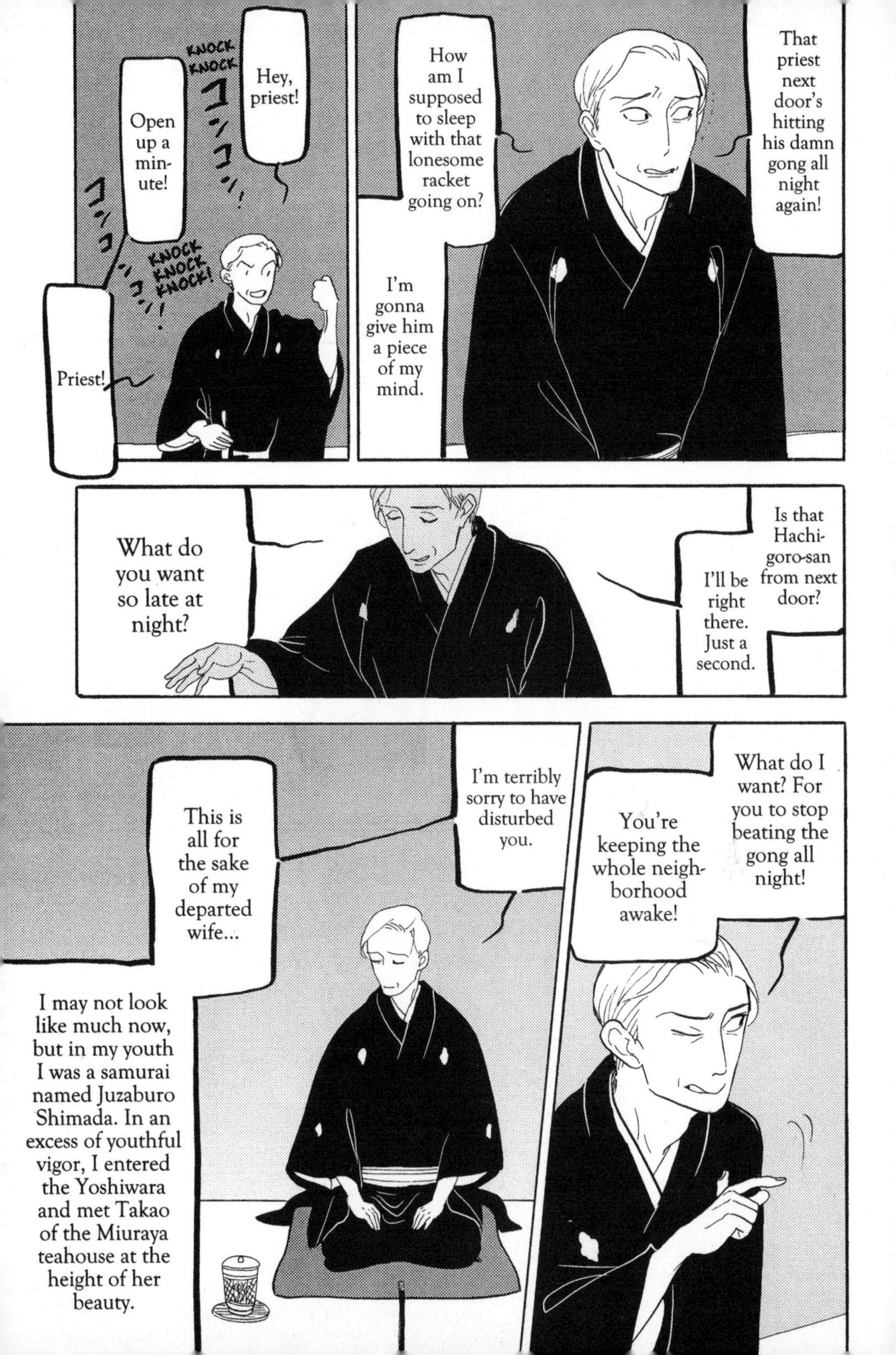
That priest next door's hitting his damn gong all night again!
How am I supposed to sleep with that lonesome racket going on?
I'm gonna give him a piece of my mind.
Hey, priest!
KNOCK KNOCK
Open up a minute!
KNOCK KNOCK KNOCK!
Priest!
Is that Hachigoro-san from next door?
I'll be right there. Just a second.
What do you want so late at night?
What do I want? For you to stop beating the gong all night!
You're keeping the whole neighborhood awake!
I'm terribly sorry to have disturbed you.
This is all for the sake of my departed wife...
I may not look like much now, but in my youth I was a samurai named Juzaburo Shimada. In an excess of youthful vigor, I entered the Yoshiwara and met Takao of the Miuraya teahouse at the height of her beauty.

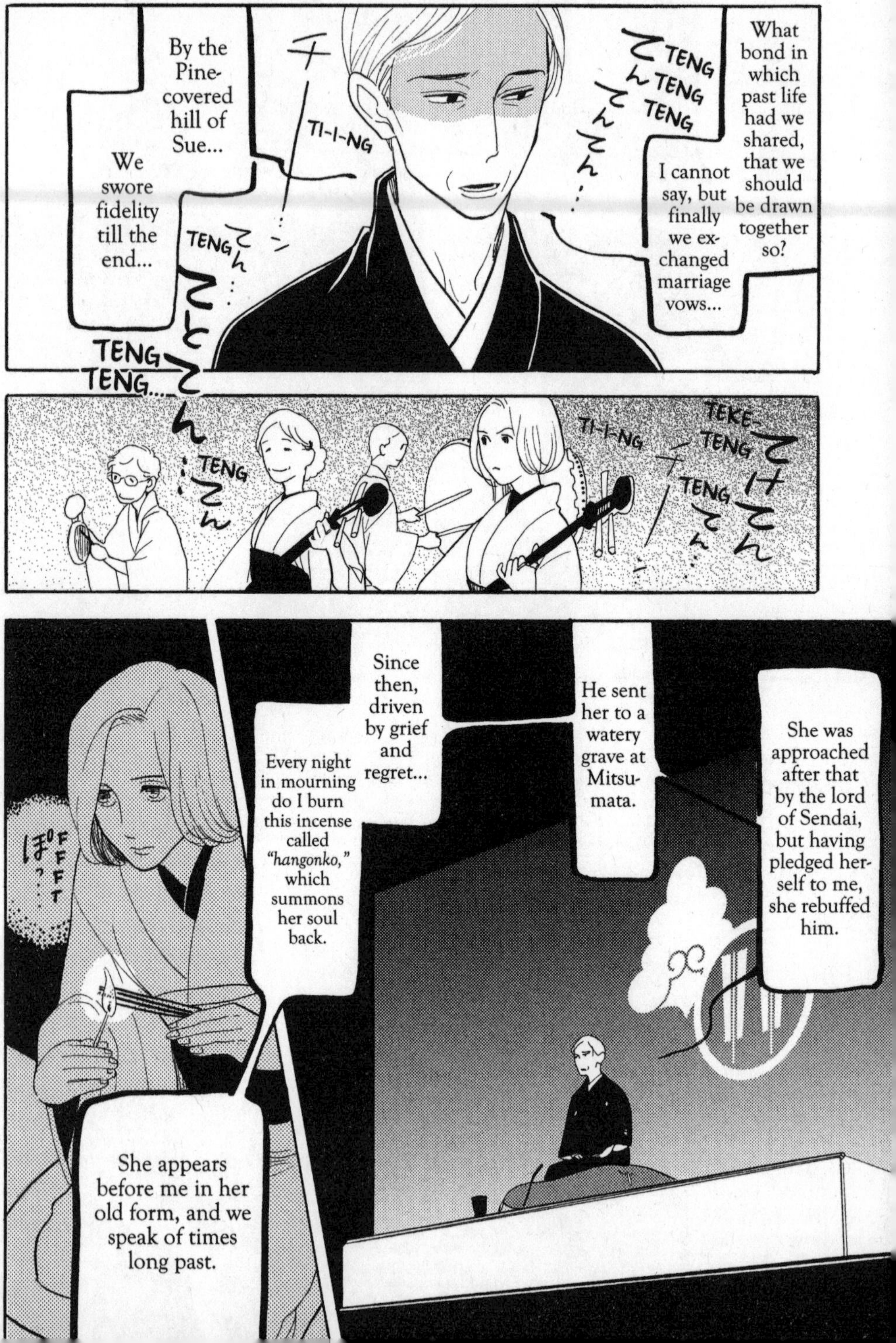

What bond in which past life had we shared, that we should be drawn together so?
TENG TENG TENG
I cannot say, but finally we exchanged marriage vows...
TI-I-NG
By the Pine-covered hill of Sue...
We swore fidelity till the end...
TENG
TENG TENG...
TEKE-TENG
TENG
TI-I-NG
TENG
She was approached after that by the lord of Sendai, but having pledged herself to me, she rebuffed him.
He sent her to a watery grave at Mitsumata.
Since then, driven by grief and regret...
Every night in mourning do I burn this incense called *"hangonko,"* which summons her soul back.
FFFT
She appears before me in her old form, and we speak of times long past.

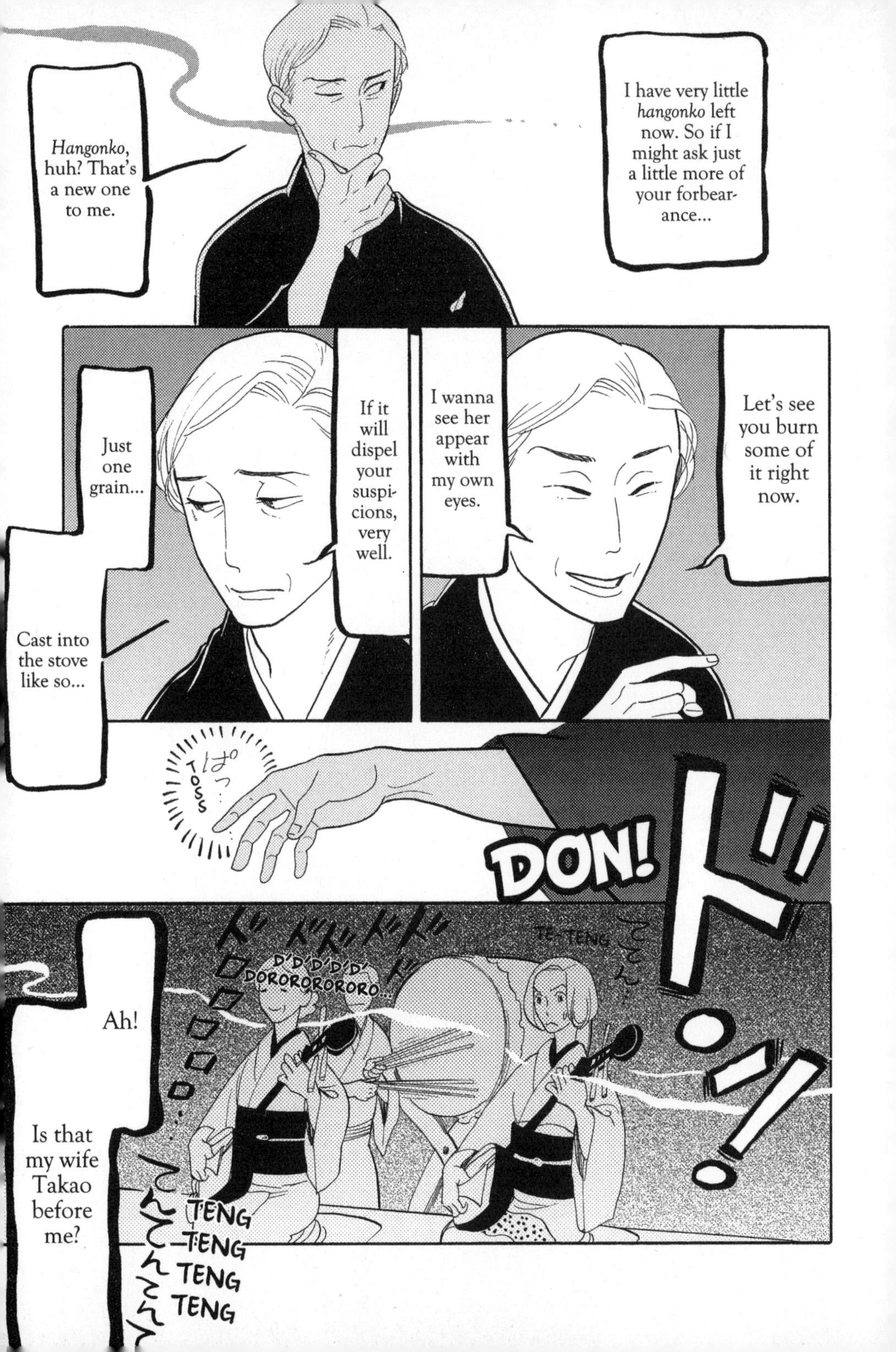

I have very little *hangonko* left now. So if I might ask just a little more of your forbearance...
Hangonko, huh? That's a new one to me.
Let's see you burn some of it right now.
I wanna see her appear with my own eyes.
If it will dispel your suspicions, very well.
Just one grain...
Cast into the stove like so...
DON!
ぱっ
TOSS
TE-TENG
D'D'D'D'D' DORORORORORO...
Ah!
Is that my wife Takao before me?
TENG
TENG
TENG
TENG

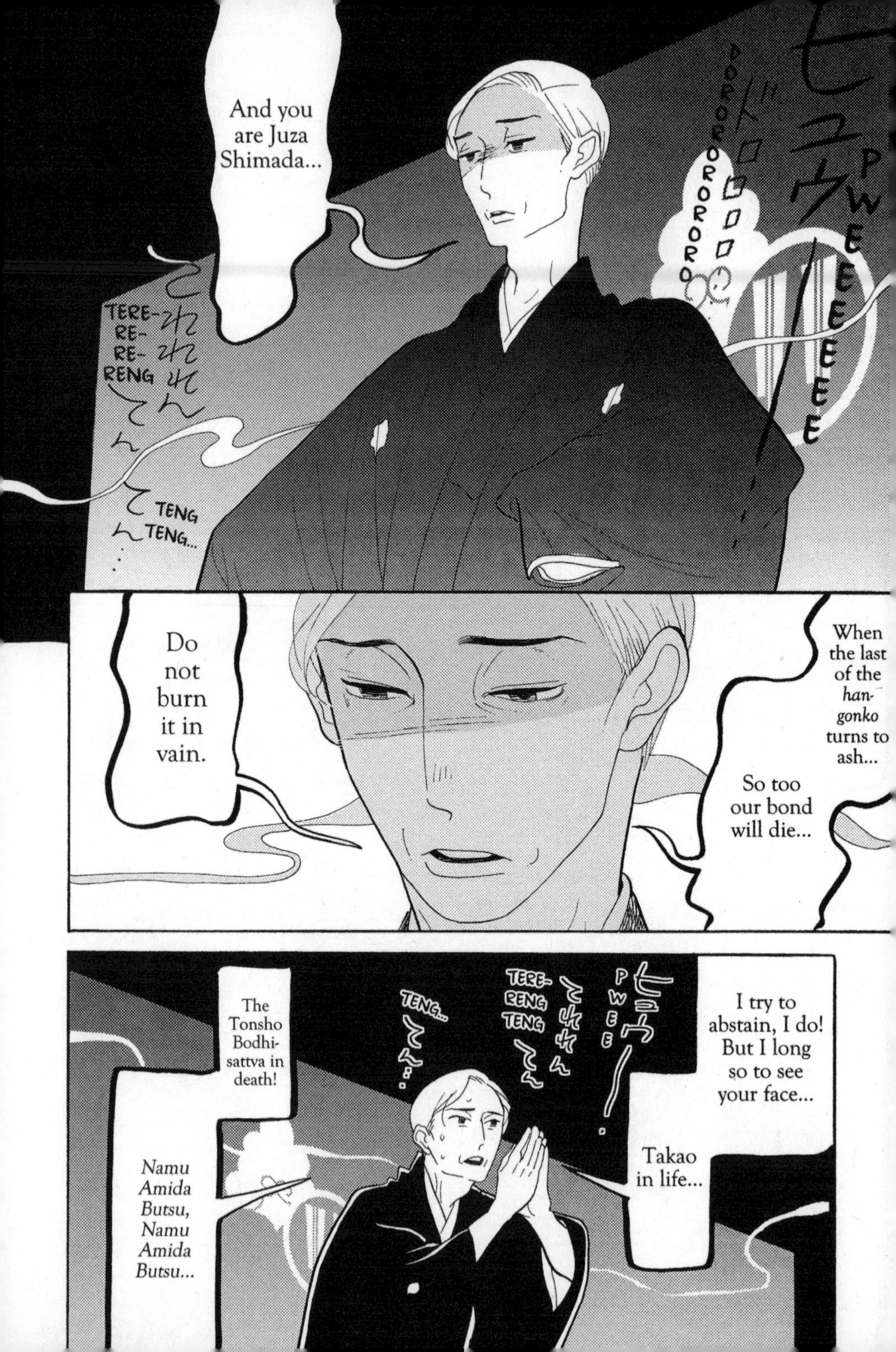
PWEEEEEEEE
DORORORORORORO
And you are Juza Shimada...
TERE-RE-RE-RENG
TENG TENG...
When the last of the *han-gonko* turns to ash...
So too our bond will die...
Do not burn it in vain.
I try to abstain, I do! But I long so to see your face...
Takao in life...
PWEE—.
TERE-RENG TENG
TENG...
The Tonsho Bodhi-sattva in death!
Namu Amida Butsu, Namu Amida Butsu...

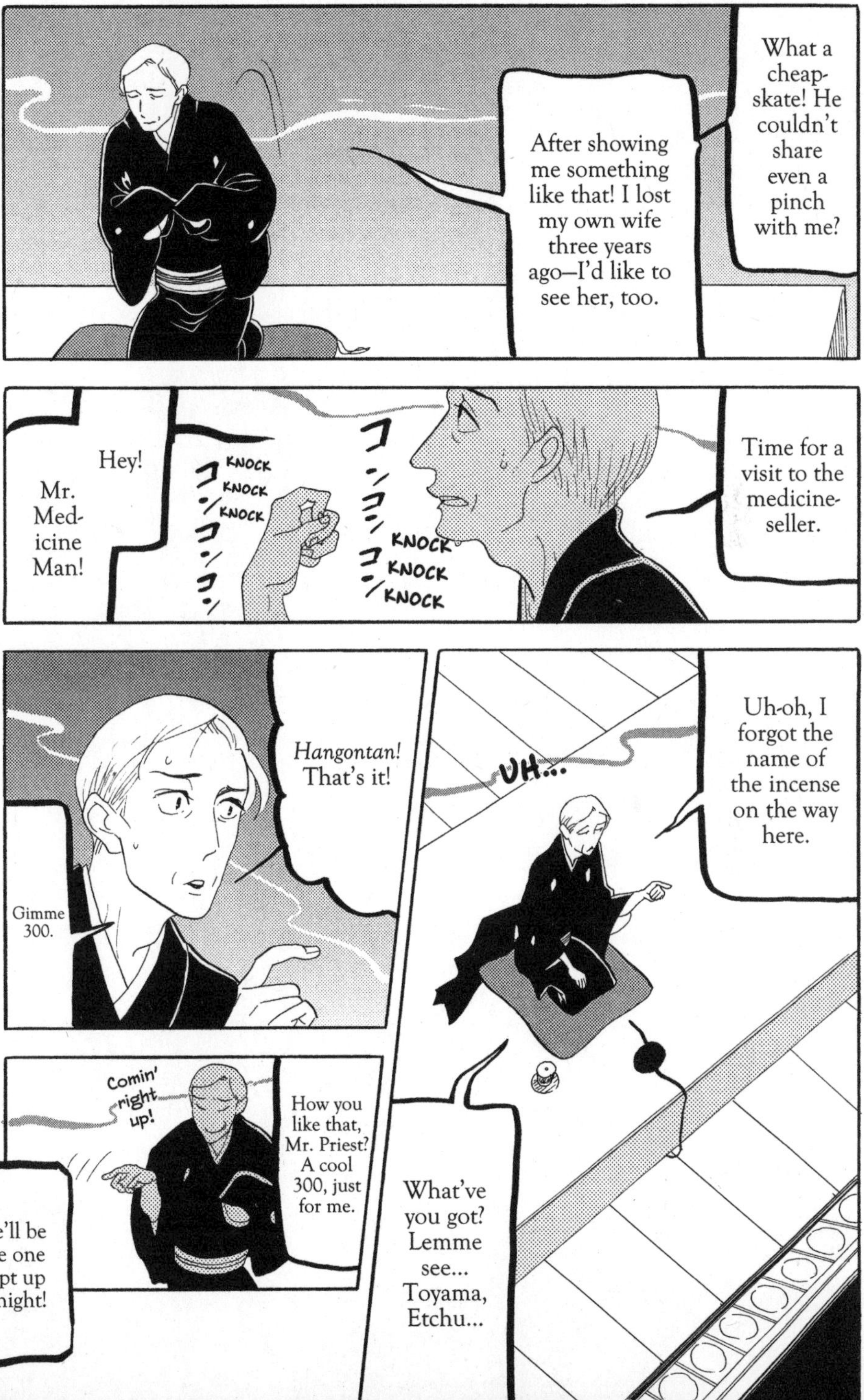
What a cheapskate! He couldn't share even a pinch with me?
After showing me something like that! I lost my own wife three years ago—I'd like to see her, too.
Time for a visit to the medicine-seller.
KNOCK KNOCK KNOCK
KNOCK KNOCK KNOCK
Hey!
Mr. Medicine Man!
Uh-oh, I forgot the name of the incense on the way here.
UH...
What've you got? Lemme see... Toyama, Etchu...
Hangontan! That's it!
Gimme 300.
Comin' right up!
How you like that, Mr. Priest? A cool 300, just for me.
He'll be the one kept up tonight!

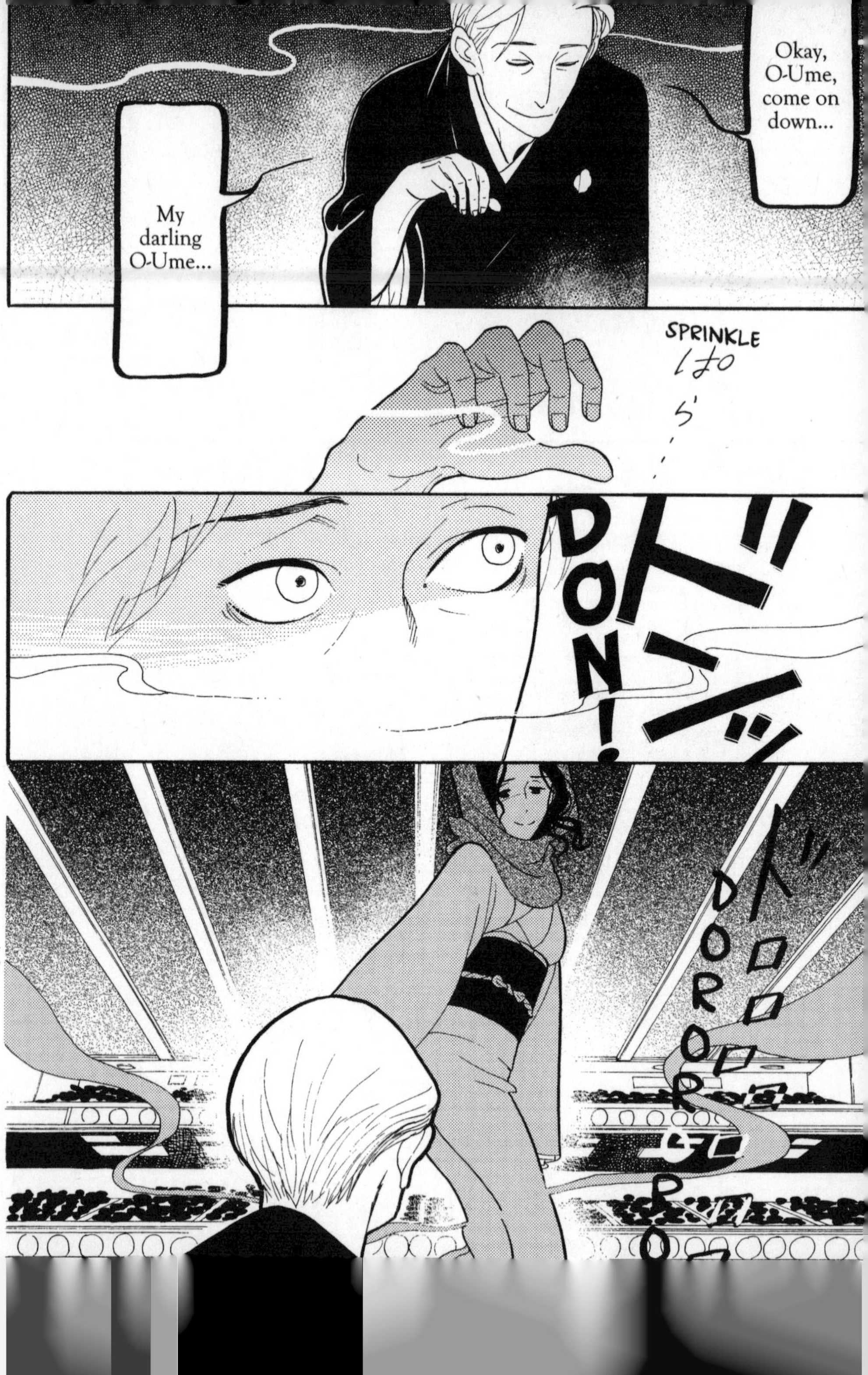
Okay, O-Ume, come on down...
My darling O-Ume...
SPRINKLE
DON!
DOROROROO

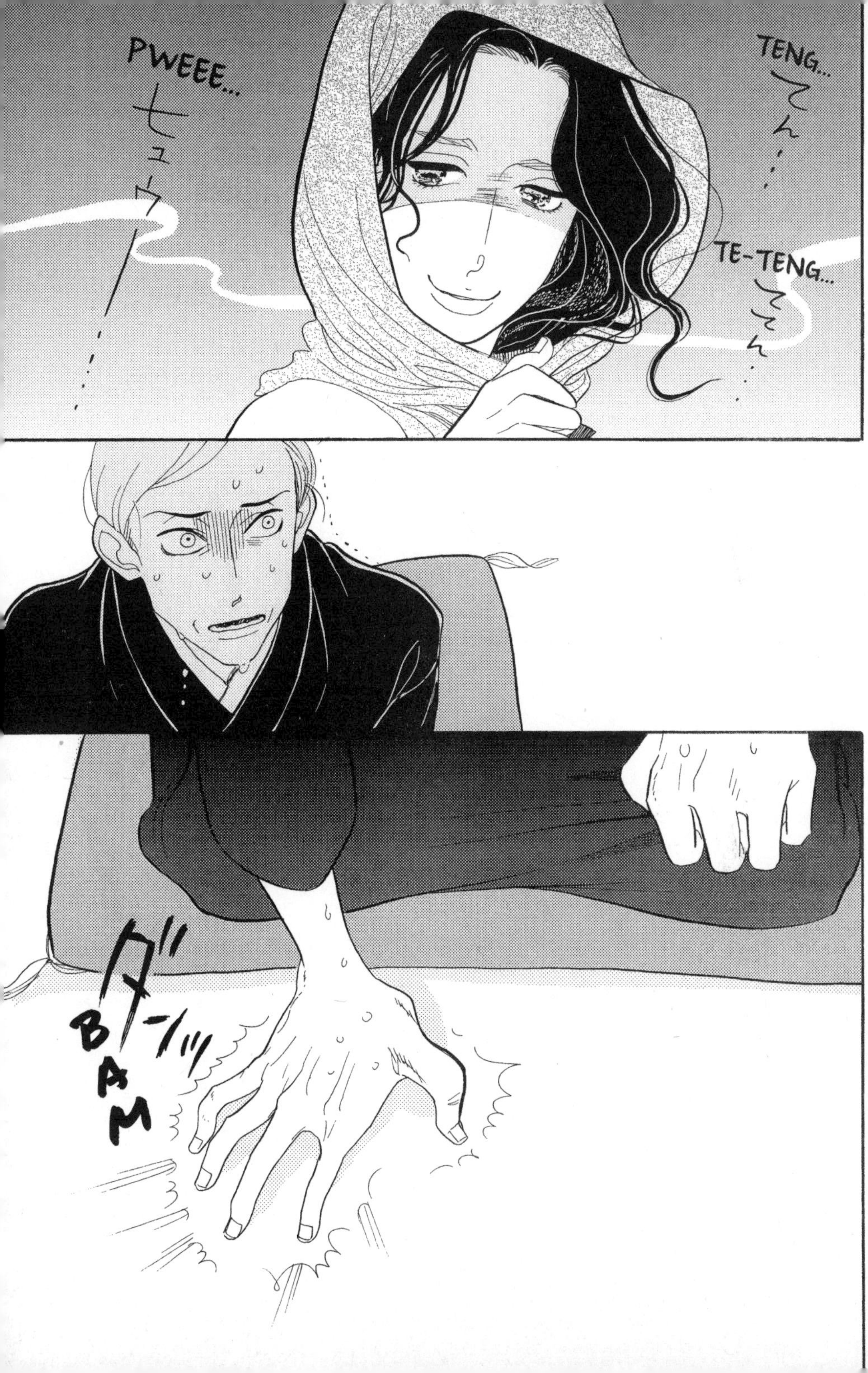
TENG...
TE-TENG...
PWEEE...
BAM

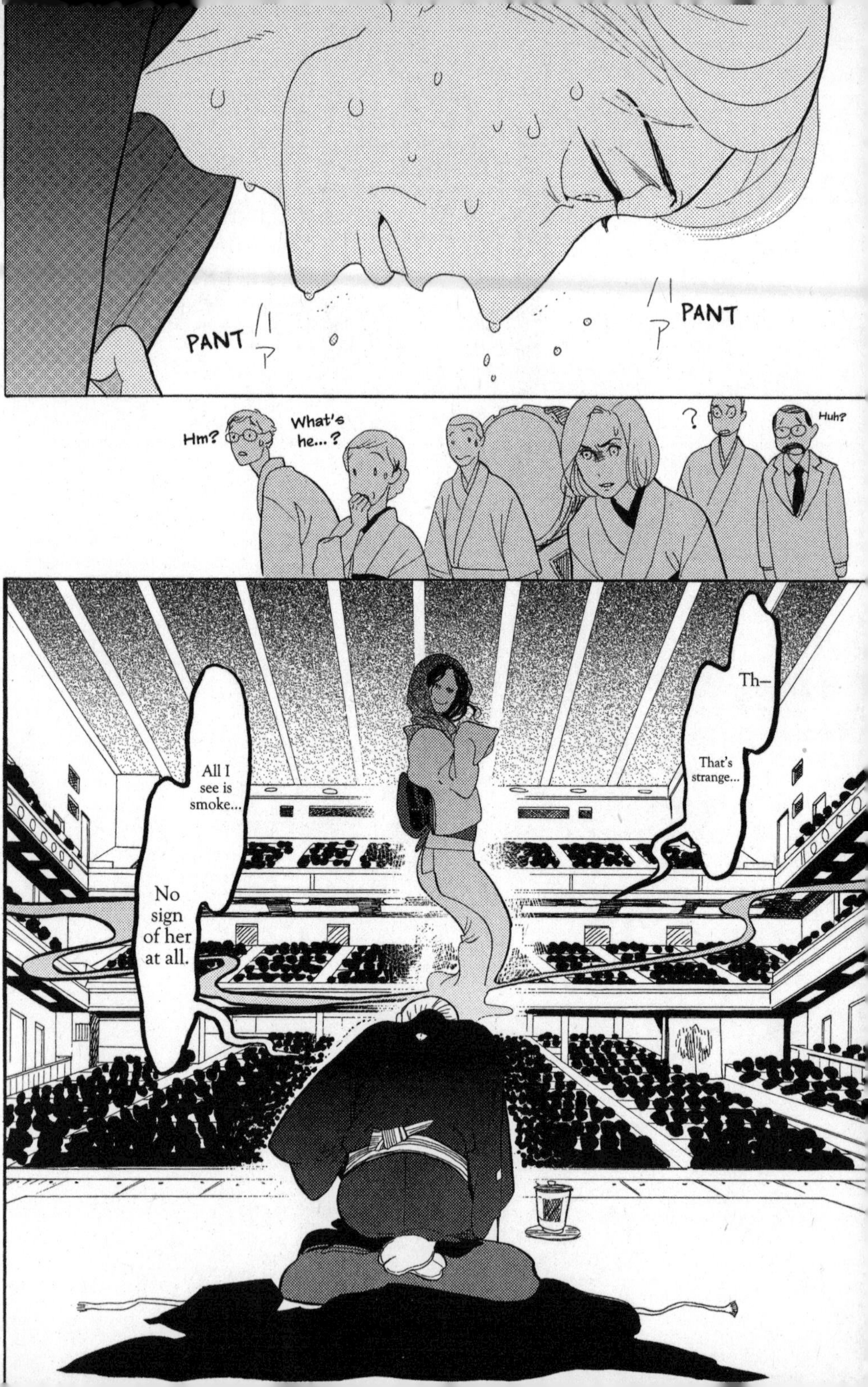

ハア PANT
PANT ハア
Huh?
?
What's he...?
Hm?
Th— That's strange...
All I see is smoke... No sign of her at all.

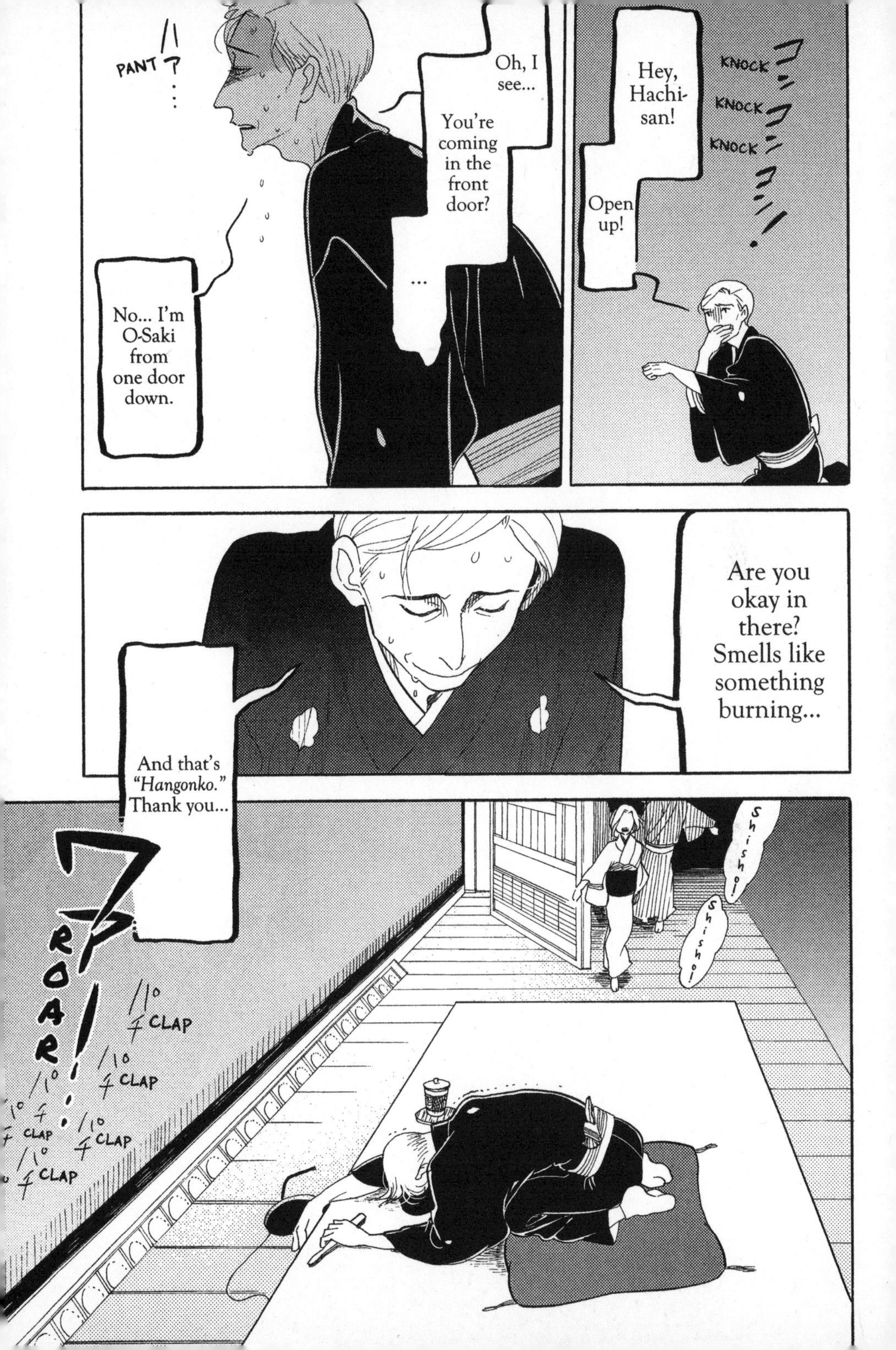
KNOCK
KNOCK
KNOCK
Hey, Hachi-san!
Open up!
Oh, I see...
You're coming in the front door?
PANT
...
...
No... I'm O-Saki from one door down.
Are you okay in there? Smells like something burning...
And that's "Hangonko." Thank you...
Shisho!
Shisho!
ROAR!
CLAP
CLAP
CLAP
CLAP
CLAP

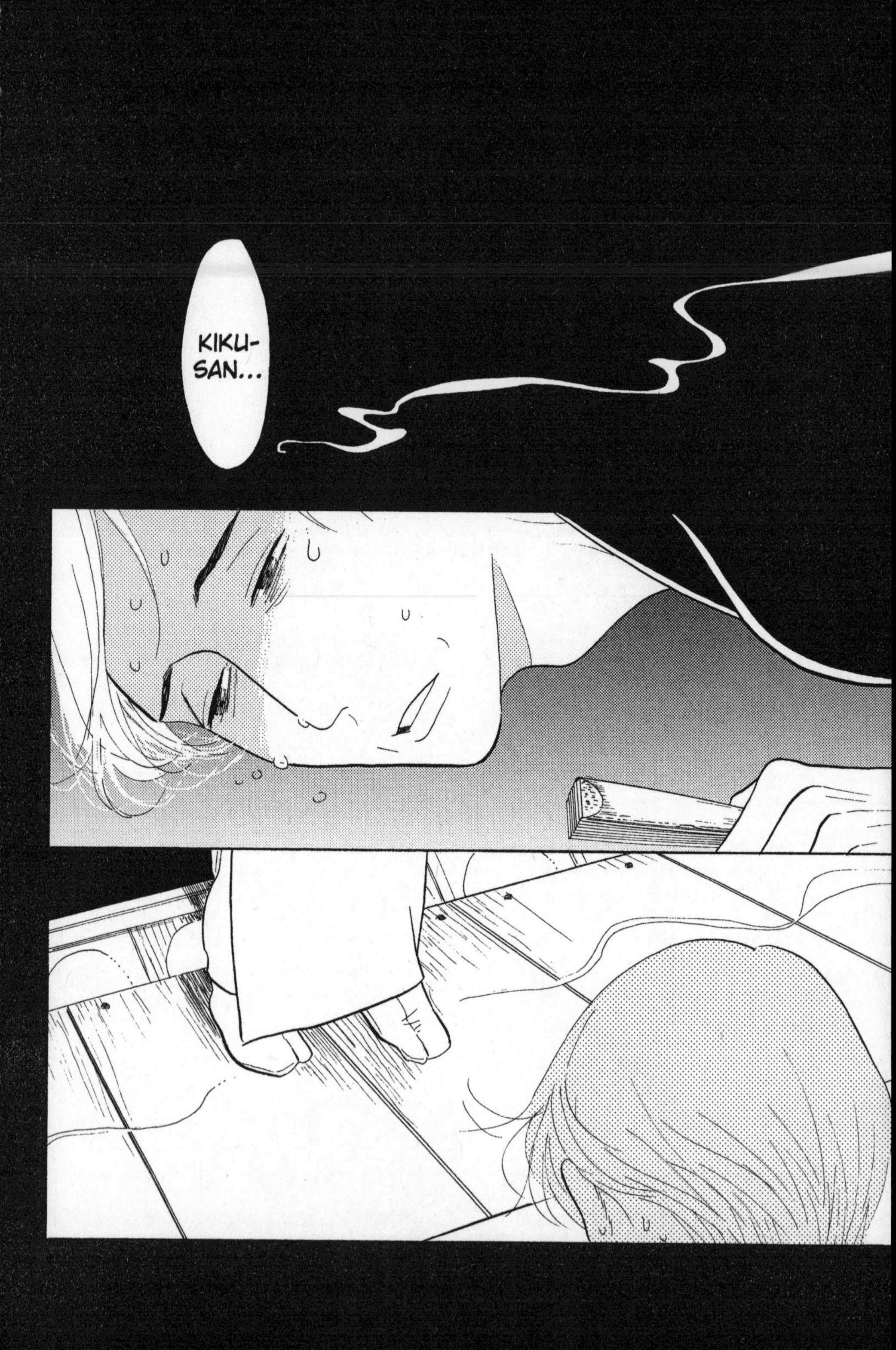
KIKU-SAN...

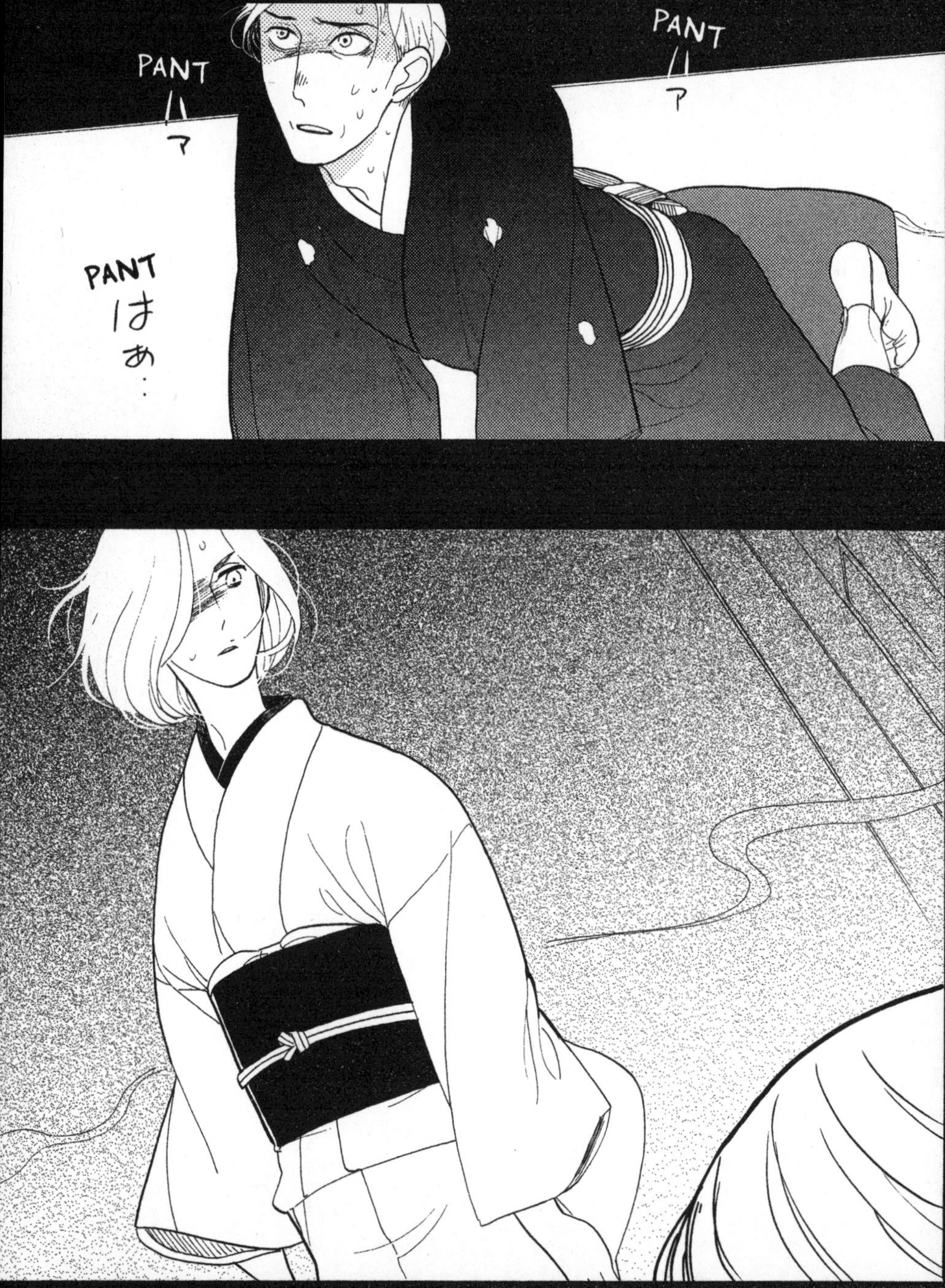
PANT
ハァ
PANT
ハァ
PANT
はぁ‥

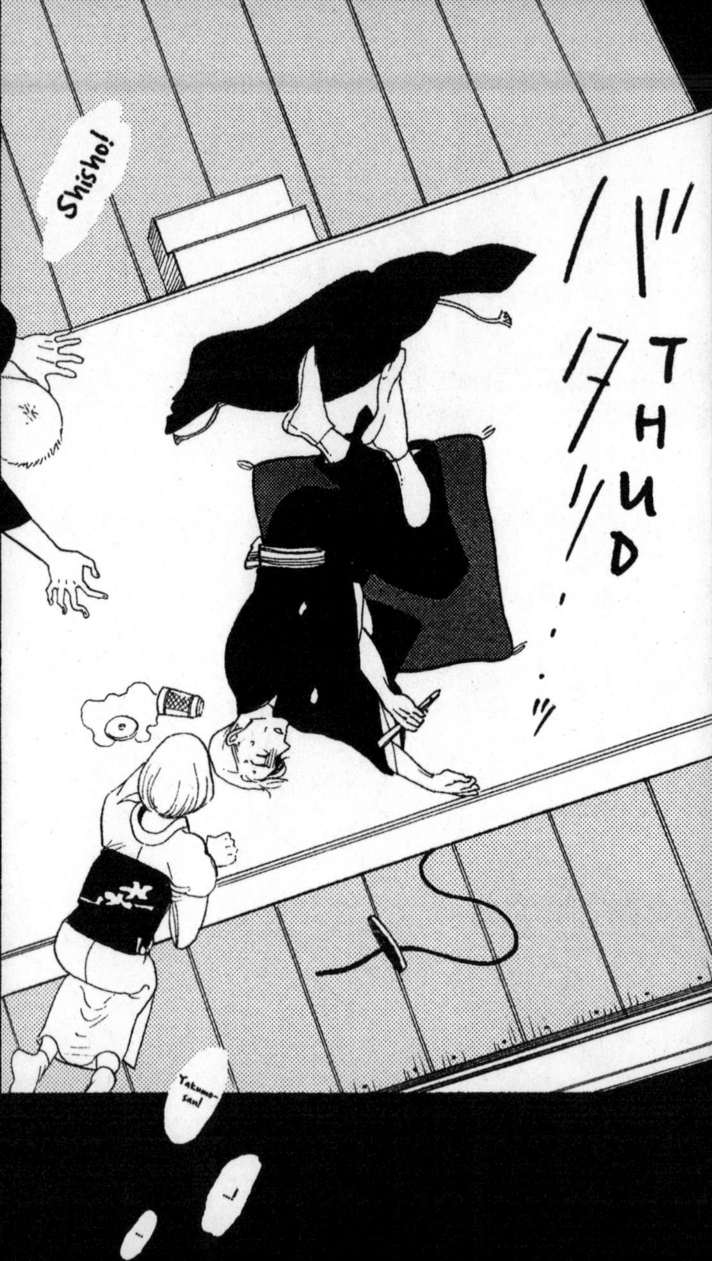
Shisho!
THUD
Takumo-san!
...!
...

DESCENDING
STORIES

SHOWA
GENROKU
RAKUGO
SHINJU

HARUKO KUMOTA

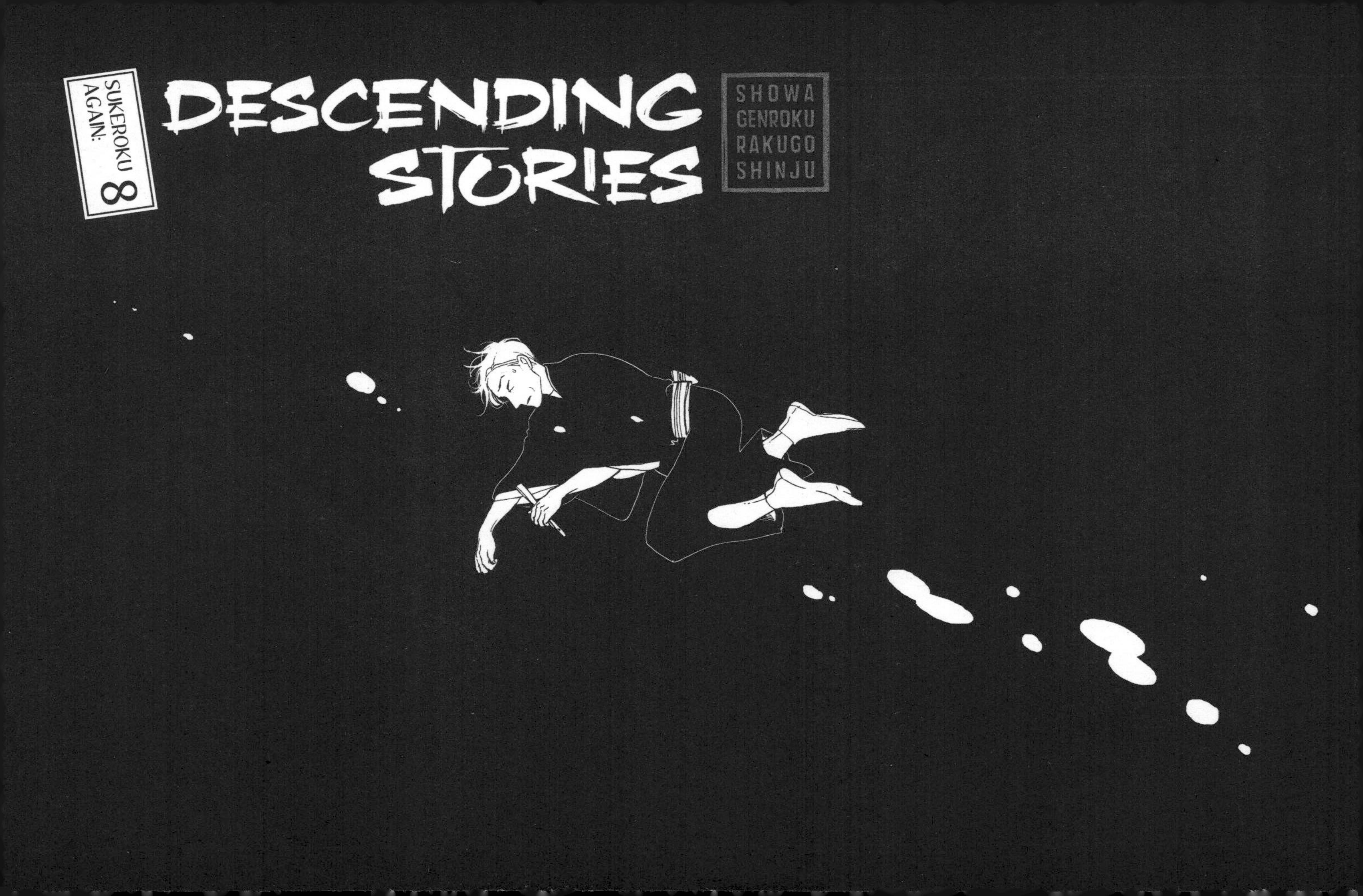
SUKEROKU AGAIN: 8
DESCENDING STORIES
SHOWA GENROKU RAKUGO SHINJU

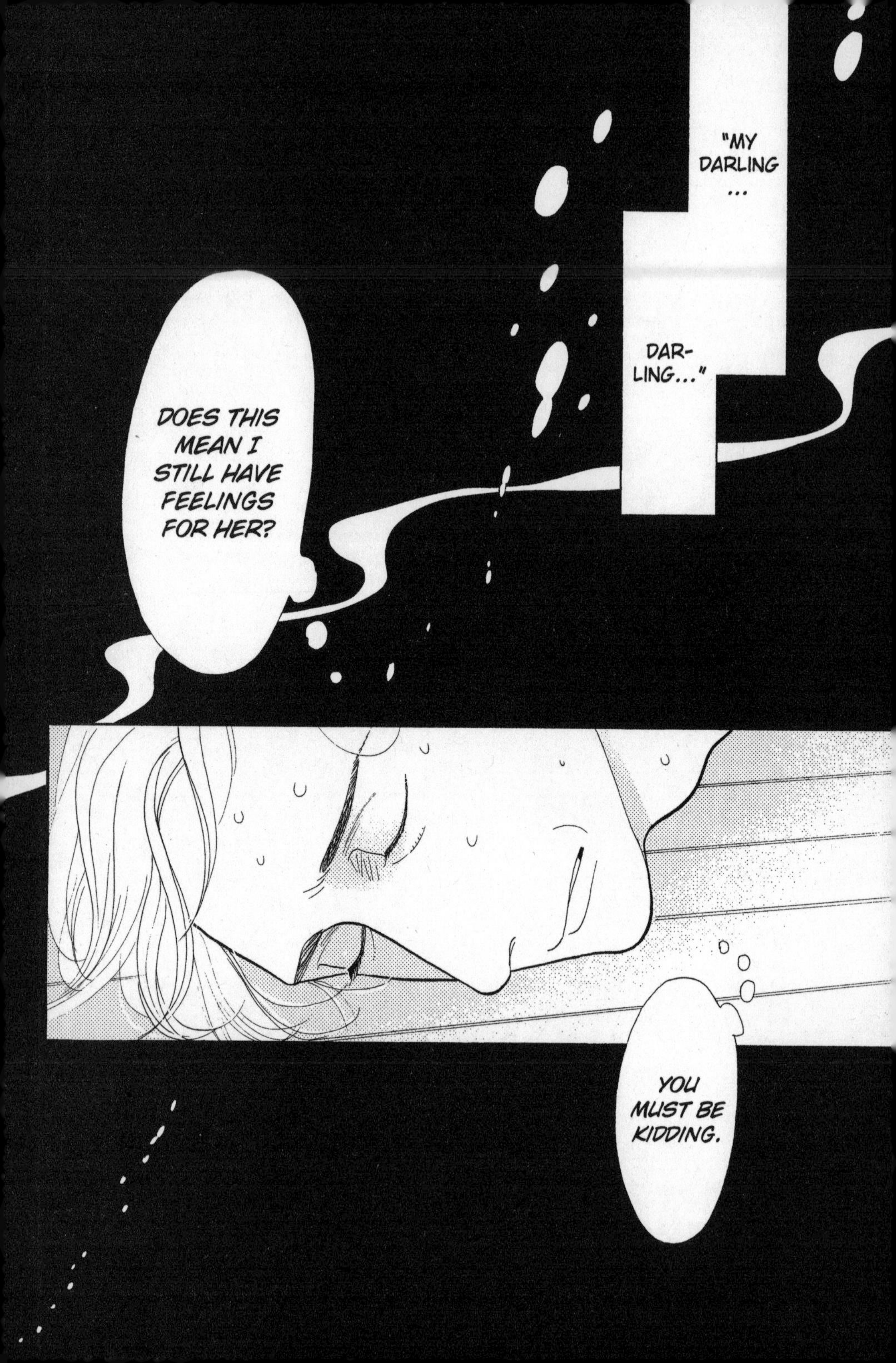
"MY DARLING ...
DAR-LING..."
DOES THIS MEAN I STILL HAVE FEELINGS FOR HER?
YOU MUST BE KIDDING.

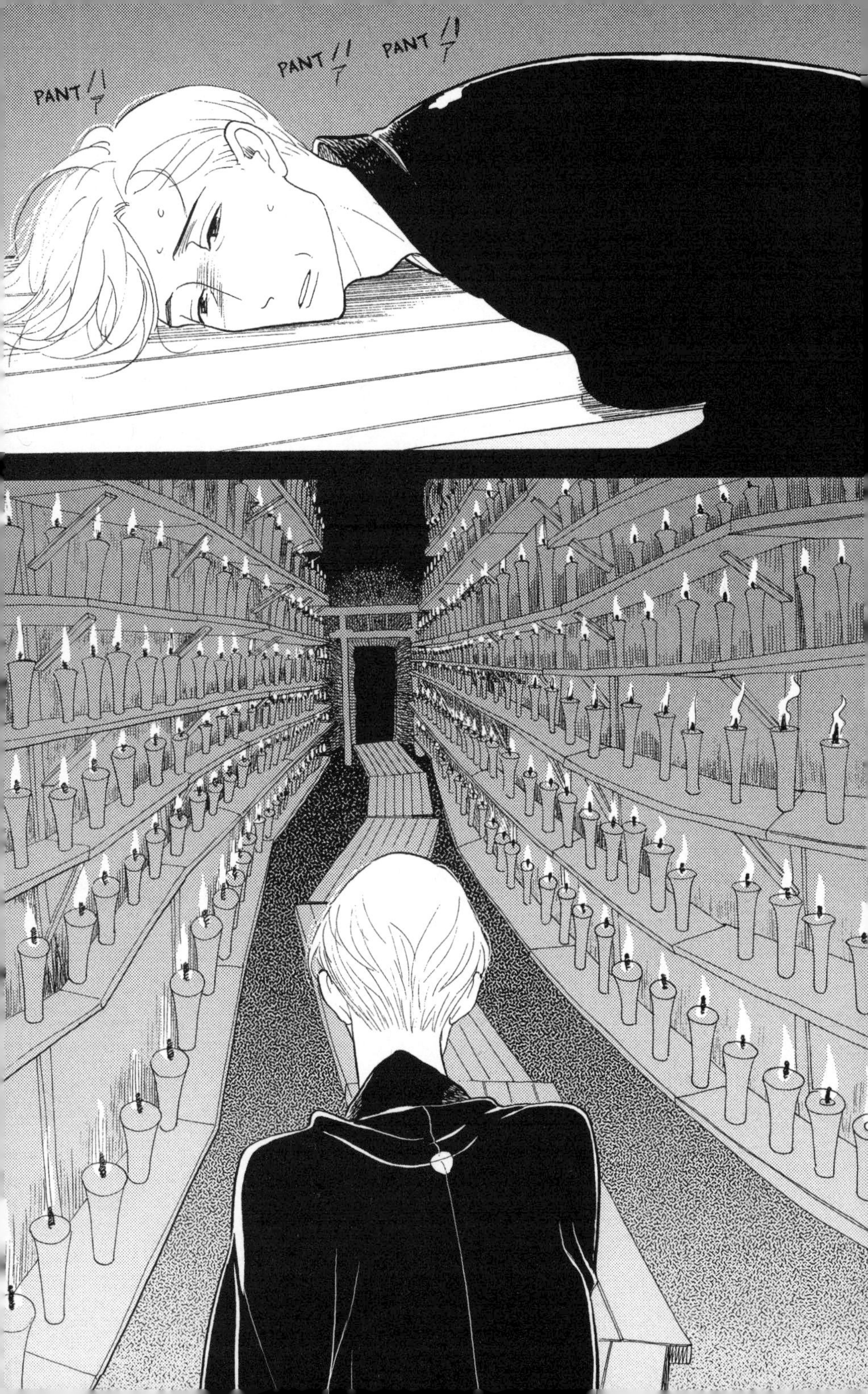
PANT
PANT
PANT

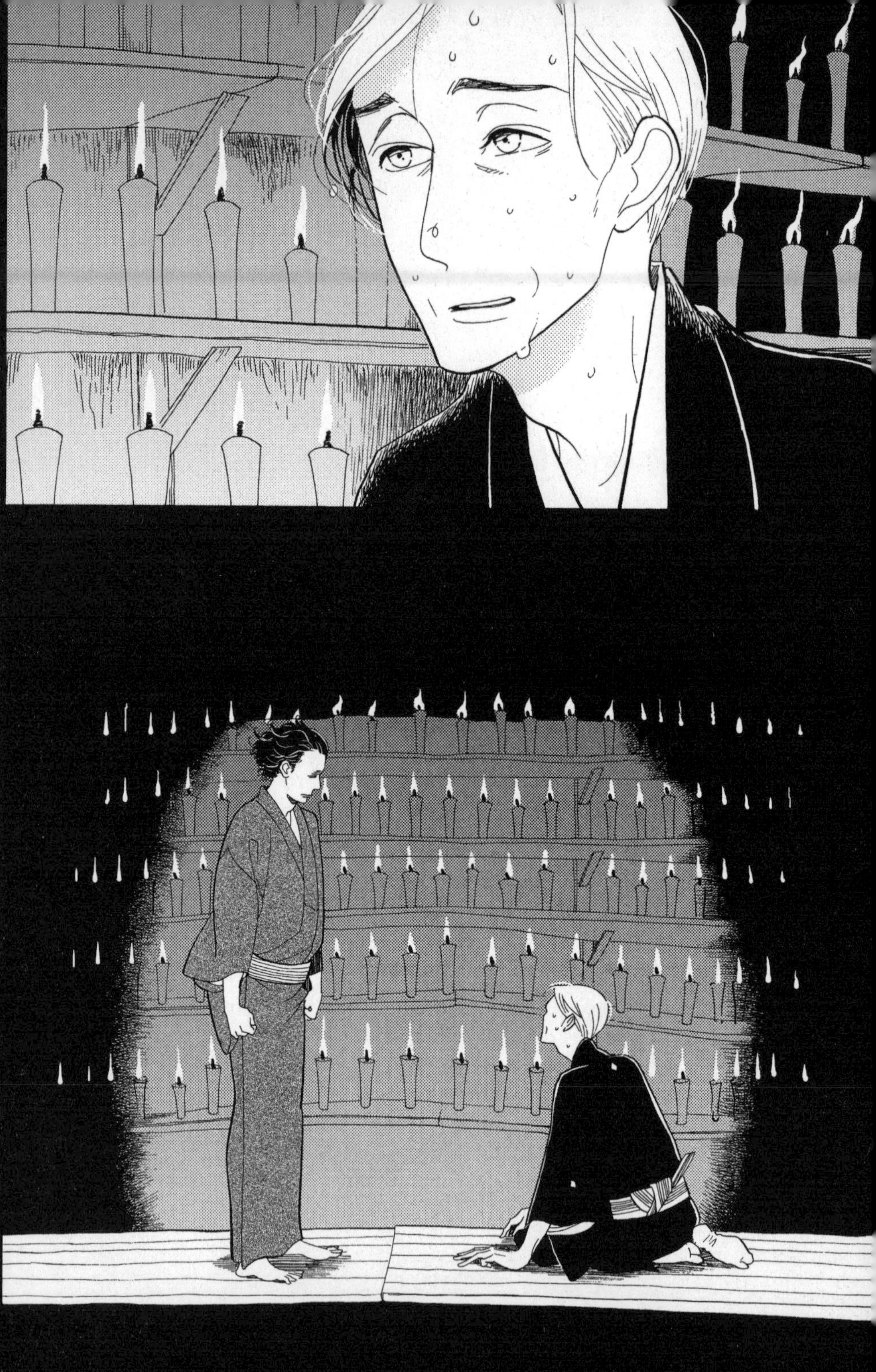

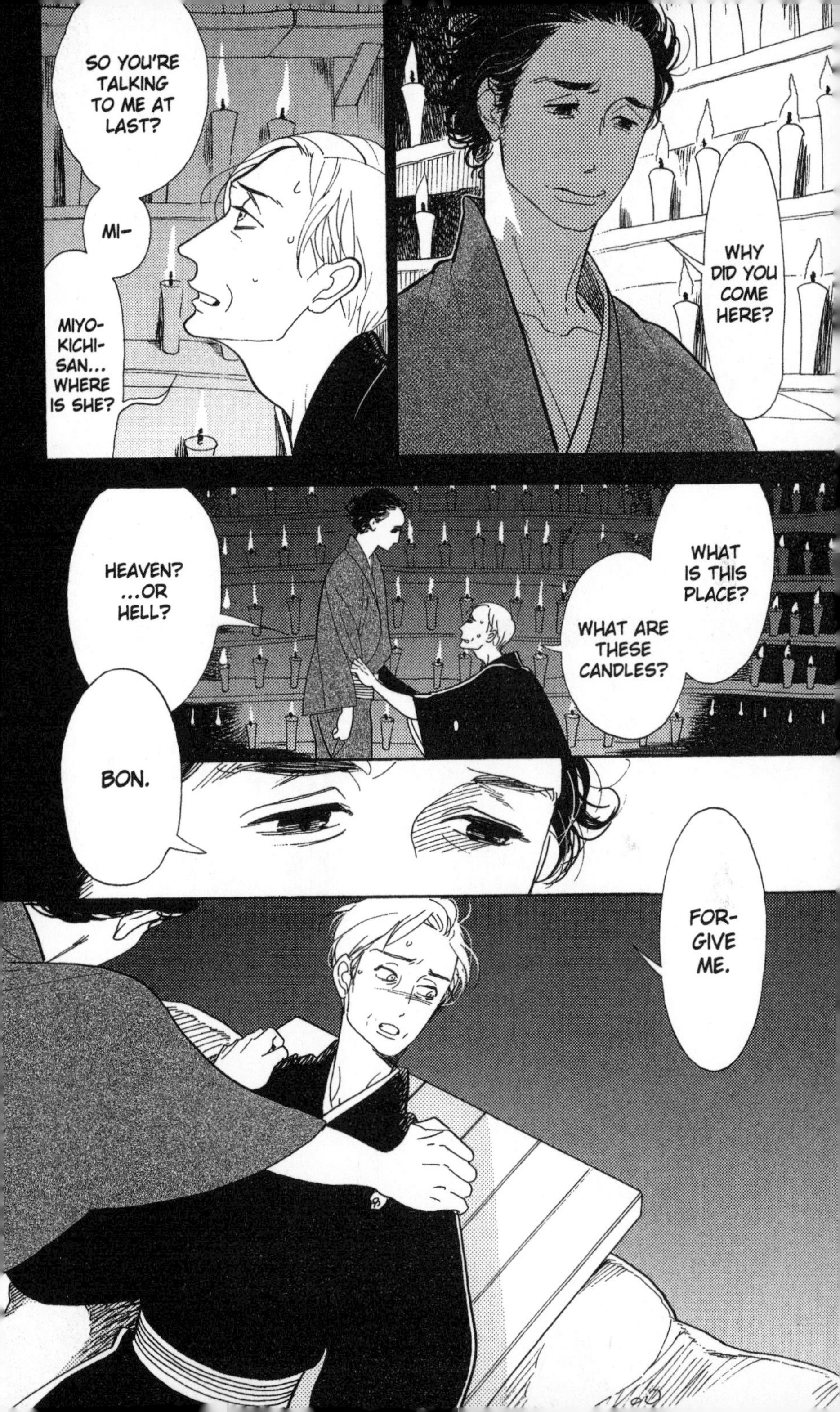
WHY DID YOU COME HERE?
SO YOU'RE TALKING TO ME AT LAST?
MI-
MIYO-KICHI-SAN... WHERE IS SHE?
WHAT IS THIS PLACE?
WHAT ARE THESE CANDLES?
HEAVEN? ...OR HELL?
BON.
FOR-GIVE ME.

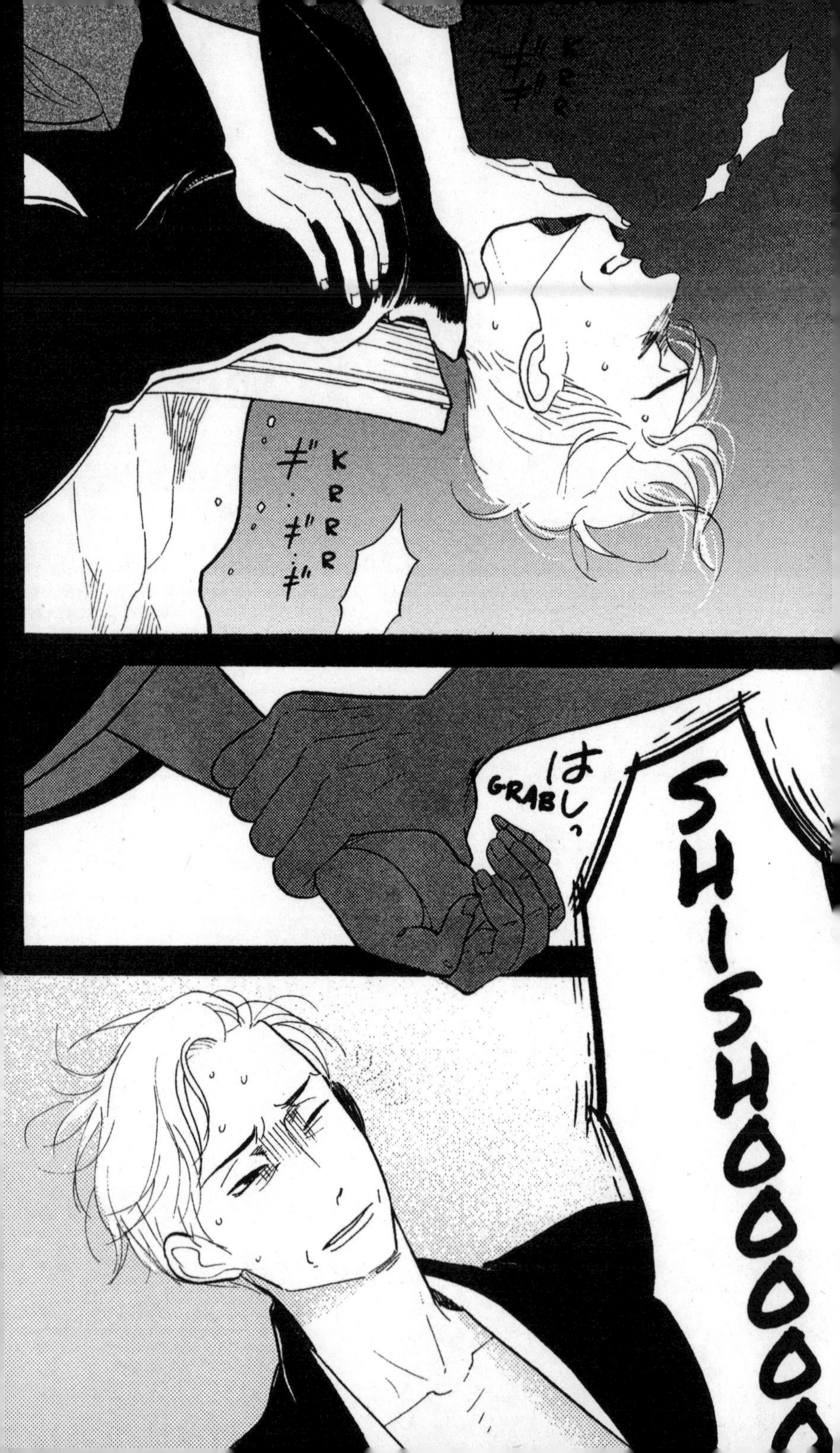

ギ ギ
KRR
ギ ギ ギ
KRRR
はしっ
GRAB
SHHOOOOO

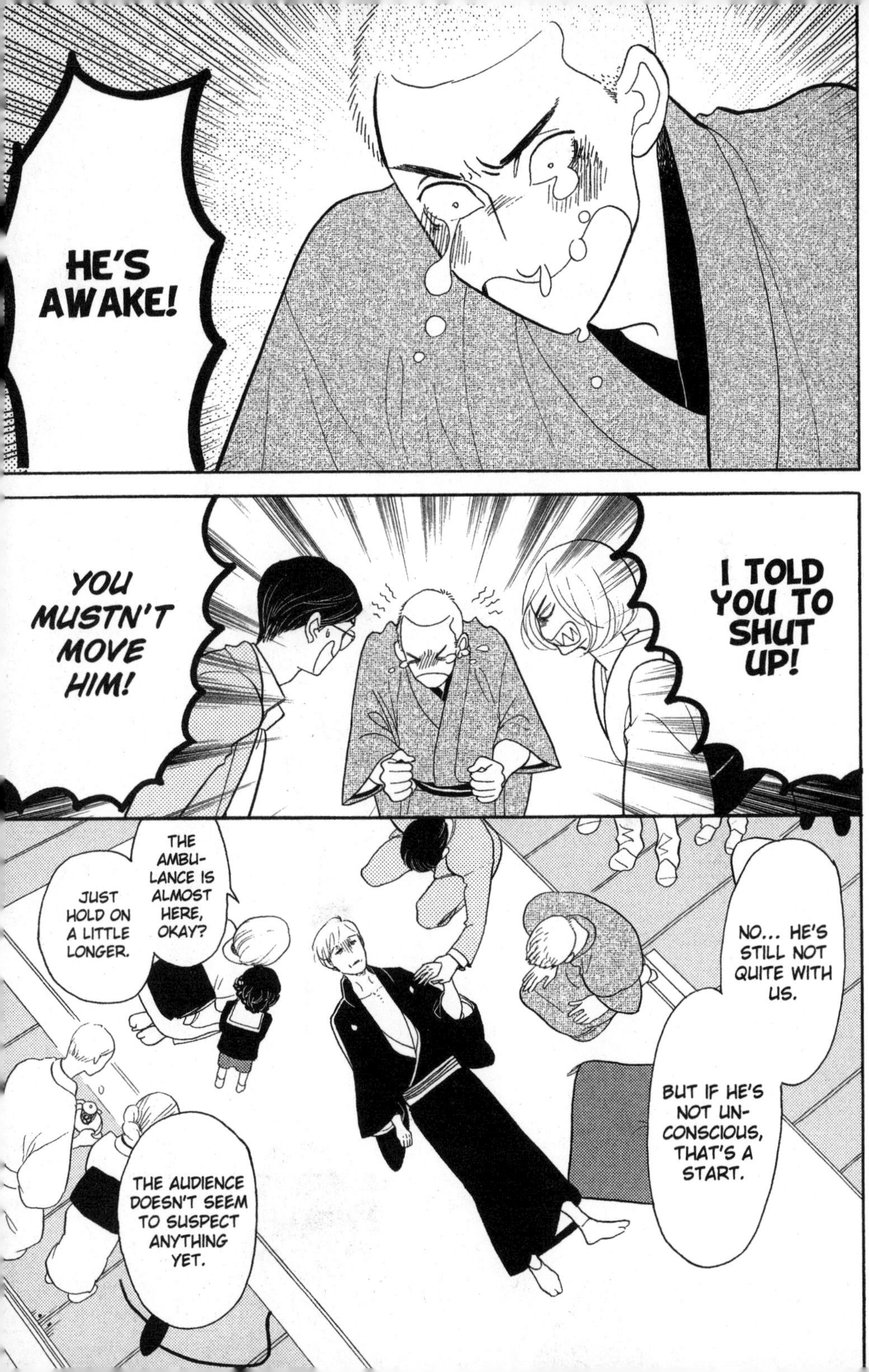
HE'S AWAKE!
I TOLD YOU TO SHUT UP!
YOU MUSTN'T MOVE HIM!
THE AMBU-LANCE IS ALMOST HERE, OKAY?
JUST HOLD ON A LITTLE LONGER.
NO... HE'S STILL NOT QUITE WITH US.
BUT IF HE'S NOT UN-CONSCIOUS, THAT'S A START.
THE AUDIENCE DOESN'T SEEM TO SUSPECT ANYTHING YET.

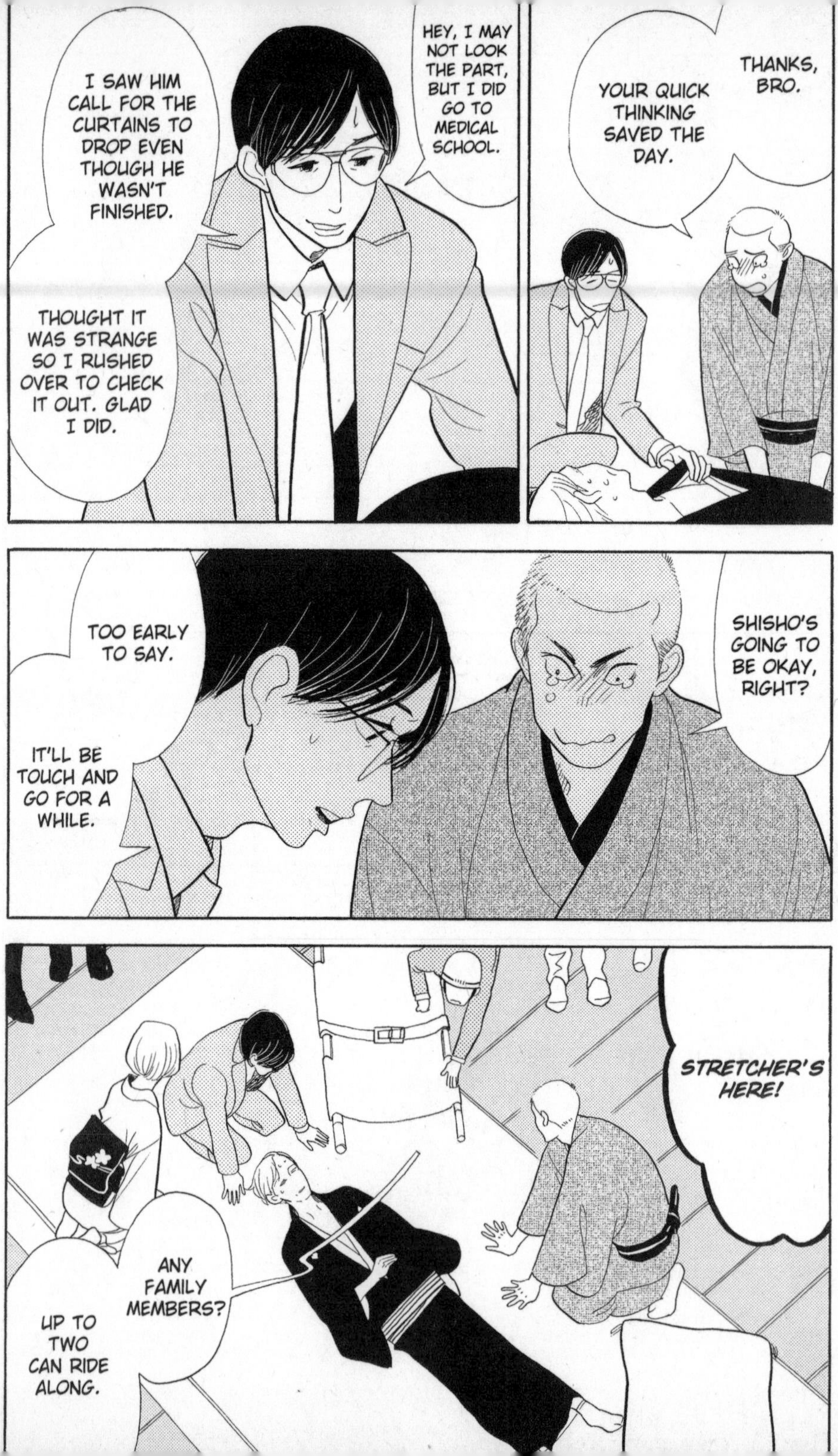
THANKS, BRO.
YOUR QUICK THINKING SAVED THE DAY.
HEY, I MAY NOT LOOK THE PART, BUT I DID GO TO MEDICAL SCHOOL.
I SAW HIM CALL FOR THE CURTAINS TO DROP EVEN THOUGH HE WASN'T FINISHED.
THOUGHT IT WAS STRANGE SO I RUSHED OVER TO CHECK IT OUT. GLAD I DID.
SHISHO'S GOING TO BE OKAY, RIGHT?
TOO EARLY TO SAY.
IT'LL BE TOUCH AND GO FOR A WHILE.
STRETCHER'S HERE!
ANY FAMILY MEMBERS?
UP TO TWO CAN RIDE ALONG.

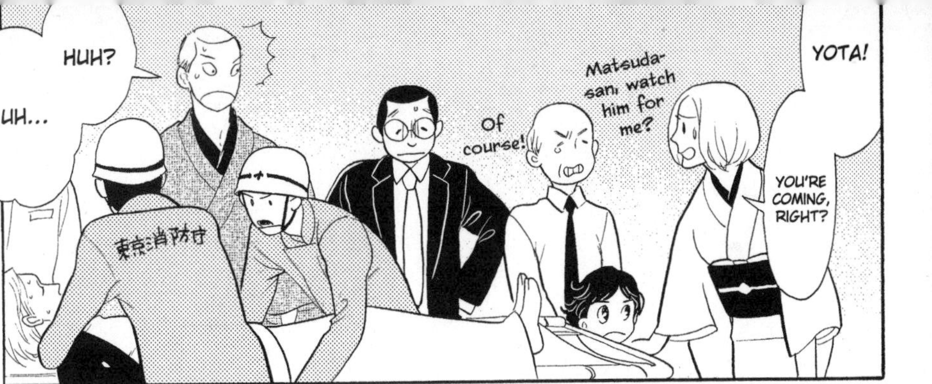
YOTA!
YOU'RE COMING, RIGHT?
Matsuda-san, watch him for me?
Of course!
HUH?
UH...
東京消防庁

Jacket: Tokyo Fire Department

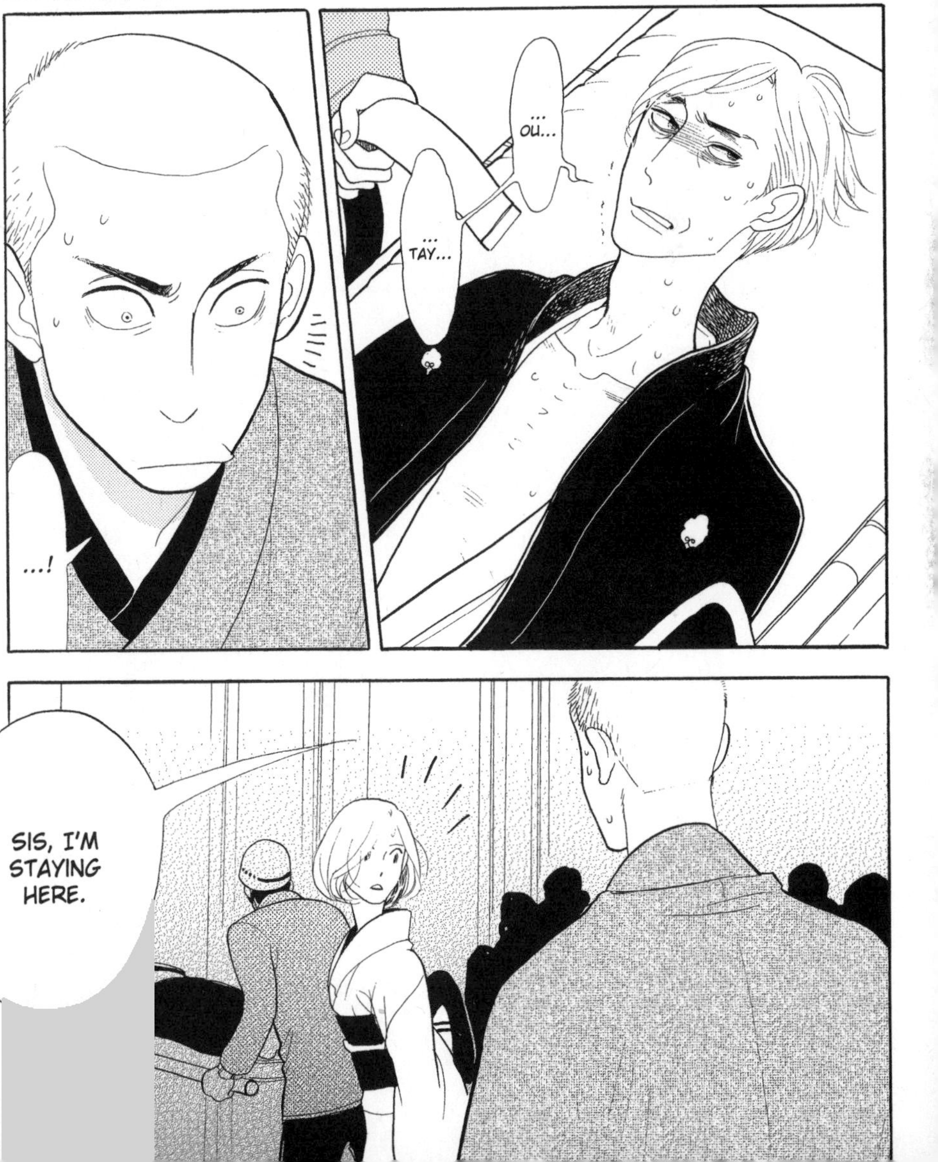
...OU...
...TAY...
...!
SIS, I'M STAYING HERE.

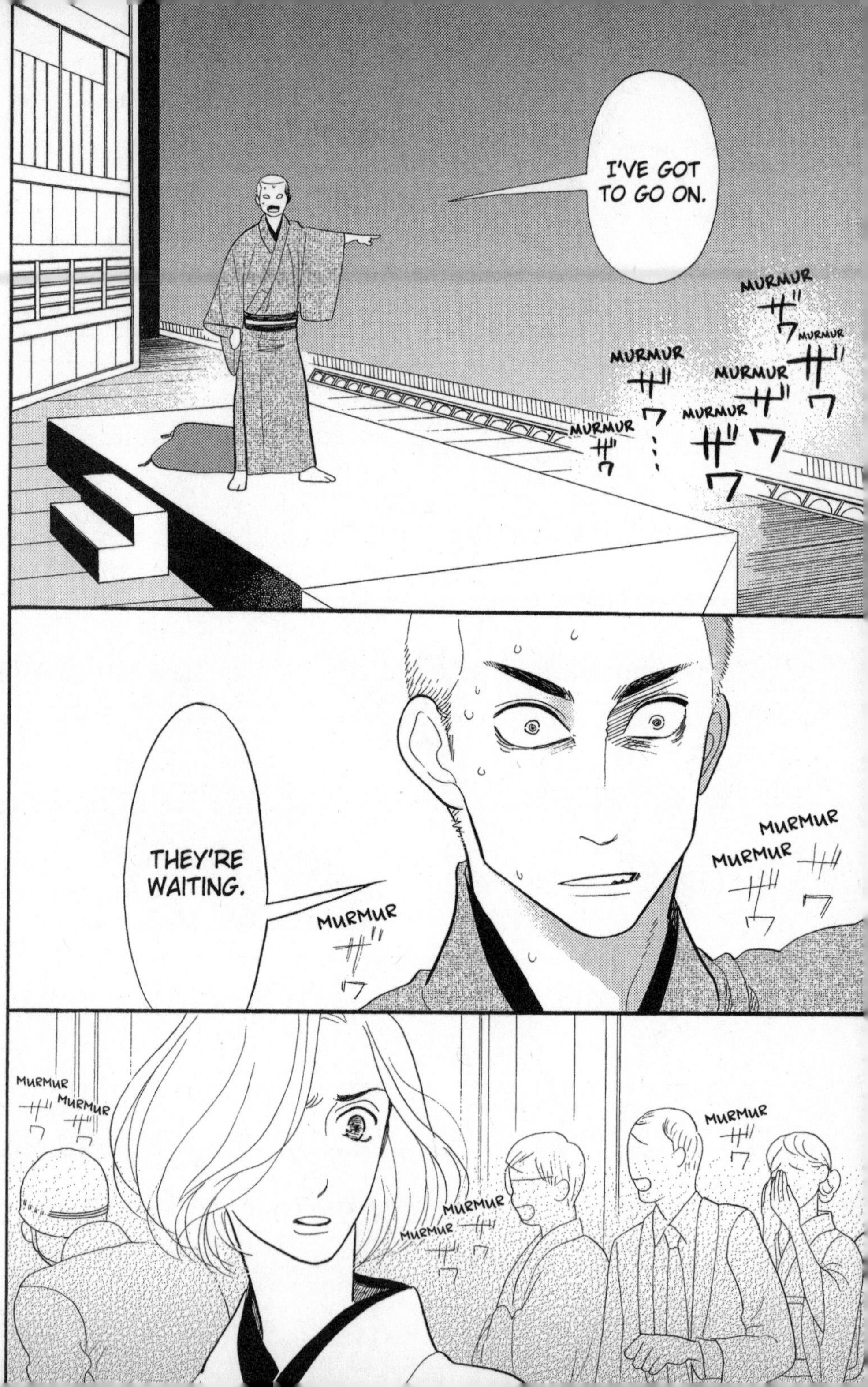
I'VE GOT TO GO ON.
MURMUR
MURMUR
MURMUR
MURMUR
MURMUR
MURMUR
MURMUR
MURMUR
THEY'RE WAITING.
MURMUR
MURMUR
MURMUR
MURMUR
MURMUR
MURMUR
MURMUR
MURMUR

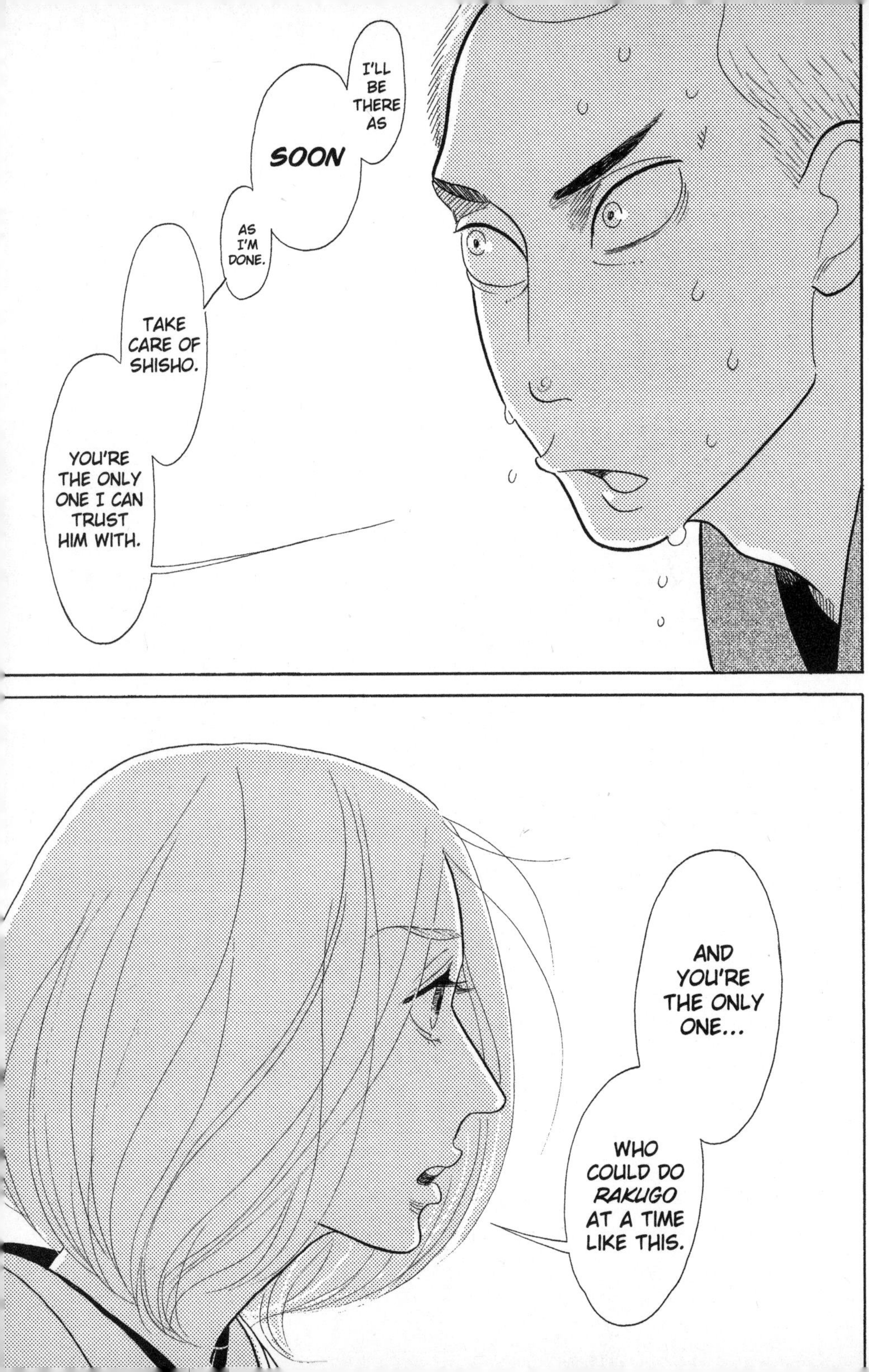
I'LL BE THERE AS
SOON
AS I'M DONE.
TAKE CARE OF SHISHO.
YOU'RE THE ONLY ONE I CAN TRUST HIM WITH.
AND YOU'RE THE ONLY ONE...
WHO COULD DO *RAKUGO* AT A TIME LIKE THIS.

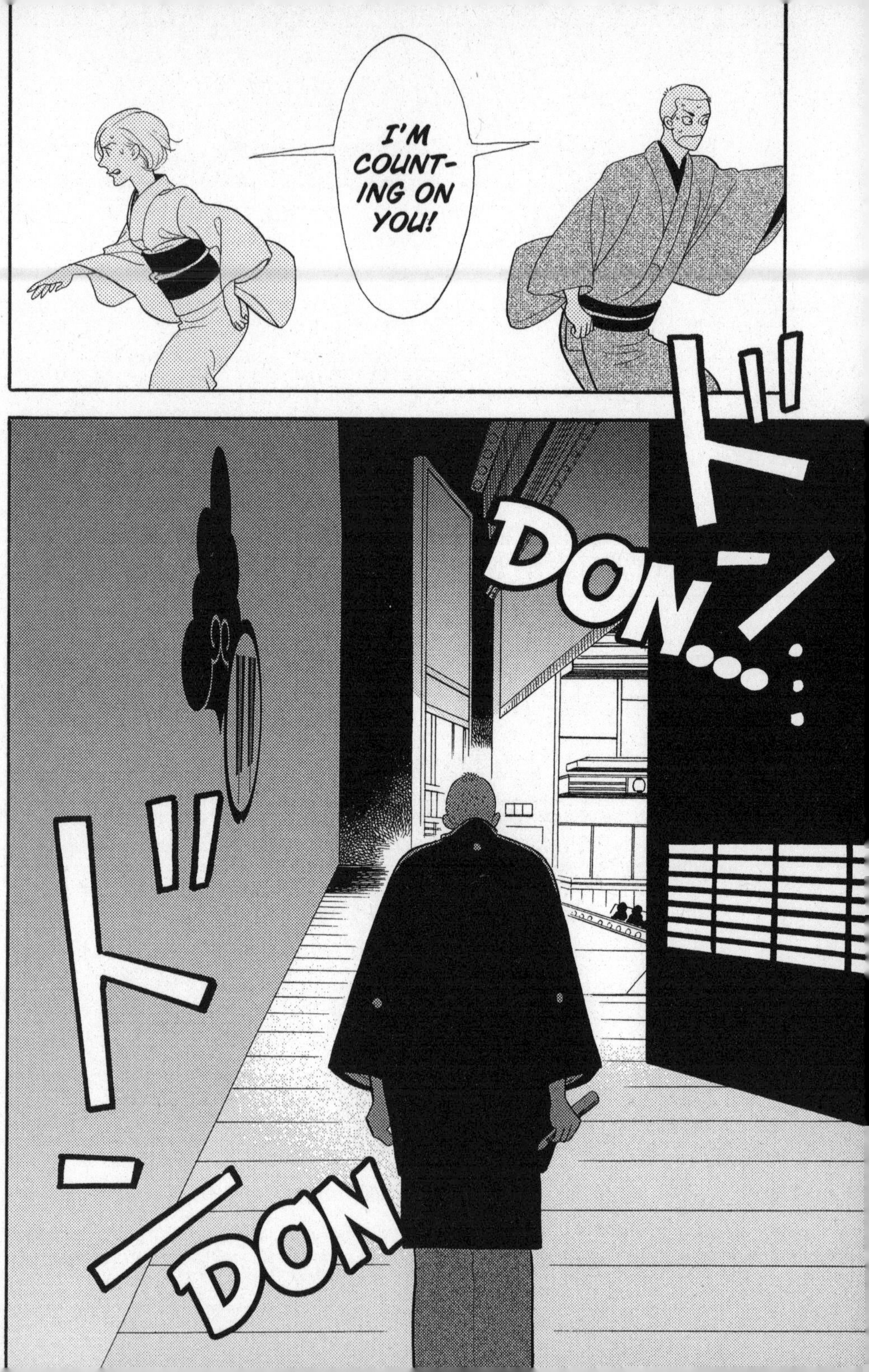
I'M COUNT-ING ON YOU!
ドーン
DON...!
ドーン
DON

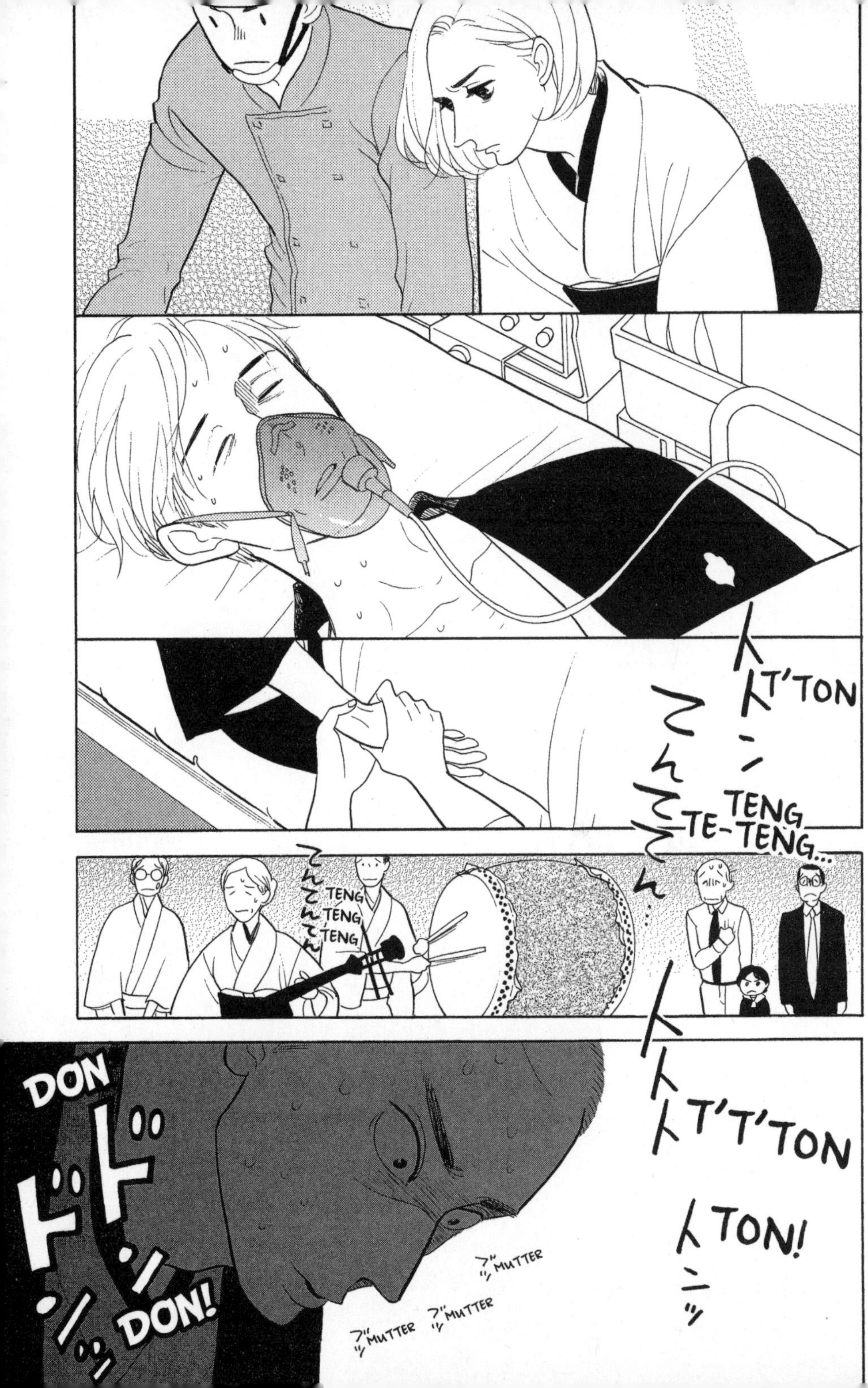
トトン T'TON
てんててん… TENG TE-TENG...
てんてんてん TENG TENG TENG
トトトン T'T'TON
トンッ TON!
ドドンッ DON DON!
ブツ MUTTER
ブツ MUTTER
ブツ MUTTER

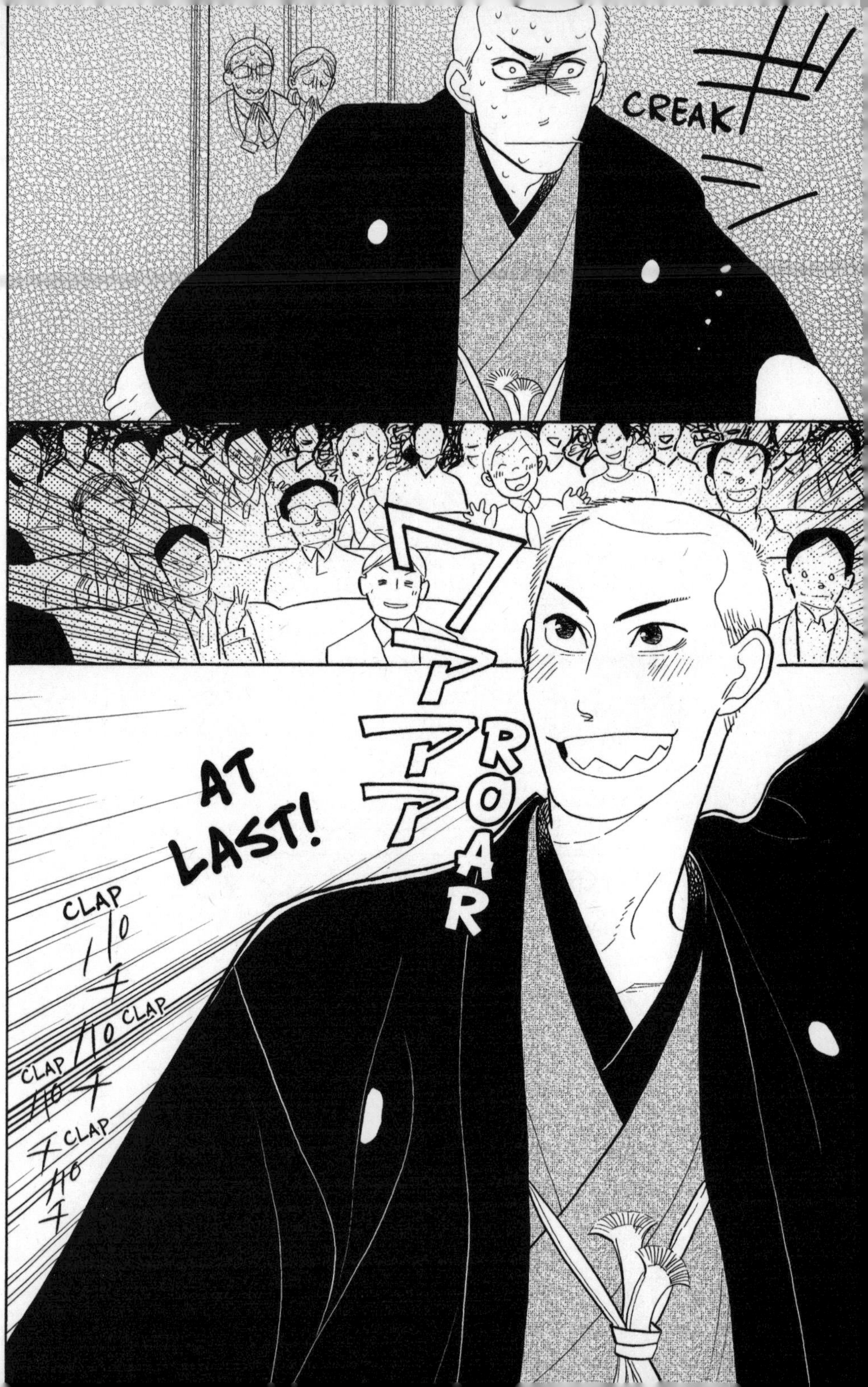
CREAK
ROAR
AT LAST!
CLAP
CLAP
CLAP
CLAP

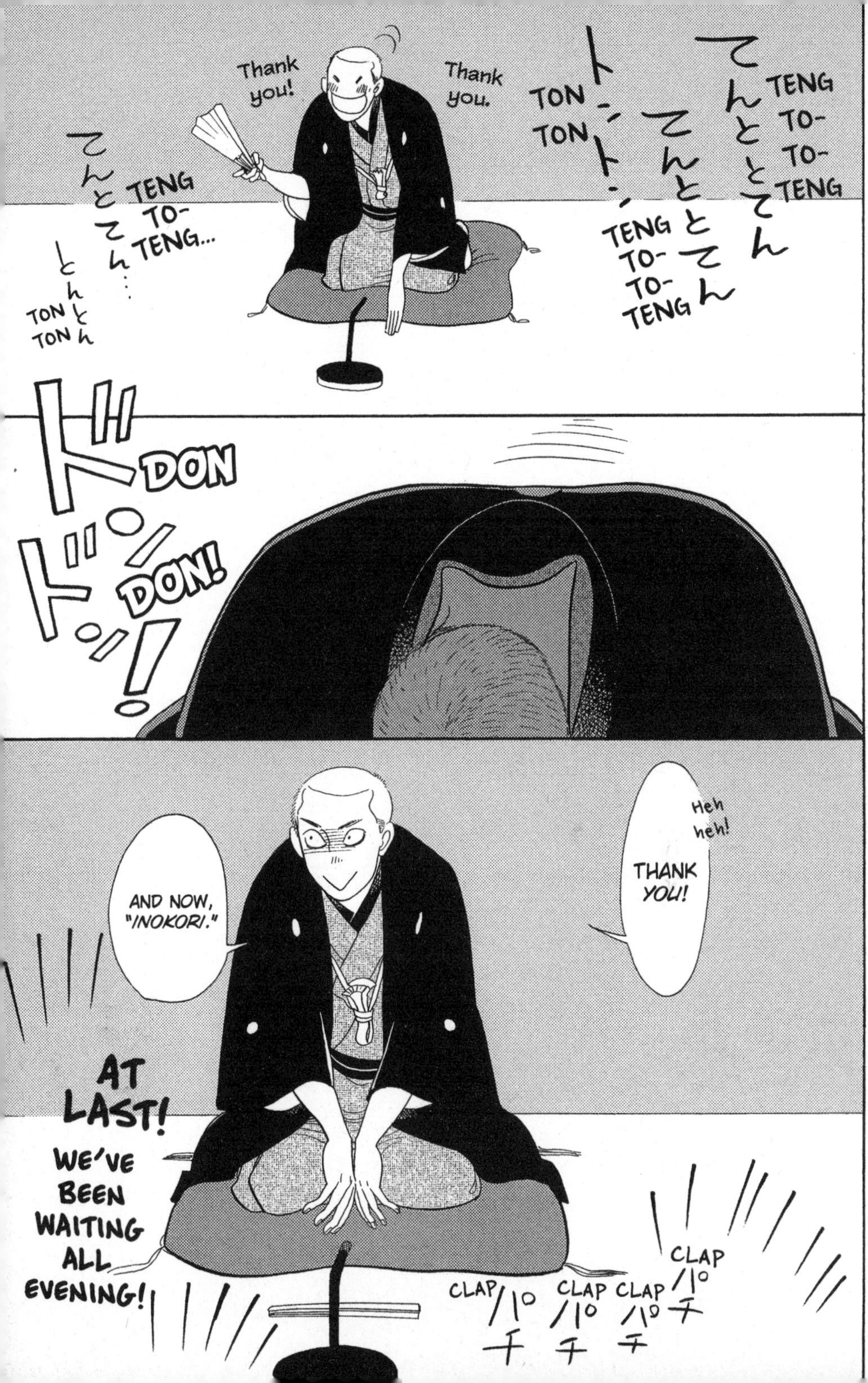
てんとてん
TENG TO-TO-TENG
トントン
TON TON
てんとてん
TENG TO-TO-TENG
Thank you.
Thank you!
てんとてん…
TENG TO-TENG...
とんとん
TON TON
ドン
DON
ドン!
DON!
Heh heh!
THANK YOU!
AND NOW, "INOKORI."
AT LAST! WE'VE BEEN WAITING ALL EVENING!
パチ
CLAP
パチ
CLAP
パチ
CLAP
パチ
CLAP

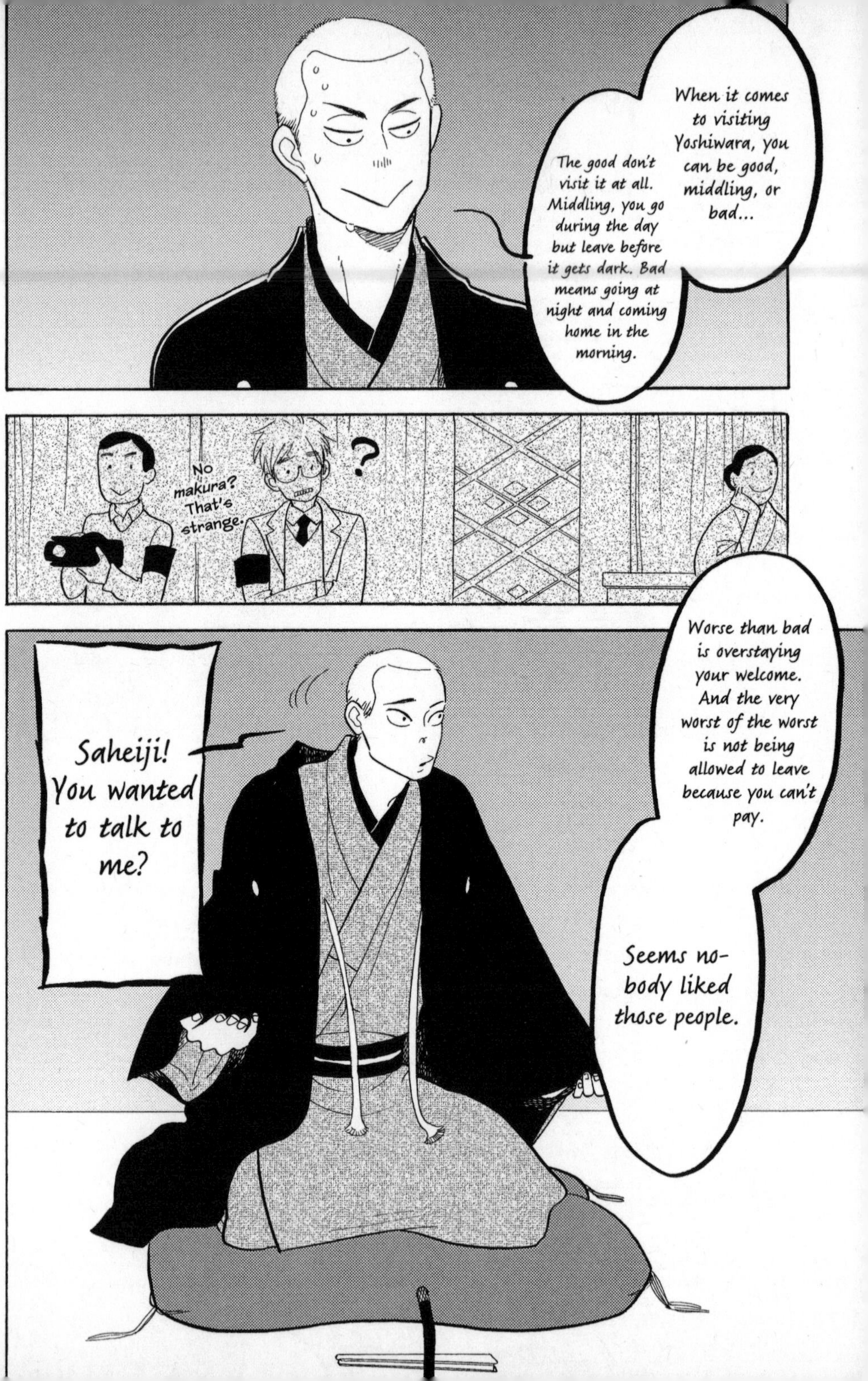
When it comes to visiting Yoshiwara, you can be good, middling, or bad...
The good don't visit it at all. Middling, you go during the day but leave before it gets dark. Bad means going at night and coming home in the morning.
No makura? That's strange.
?
Worse than bad is overstaying your welcome. And the very worst of the worst is not being allowed to leave because you can't pay.
Seems no-body liked those people.
Saheiji! You wanted to talk to me?

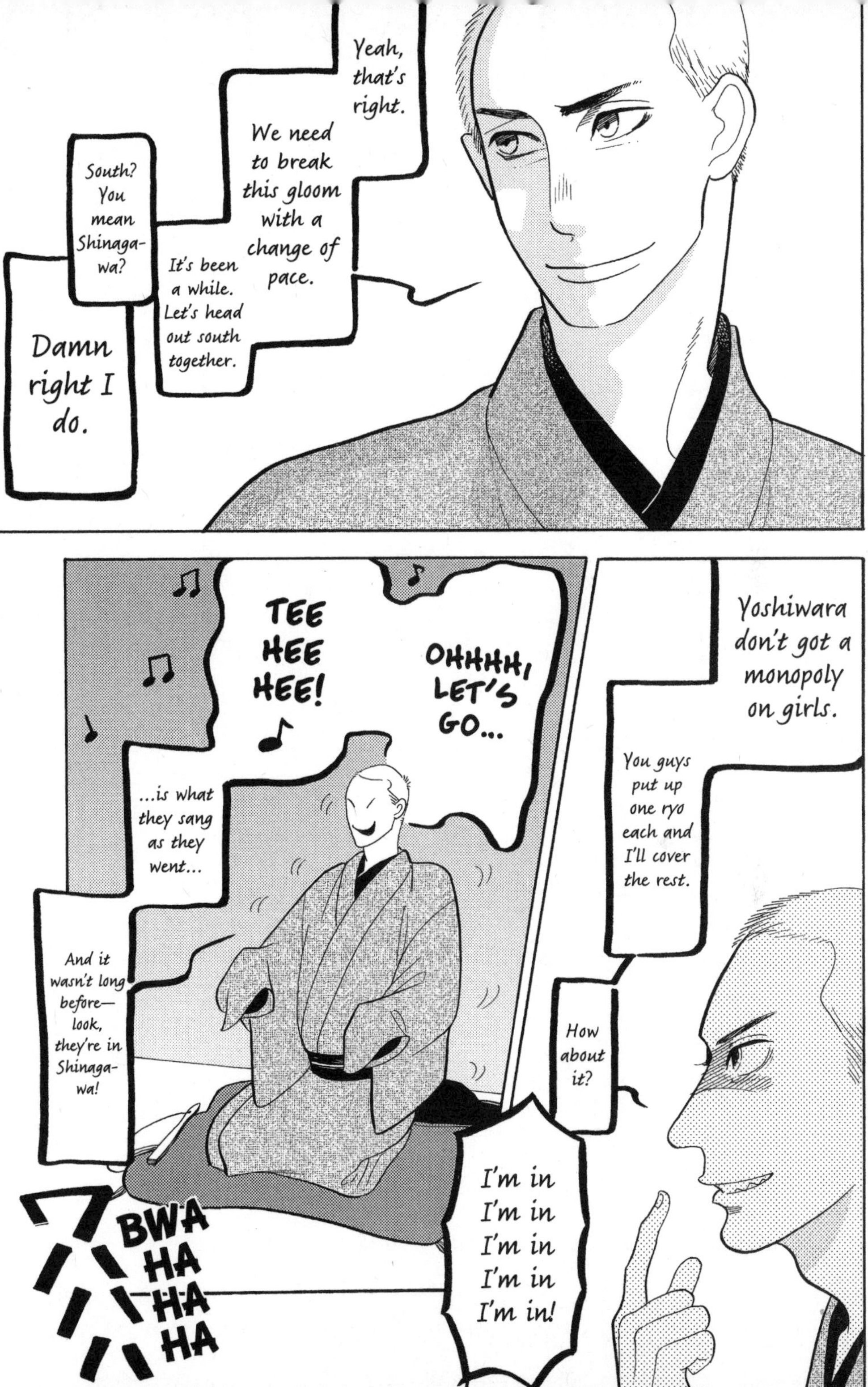

Yeah, that's right.
We need to break this gloom with a change of pace.
It's been a while. Let's head out south together.
South? You mean Shinaga-wa?
Damn right I do.
Yoshiwara don't got a monopoly on girls.
You guys put up one ryo each and I'll cover the rest.
How about it?
I'm in I'm in I'm in I'm in I'm in!
OHHHH, LET'S GO...
TEE HEE HEE!
...is what they sang as they went...
And it wasn't long before—look, they're in Shinaga-wa!
BWA HA HA HA

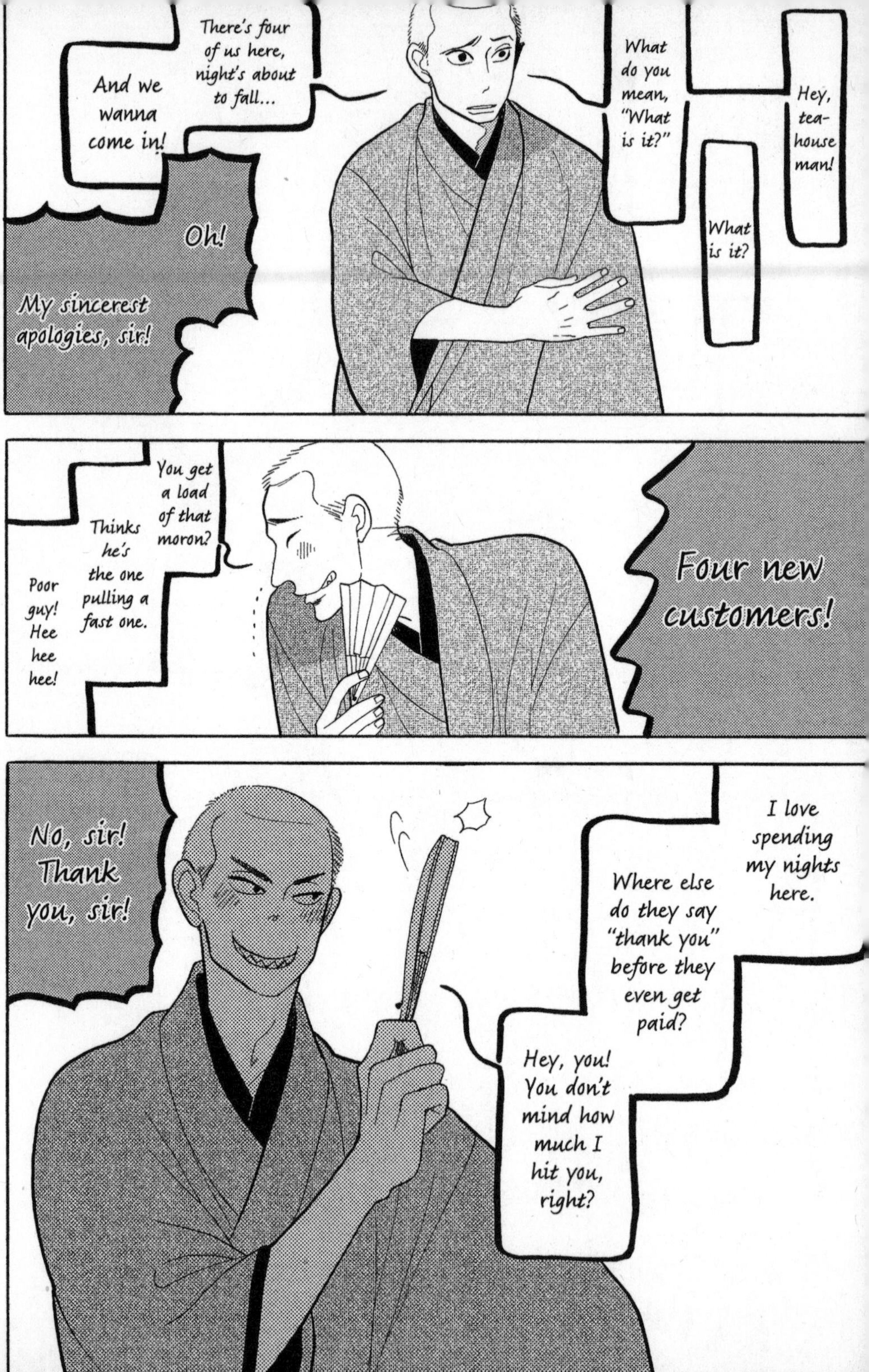
Hey, teahouse man!
What is it?
What do you mean, "What is it?"
There's four of us here, night's about to fall...
And we wanna come in!
Oh!
My sincerest apologies, sir!
Four new customers!
You get a load of that moron?
Thinks he's the one pulling a fast one.
Poor guy! Hee hee hee!
I love spending my nights here.
Where else do they say "thank you" before they even get paid?
Hey, you! You don't mind how much I hit you, right?
No, sir! Thank you, sir!

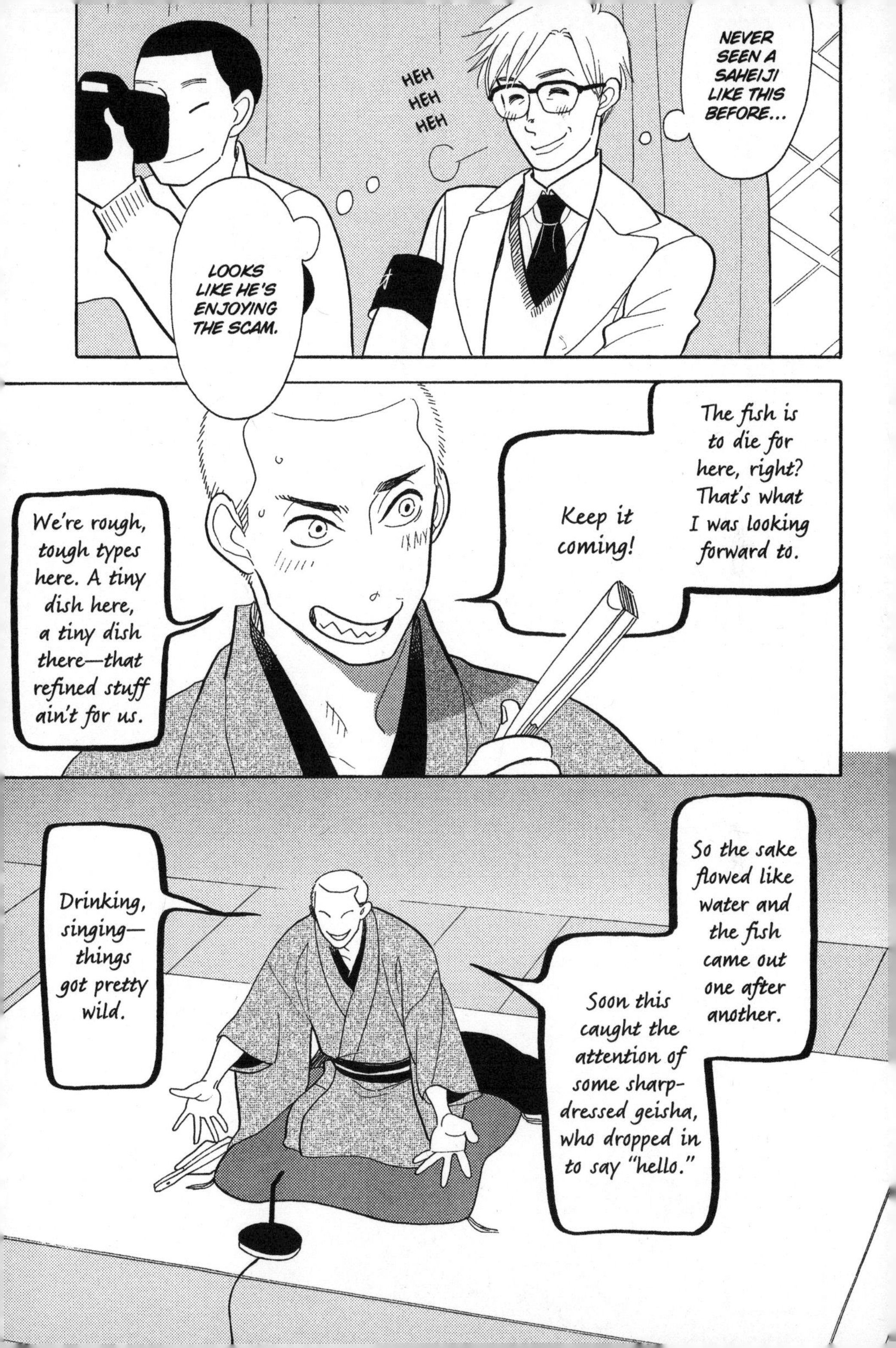
NEVER SEEN A SAHEIJI LIKE THIS BEFORE...
HEH HEH HEH
LOOKS LIKE HE'S ENJOYING THE SCAM.
The fish is to die for here, right? That's what I was looking forward to.
Keep it coming!
We're rough, tough types here. A tiny dish here, a tiny dish there—that refined stuff ain't for us.
So the sake flowed like water and the fish came out one after another.
Soon this caught the attention of some sharp-dressed geisha, who dropped in to say "hello."
Drinking, singing—things got pretty wild.

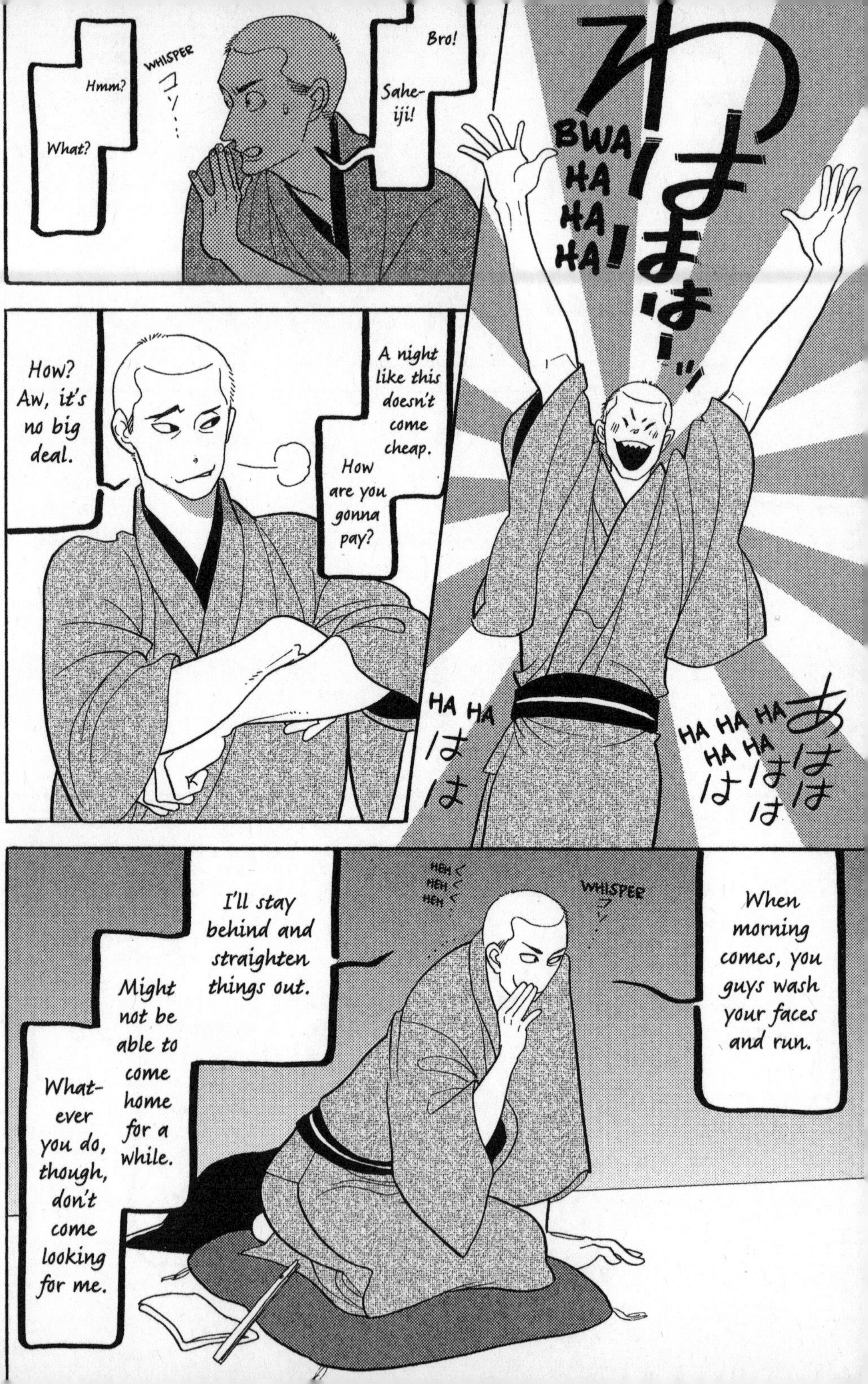

わっはっは!!
BWA HA HA HA!
あははは
HA HA HA HA HA
はは
HA HA
Bro!
Sahe-iji!
WHISPER
コソ…
Hmm?
What?
A night like this doesn't come cheap.
How are you gonna pay?
How? Aw, it's no big deal.
When morning comes, you guys wash your faces and run.
WHISPER
コソ
HEH HEH HEH
I'll stay behind and straighten things out.
Might not be able to come home for a while.
What-ever you do, though, don't come looking for me.

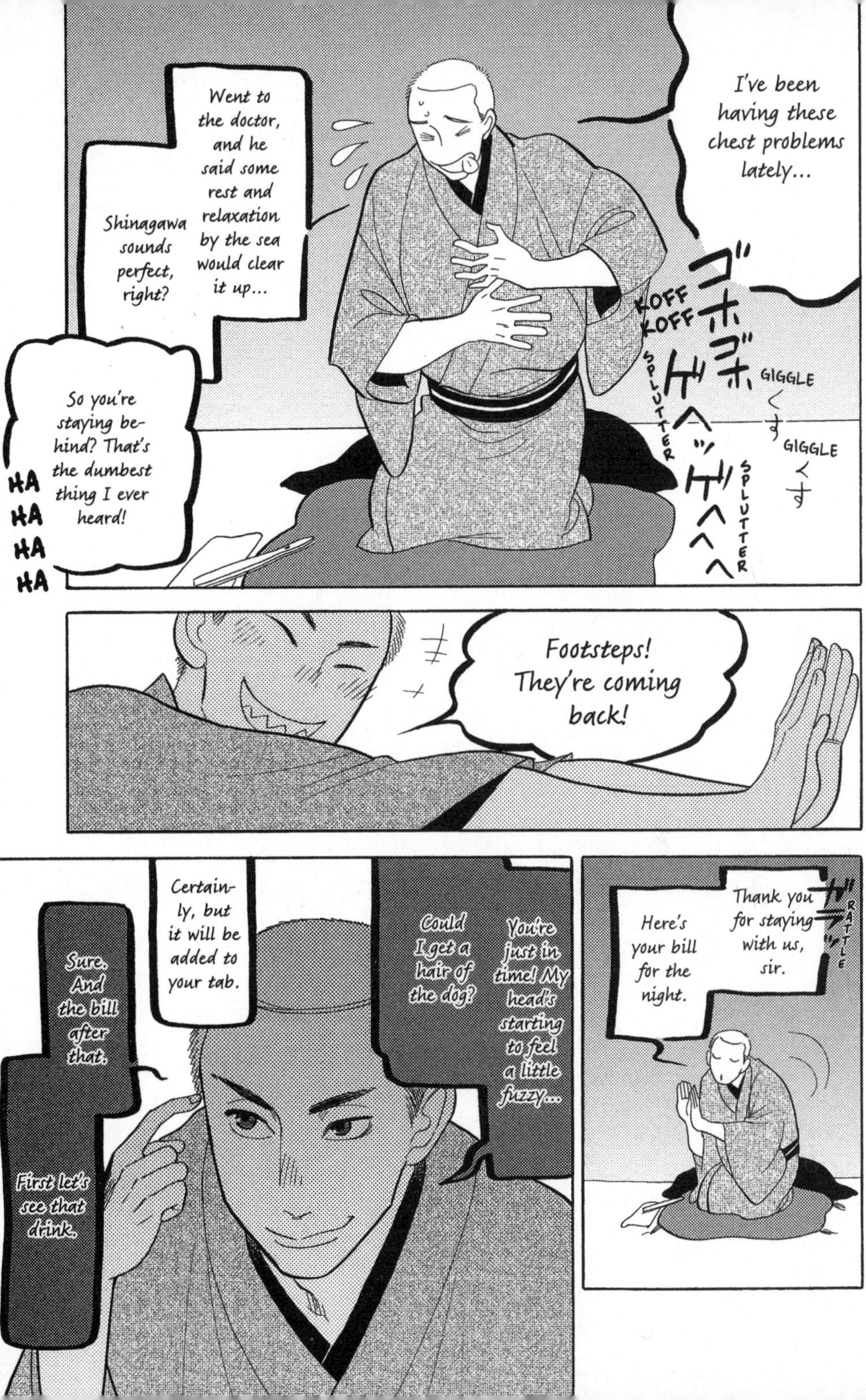
I've been having these chest problems lately...
Went to the doctor, and he said some rest and relaxation by the sea would clear it up...
Shinagawa sounds perfect, right?
ゴホゴホ KOFF KOFF
ゲヘッゲヘヘヘ SPLUTTER SPLUTTER
くす GIGGLE
くす GIGGLE
So you're staying be-hind? That's the dumbest thing I ever heard!
HA HA HA HA
Footsteps! They're coming back!
ガラッ RATTLE
Thank you for staying with us, sir.
Here's your bill for the night.
You're just in time! My head's starting to feel a little fuzzy...
Could I get a hair of the dog?
Certain-ly, but it will be added to your tab.
Sure. And the bill after that.
First let's see that drink.

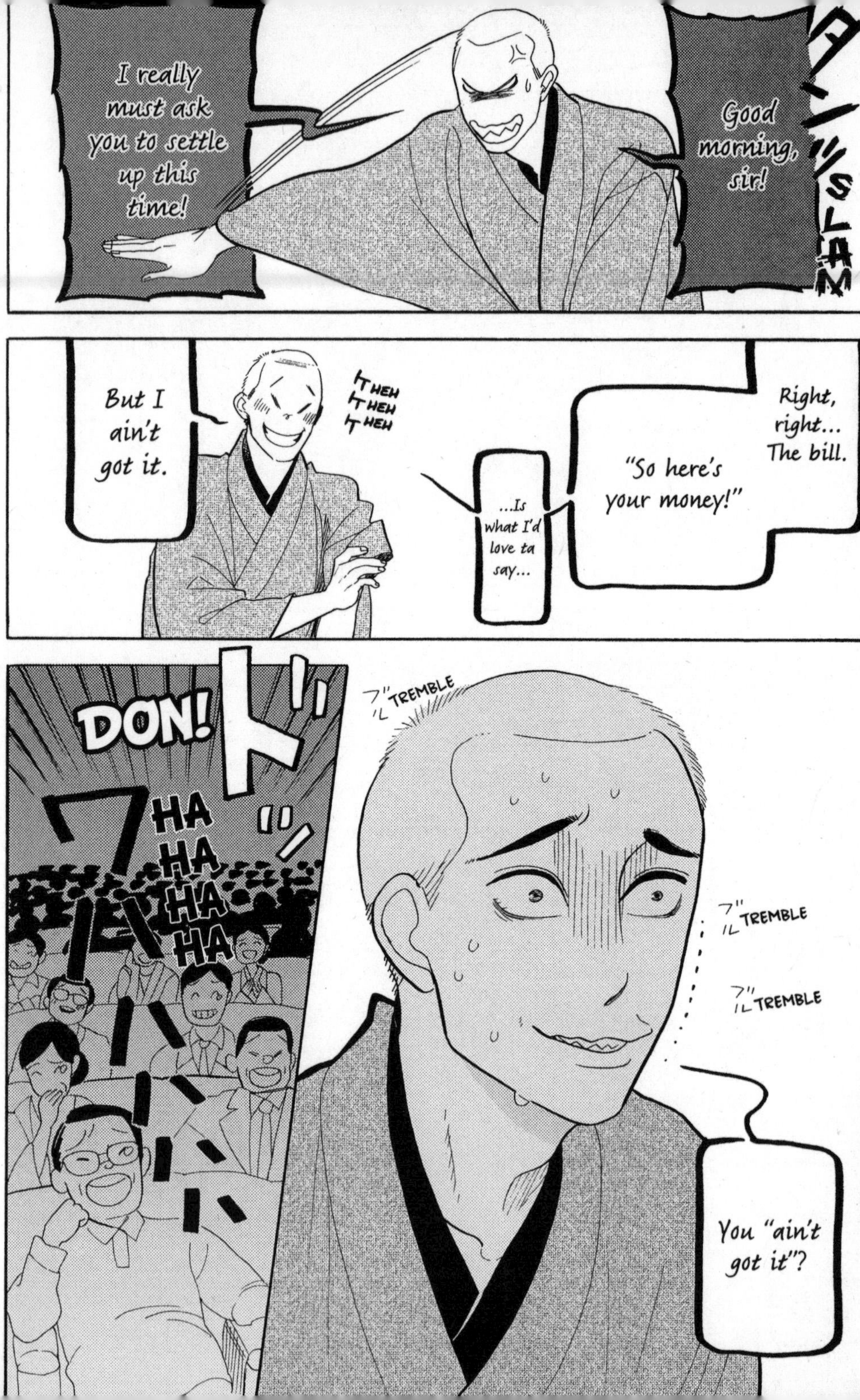
Good morning, sir!
SLAM
I really must ask you to settle up this time!
Right, right... The bill.
"So here's your money!"
...Is what I'd love ta say...
HEH HEH HEH
But I ain't got it.
TREMBLE
TREMBLE
TREMBLE
You "ain't got it"?
DON!
HA HA HA HA

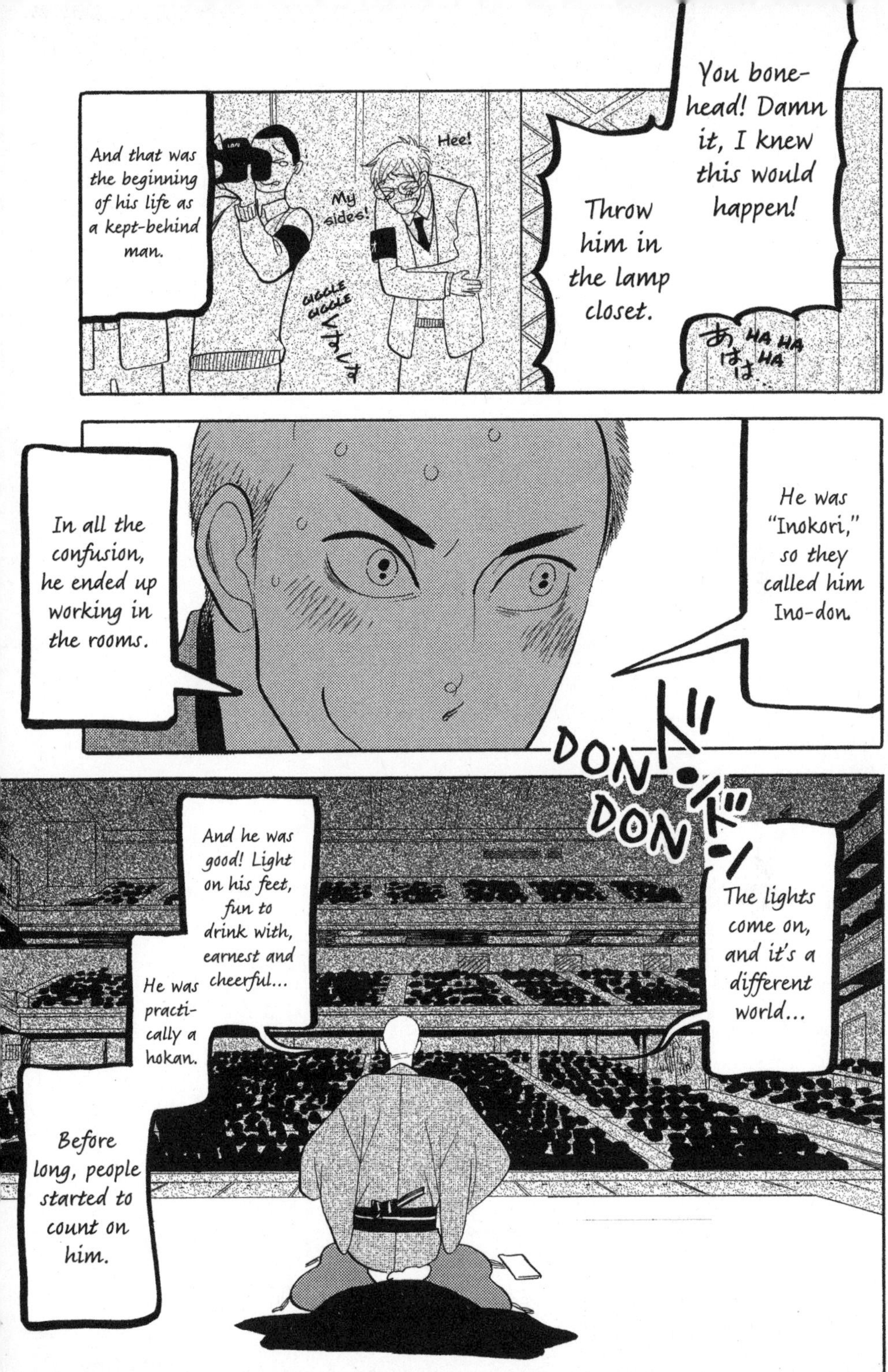
You bone-head! Damn it, I knew this would happen!
Throw him in the lamp closet.
あはは HA HA HA
Hee!
My sides!
GIGGLE GIGGLE くすくす
And that was the beginning of his life as a kept-behind man.
He was "Inokori," so they called him Ino-don.
In all the confusion, he ended up working in the rooms.
DON DON ドン ドン
The lights come on, and it's a different world...
And he was good! Light on his feet, fun to drink with, earnest and cheerful...
He was practically a hokan.
Before long, people started to count on him.

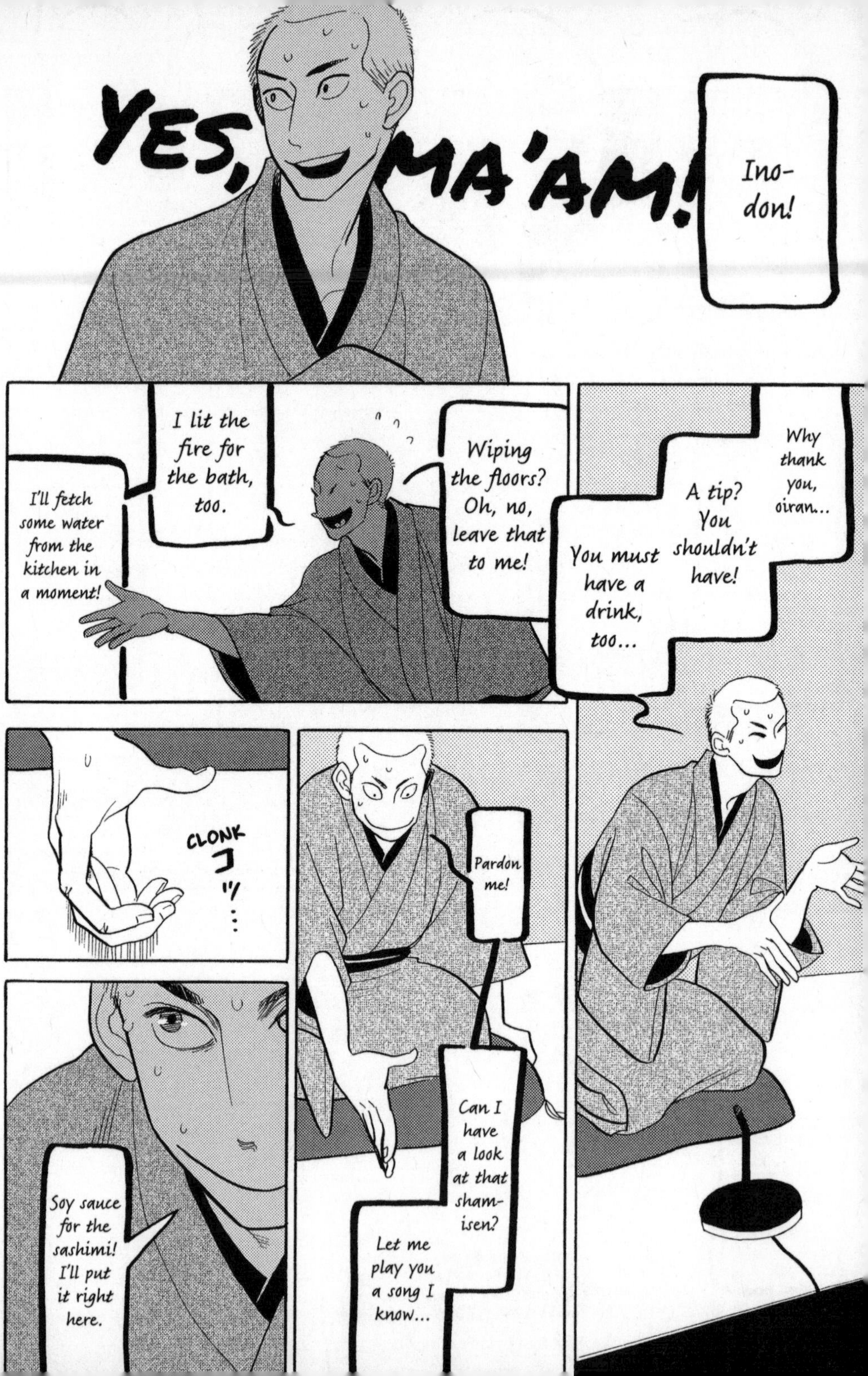
Ino-don!
YES, MA'AM!
Why thank you, oiran...
A tip? You shouldn't have!
You must have a drink, too...
Wiping the floors? Oh, no, leave that to me!
I lit the fire for the bath, too.
I'll fetch some water from the kitchen in a moment!
Pardon me!
Can I have a look at that shamisen?
Let me play you a song I know...
CLONK
コツ…
Soy sauce for the sashimi! I'll put it right here.

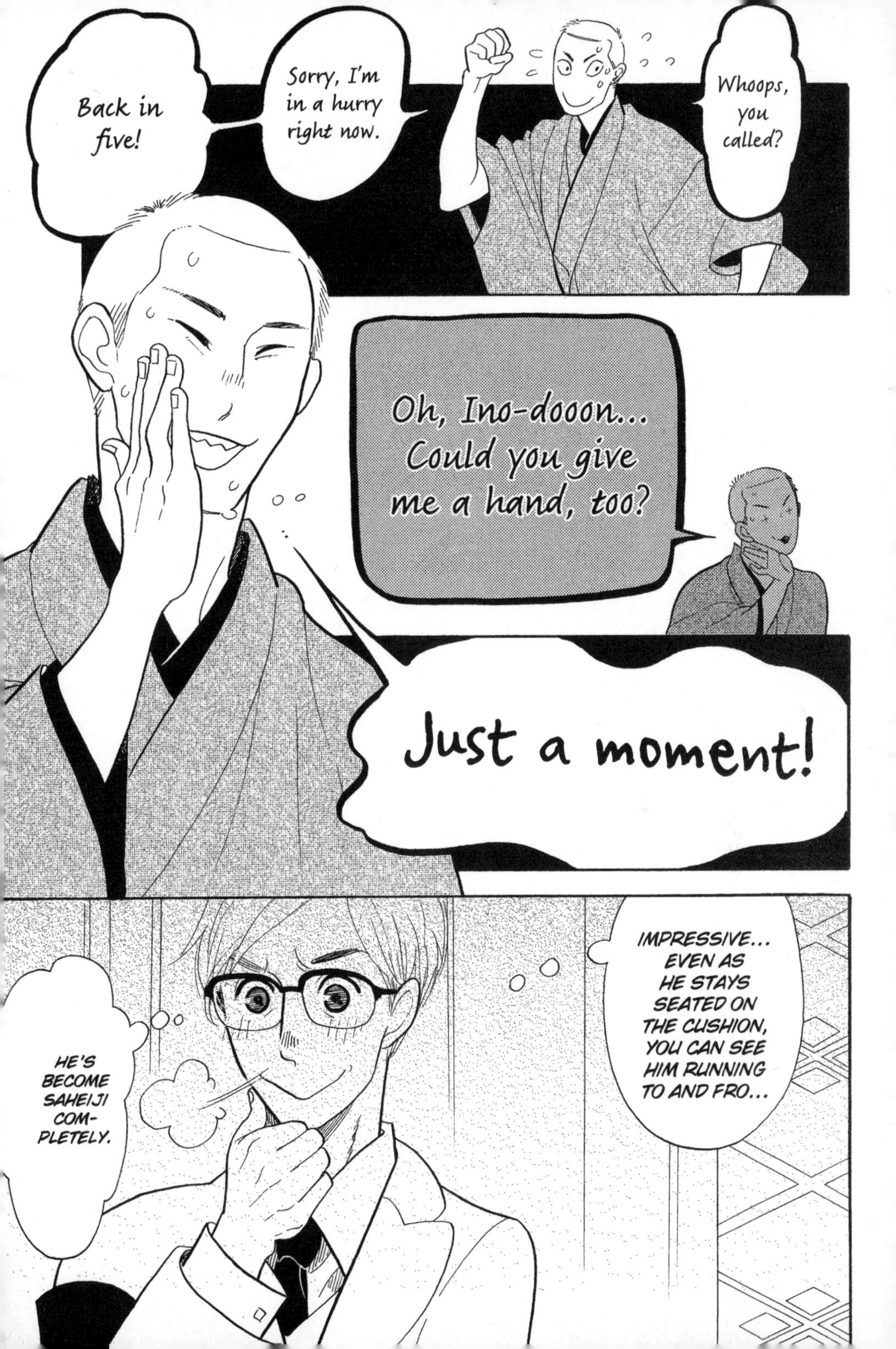

Whoops, you called?
Sorry, I'm in a hurry right now.
Back in five!
Oh, Ino-dooon... Could you give me a hand, too?
Just a moment!
IMPRESSIVE... EVEN AS HE STAYS SEATED ON THE CUSHION, YOU CAN SEE HIM RUNNING TO AND FRO...
HE'S BECOME SAHEIJI COM-PLETELY.

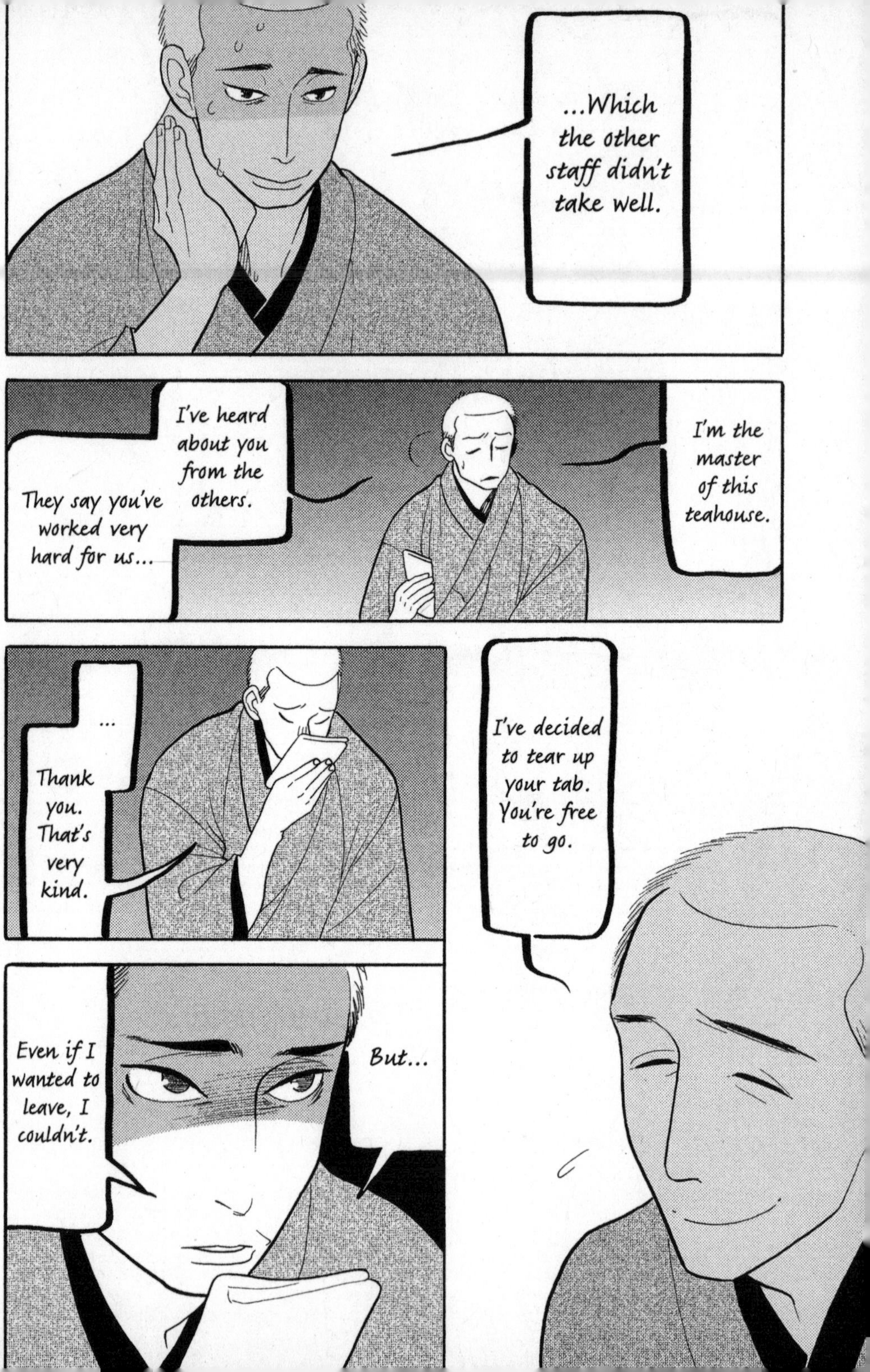
...Which the other staff didn't take well.
I'm the master of this teahouse.
I've heard about you from the others.
They say you've worked very hard for us...
I've decided to tear up your tab. You're free to go.
...
Thank you. That's very kind.
But...
Even if I wanted to leave, I couldn't.

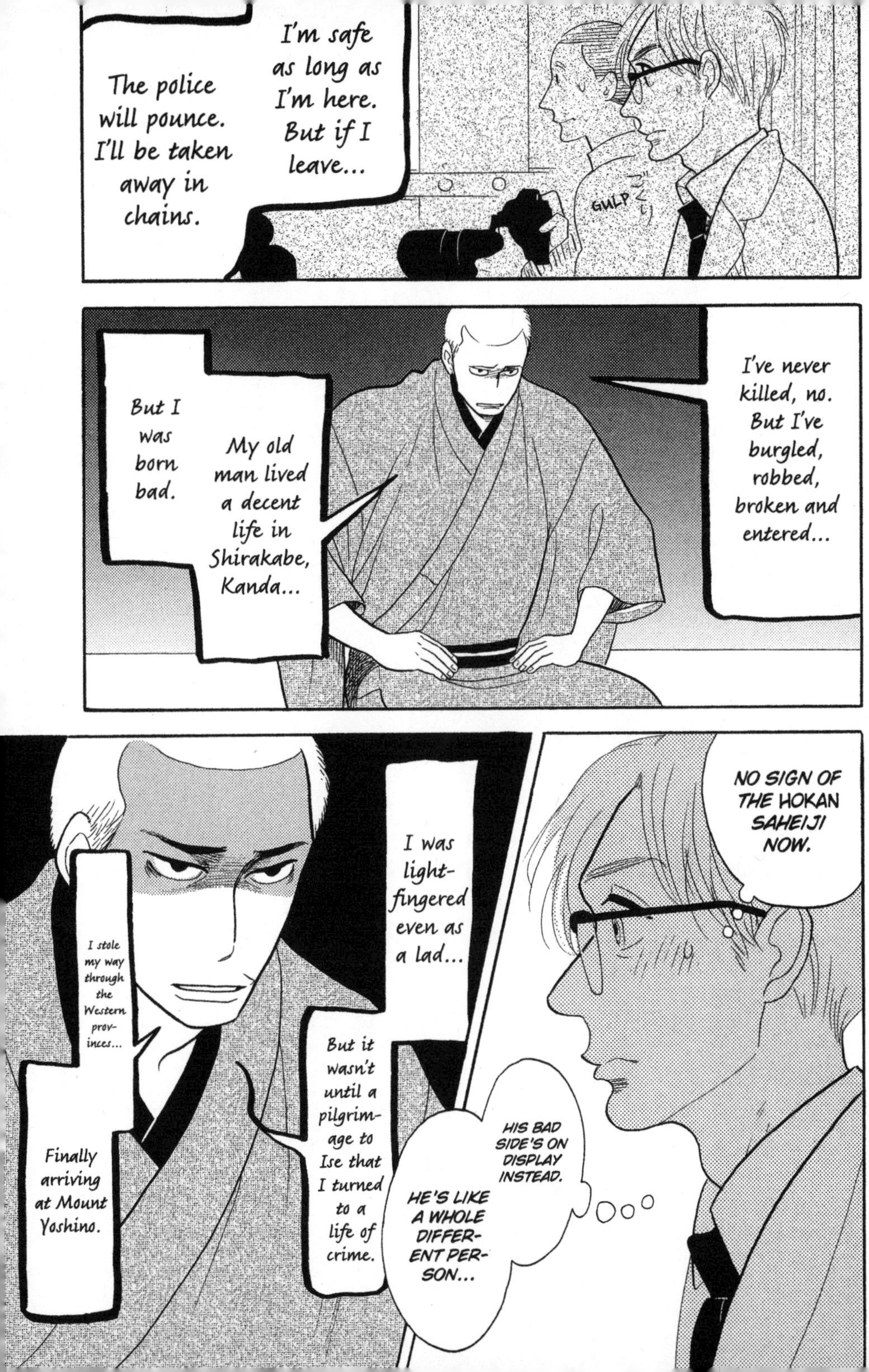
I'm safe as long as I'm here. But if I leave...
The police will pounce. I'll be taken away in chains.
GULP
I've never killed, no. But I've burgled, robbed, broken and entered...
My old man lived a decent life in Shirakabe, Kanda...
But I was born bad.
NO SIGN OF THE HOKAN SAHEIJI NOW.
HIS BAD SIDE'S ON DISPLAY INSTEAD.
HE'S LIKE A WHOLE DIFFER-ENT PER-SON...
I was light-fingered even as a lad...
But it wasn't until a pilgrim-age to Ise that I turned to a life of crime.
I stole my way through the Western prov-inces...
Finally arriving at Mount Yoshino.

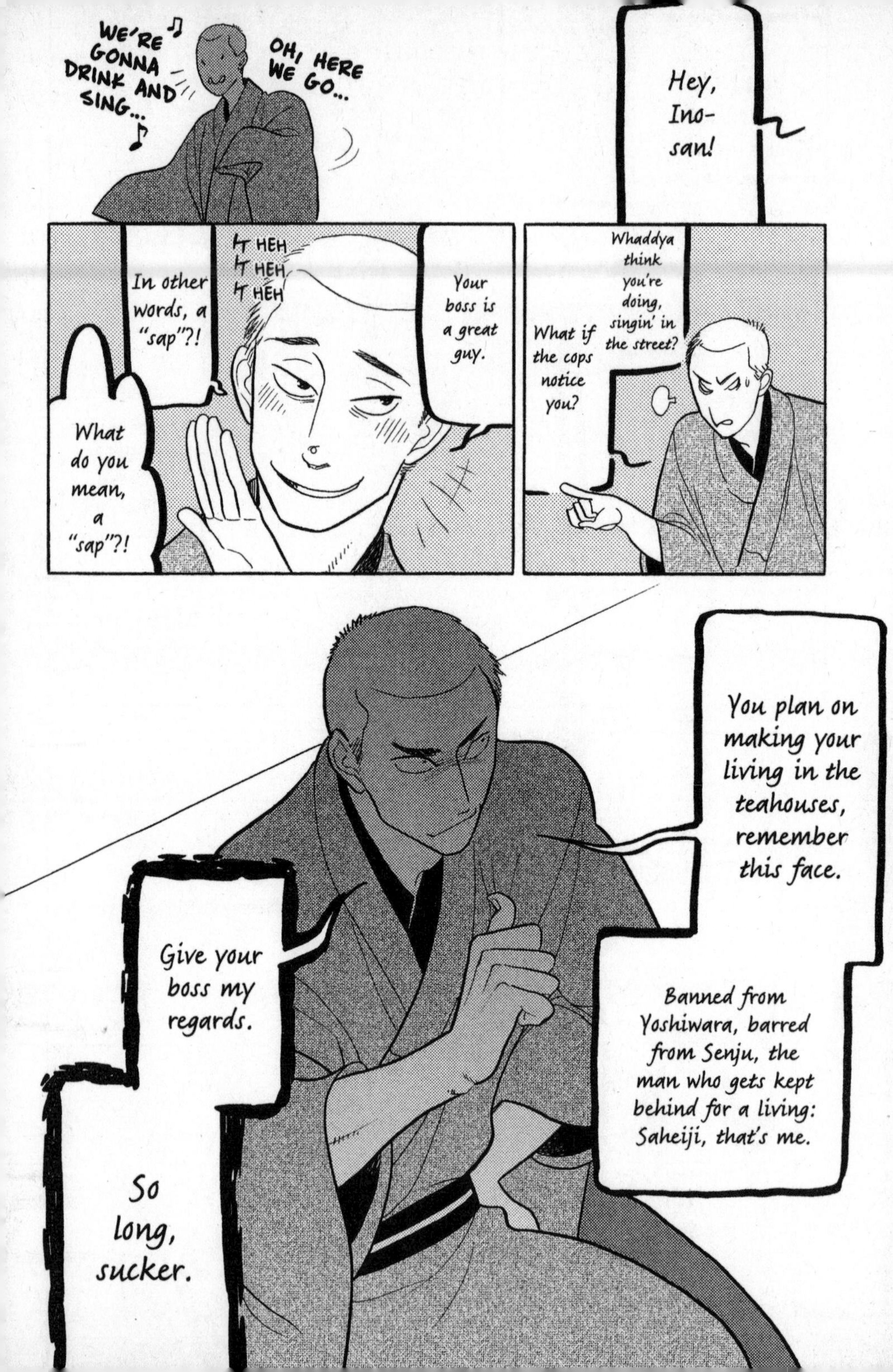
Hey, Ino-san!
OH, HERE WE GO...
WE'RE GONNA DRINK AND SING... ♪
Whaddya think you're doing, singin' in the street?
What if the cops notice you?
Your boss is a great guy.
HEH HEH HEH
In other words, a "sap"?!
What do you mean, a "sap"?!
You plan on making your living in the teahouses, remember this face.
Banned from Yoshiwara, barred from Senju, the man who gets kept behind for a living: Saheiji, that's me.
Give your boss my regards.
So long, sucker.

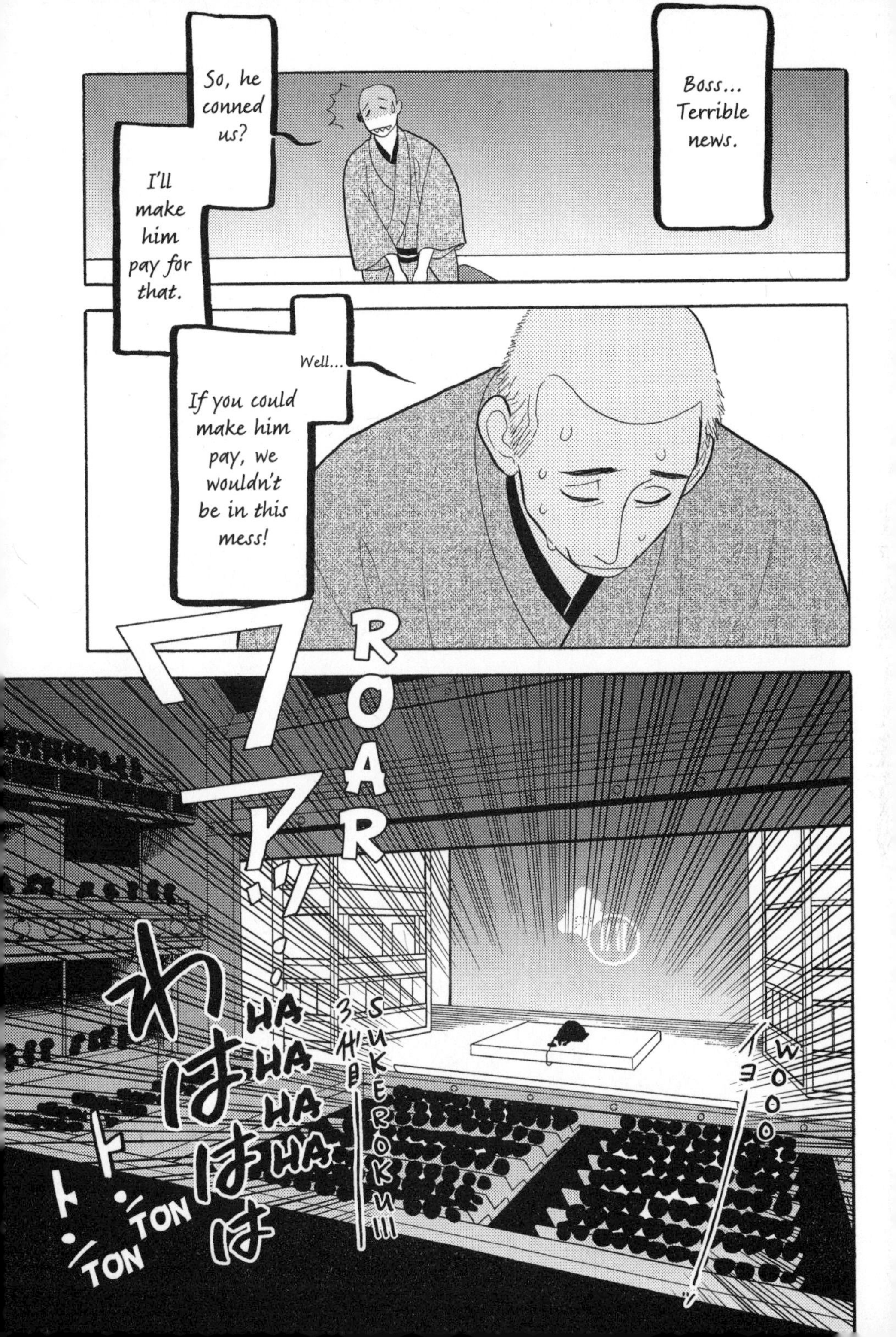
Boss... Terrible news.
So, he conned us?
I'll make him pay for that.
Well...
If you could make him pay, we wouldn't be in this mess!
ROAR
WOOO
SUKEROKU!!!
HA HA HA HA
わははは
TON TON TON

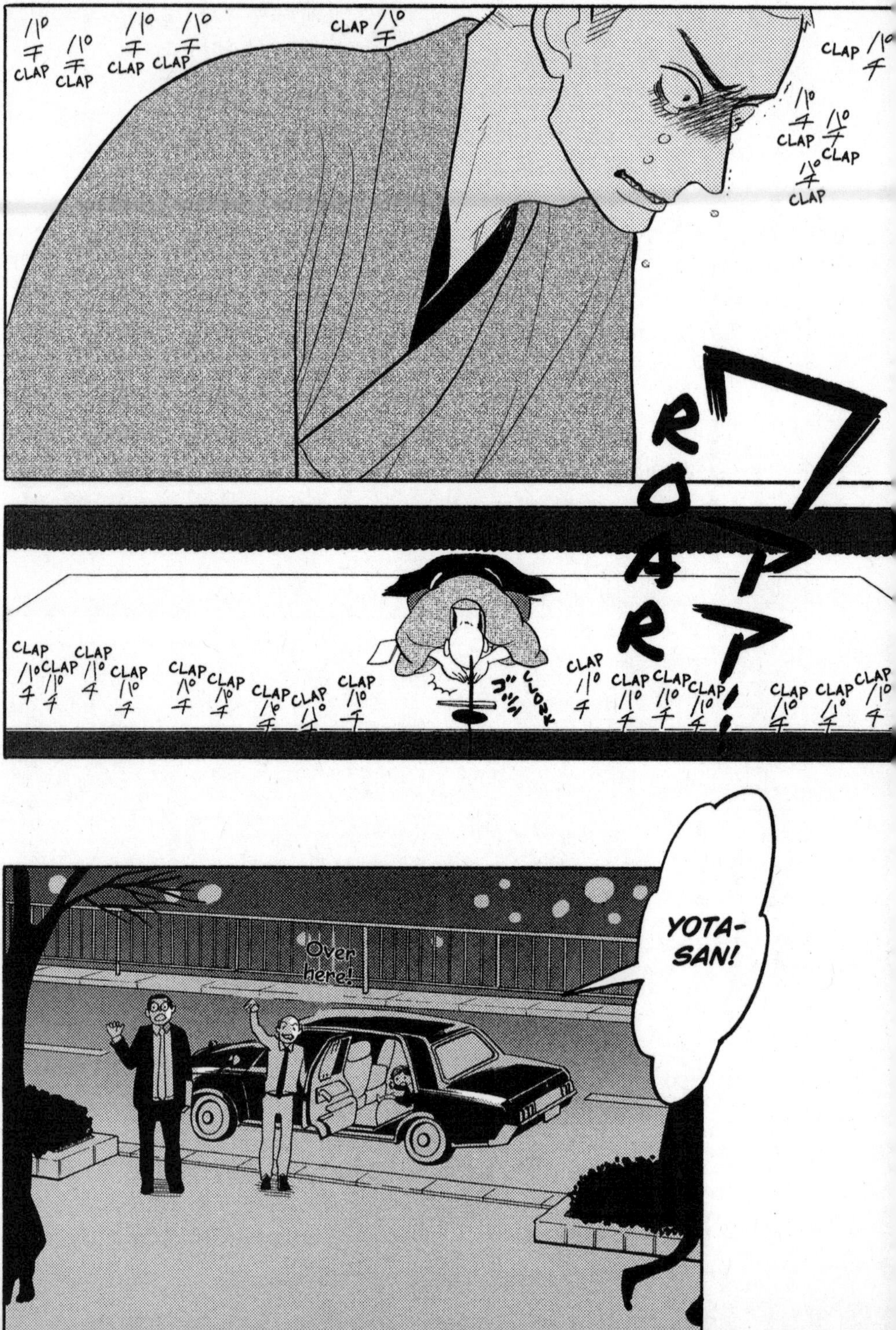

パチ CLAP
パチ CLAP
パチ CLAP
パチ CLAP
パチ CLAP
パチ CLAP
パチ CLAP
パチ CLAP
パチ CLAP
ROAR!
ワァ!
ゴツン CLONK
CLAP
YOTA-SAN!
Over here!

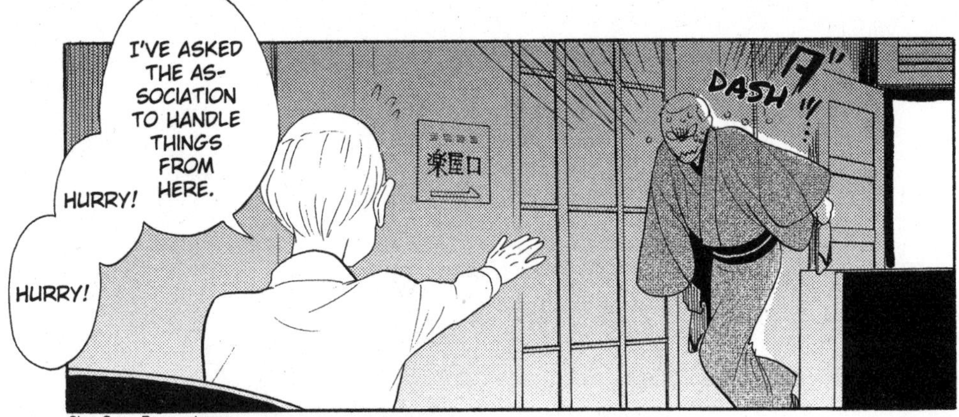
ダッ
DASH
I'VE ASKED THE ASSOCIATION TO HANDLE THINGS FROM HERE.
HURRY!
HURRY!

Sign: Green Room entrance

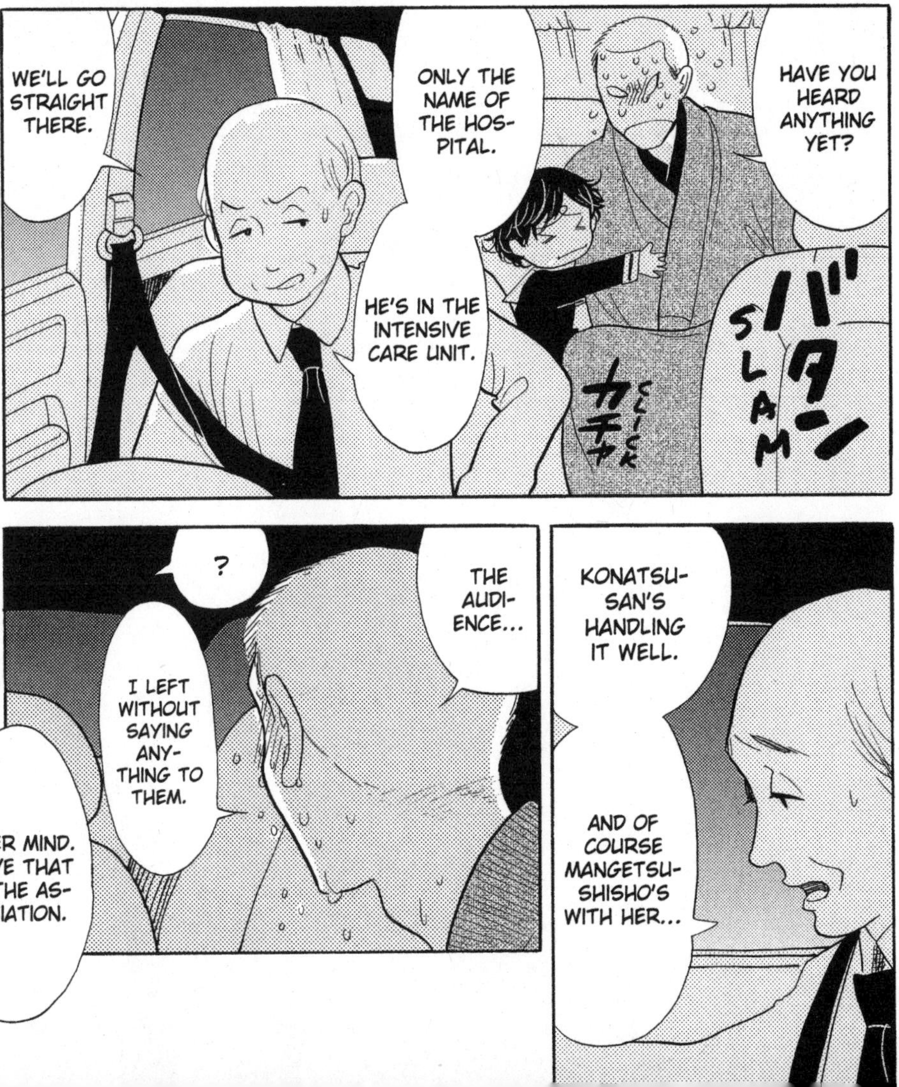
HAVE YOU HEARD ANYTHING YET?
バタン
SLAM
カチャ
CLICK
ONLY THE NAME OF THE HOSPITAL.
HE'S IN THE INTENSIVE CARE UNIT.
WE'LL GO STRAIGHT THERE.
KONATSU-SAN'S HANDLING IT WELL.
AND OF COURSE MANGETSU-SHISHO'S WITH HER...
THE AUDIENCE...
?
I LEFT WITHOUT SAYING ANYTHING TO THEM.
NEVER MIND. LEAVE THAT TO THE ASSOCIATION.

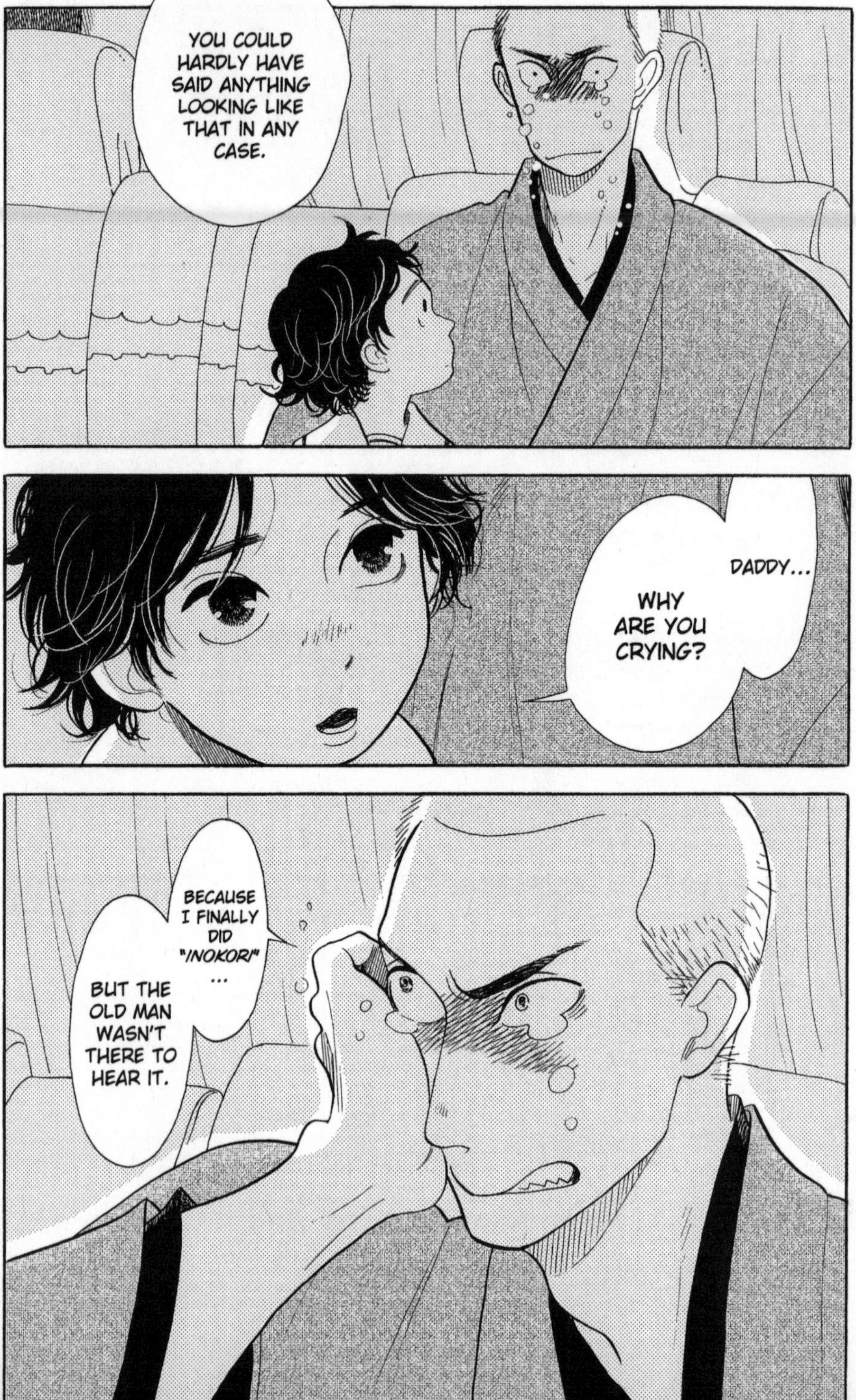
YOU COULD HARDLY HAVE SAID ANYTHING LOOKING LIKE THAT IN ANY CASE.
DADDY...
WHY ARE YOU CRYING?
BECAUSE I FINALLY DID "INOKORI"...
BUT THE OLD MAN WASN'T THERE TO HEAR IT.

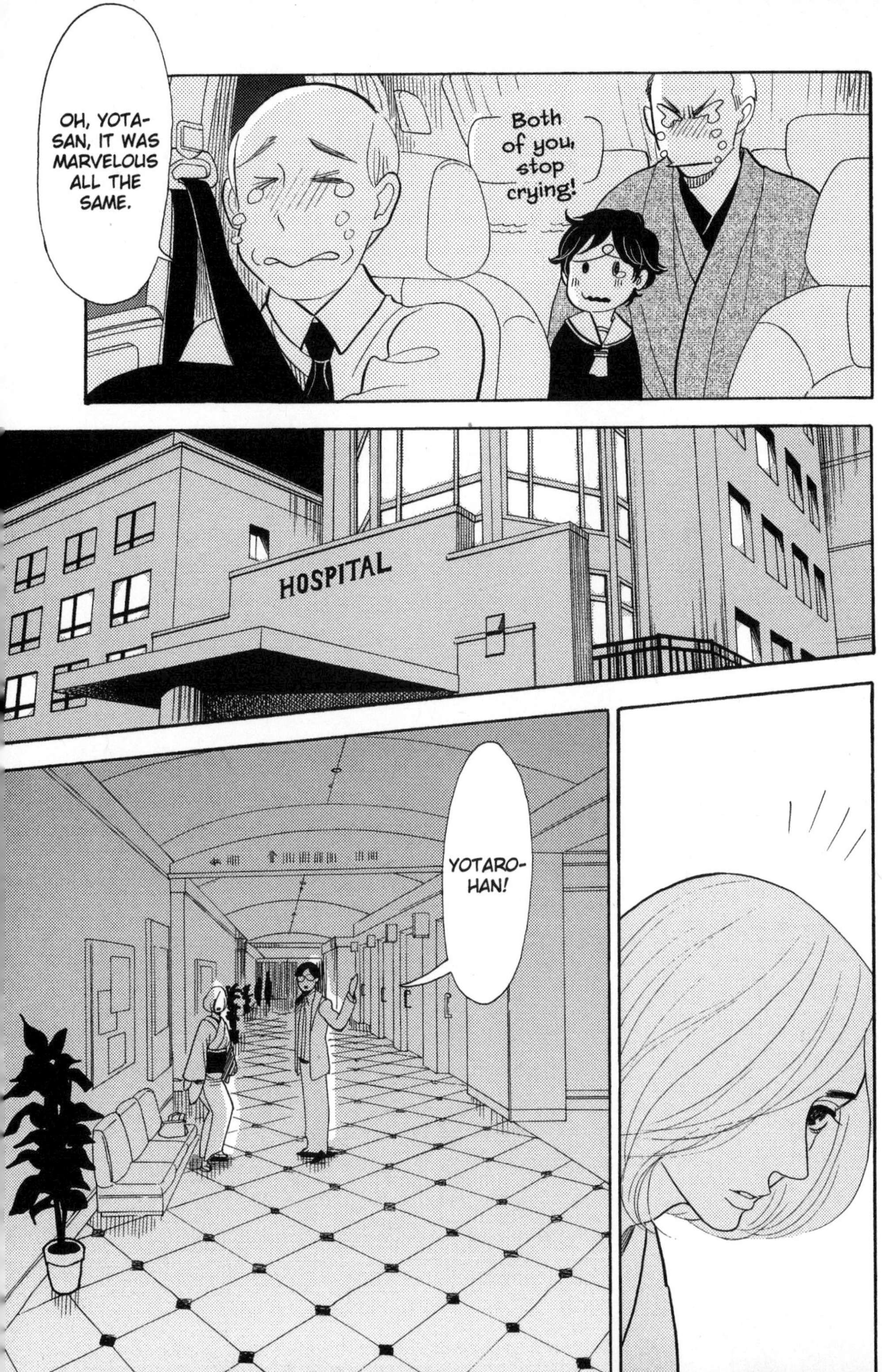
OH, YOTA-SAN, IT WAS MARVELOUS ALL THE SAME.
Both of you, stop crying!
HOSPITAL
YOTARO-HAN!

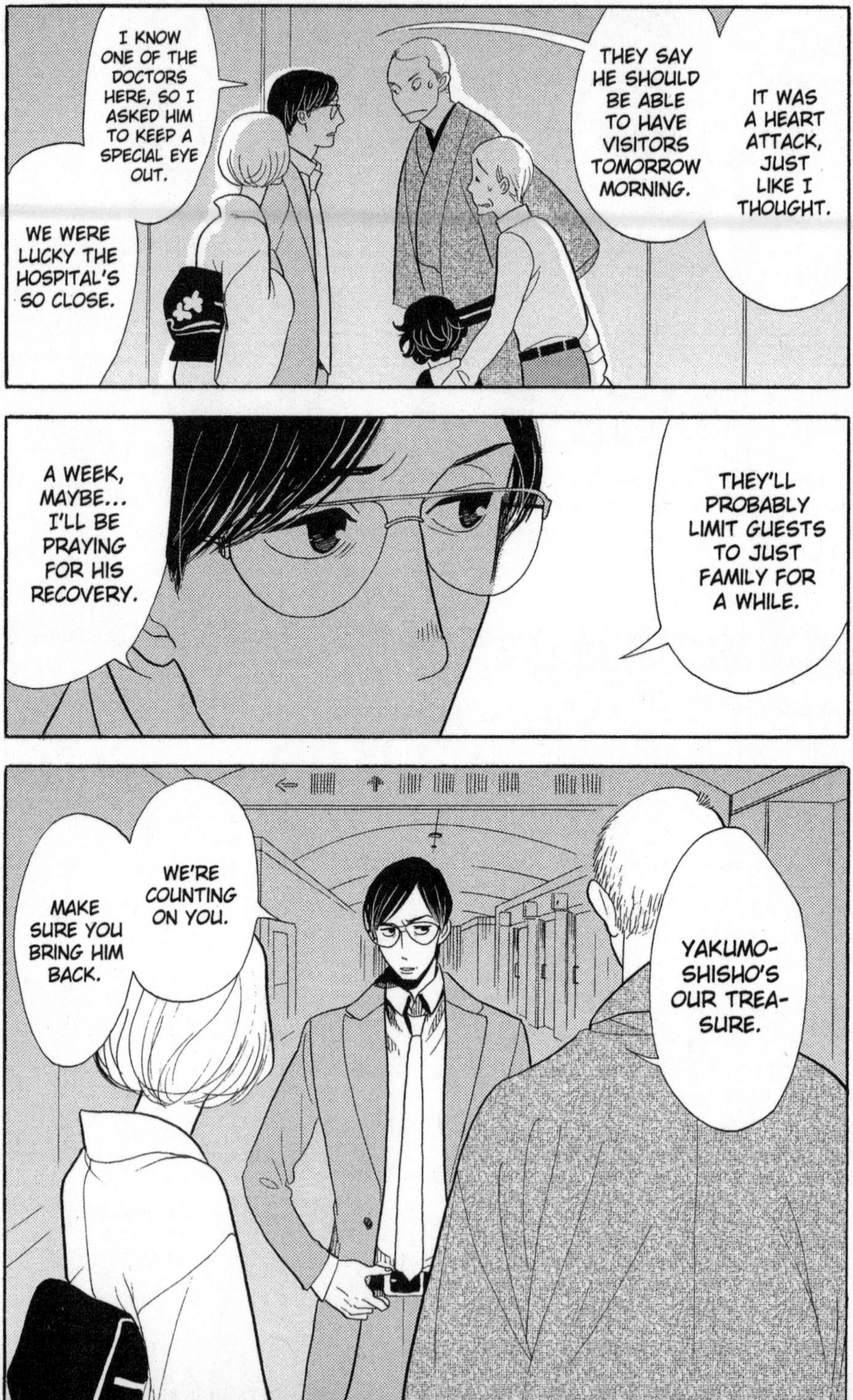
IT WAS A HEART ATTACK, JUST LIKE I THOUGHT.
THEY SAY HE SHOULD BE ABLE TO HAVE VISITORS TOMORROW MORNING.
I KNOW ONE OF THE DOCTORS HERE, SO I ASKED HIM TO KEEP A SPECIAL EYE OUT.
WE WERE LUCKY THE HOSPITAL'S SO CLOSE.
THEY'LL PROBABLY LIMIT GUESTS TO JUST FAMILY FOR A WHILE.
A WEEK, MAYBE... I'LL BE PRAYING FOR HIS RECOVERY.
YAKUMO-SHISHO'S OUR TREA-SURE.
WE'RE COUNTING ON YOU.
MAKE SURE YOU BRING HIM BACK.

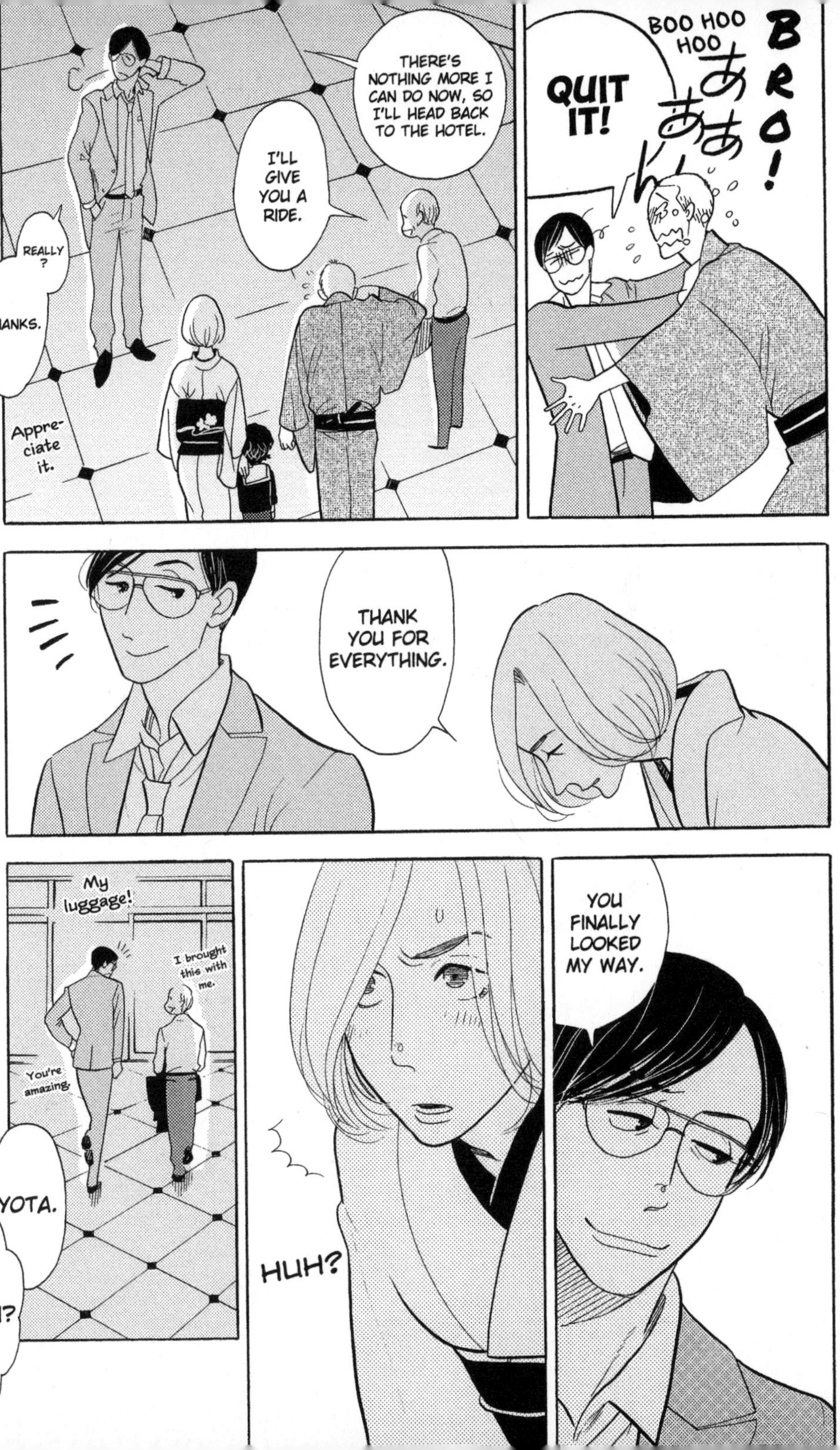
BRO!
BOO HOO HOO
あああん
QUIT IT!
THERE'S NOTHING MORE I CAN DO NOW, SO I'LL HEAD BACK TO THE HOTEL.
I'LL GIVE YOU A RIDE.
REALLY?
THANKS.
Appreciate it.
THANK YOU FOR EVERYTHING.
YOU FINALLY LOOKED MY WAY.
HUH?
My luggage!
I brought this with me.
You're amazing.
YOTA.
YEAH?

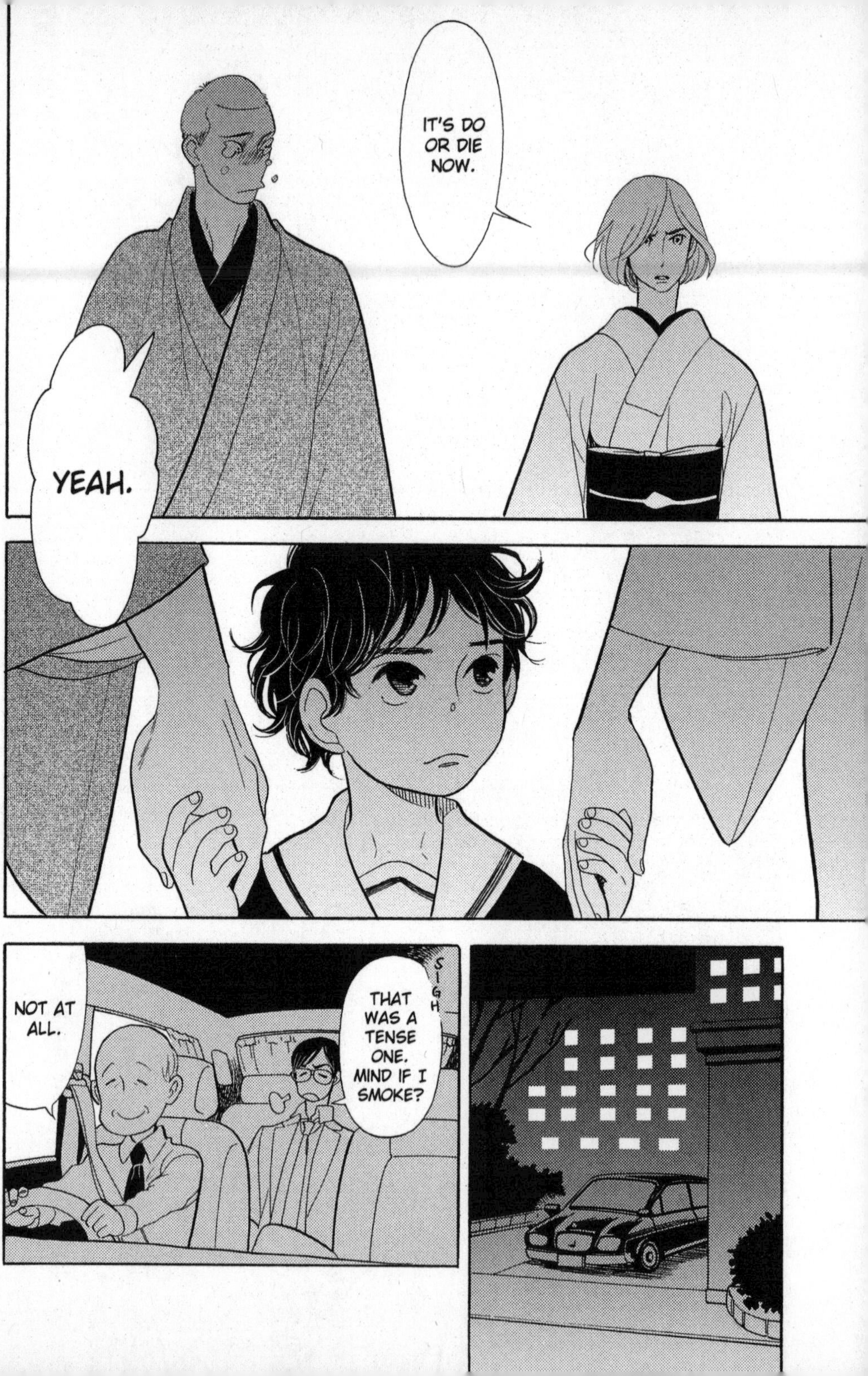
IT'S DO OR DIE NOW.
YEAH.
SIGH
THAT WAS A TENSE ONE. MIND IF I SMOKE?
NOT AT ALL.

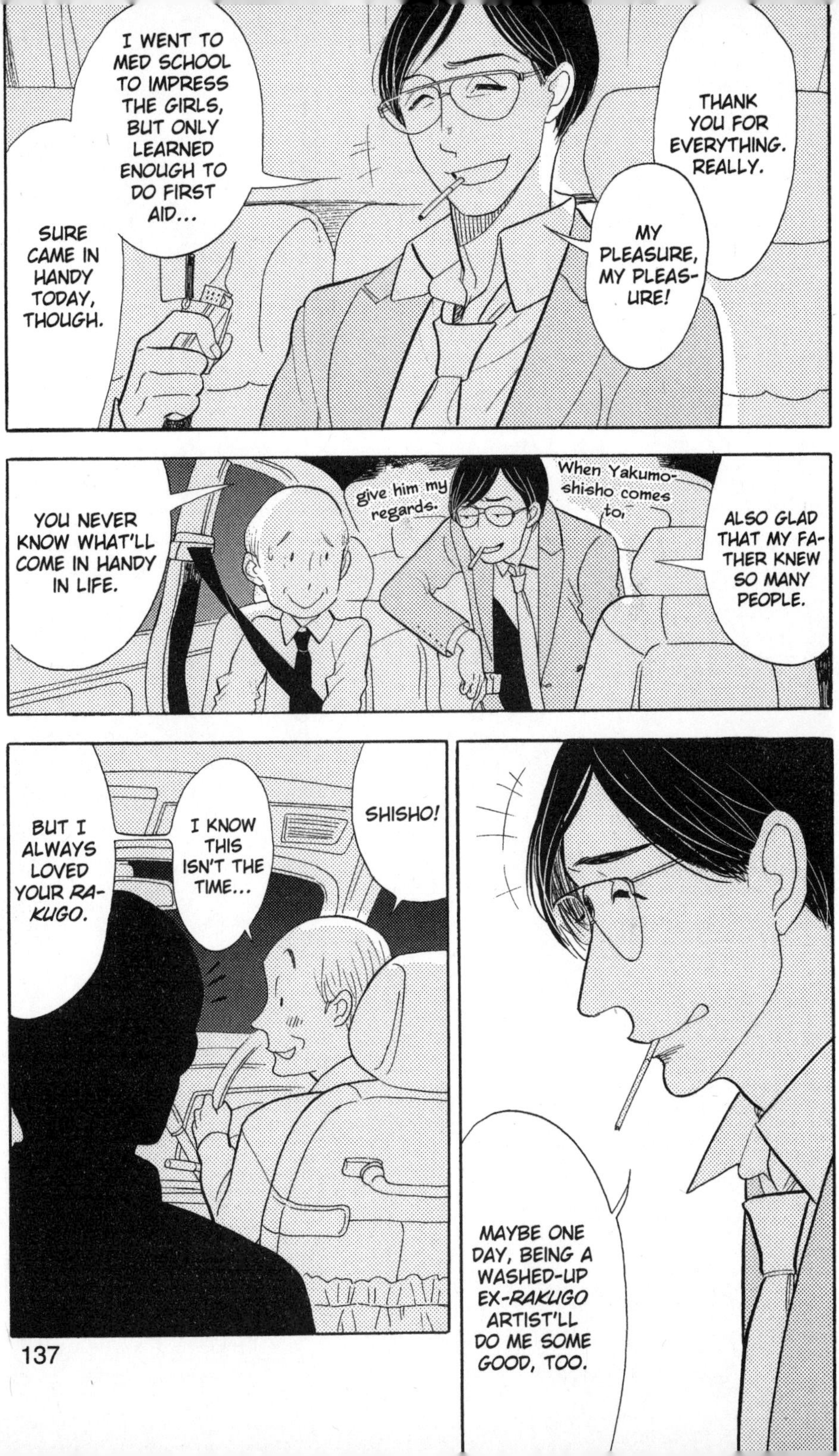
THANK YOU FOR EVERYTHING. REALLY.
MY PLEASURE, MY PLEASURE!
I WENT TO MED SCHOOL TO IMPRESS THE GIRLS, BUT ONLY LEARNED ENOUGH TO DO FIRST AID...
SURE CAME IN HANDY TODAY, THOUGH.
ALSO GLAD THAT MY FATHER KNEW SO MANY PEOPLE.
When Yakumo-shisho comes to,
give him my regards.
YOU NEVER KNOW WHAT'LL COME IN HANDY IN LIFE.
MAYBE ONE DAY, BEING A WASHED-UP EX-*RAKUGO* ARTIST'LL DO ME SOME GOOD, TOO.
SHISHO!
I KNOW THIS ISN'T THE TIME...
BUT I ALWAYS LOVED YOUR *RAKUGO*.

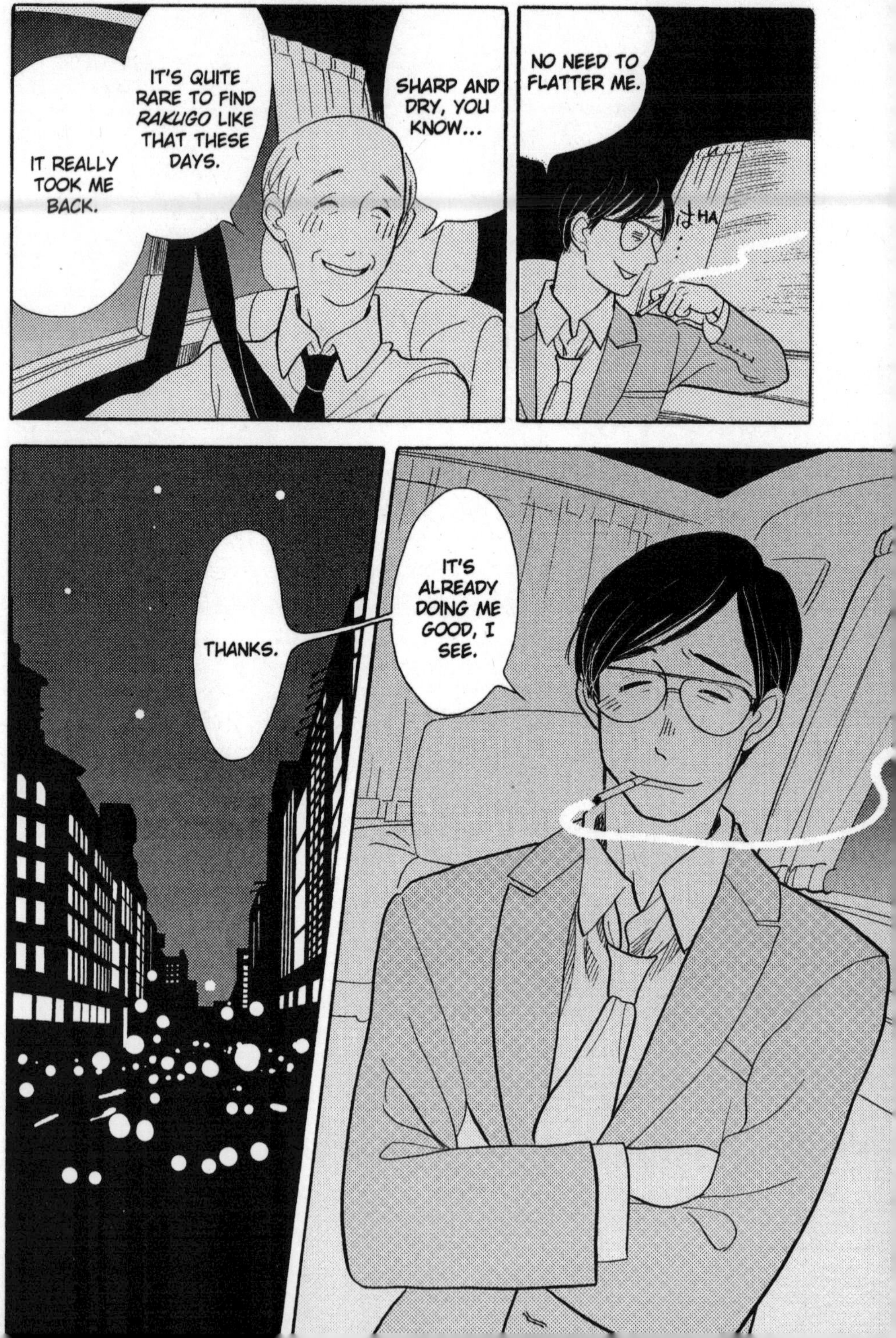
NO NEED TO FLATTER ME.
HA
SHARP AND DRY, YOU KNOW...
IT'S QUITE RARE TO FIND *RAKUGO* LIKE THAT THESE DAYS.
IT REALLY TOOK ME BACK.
IT'S ALREADY DOING ME GOOD, I SEE.
THANKS.

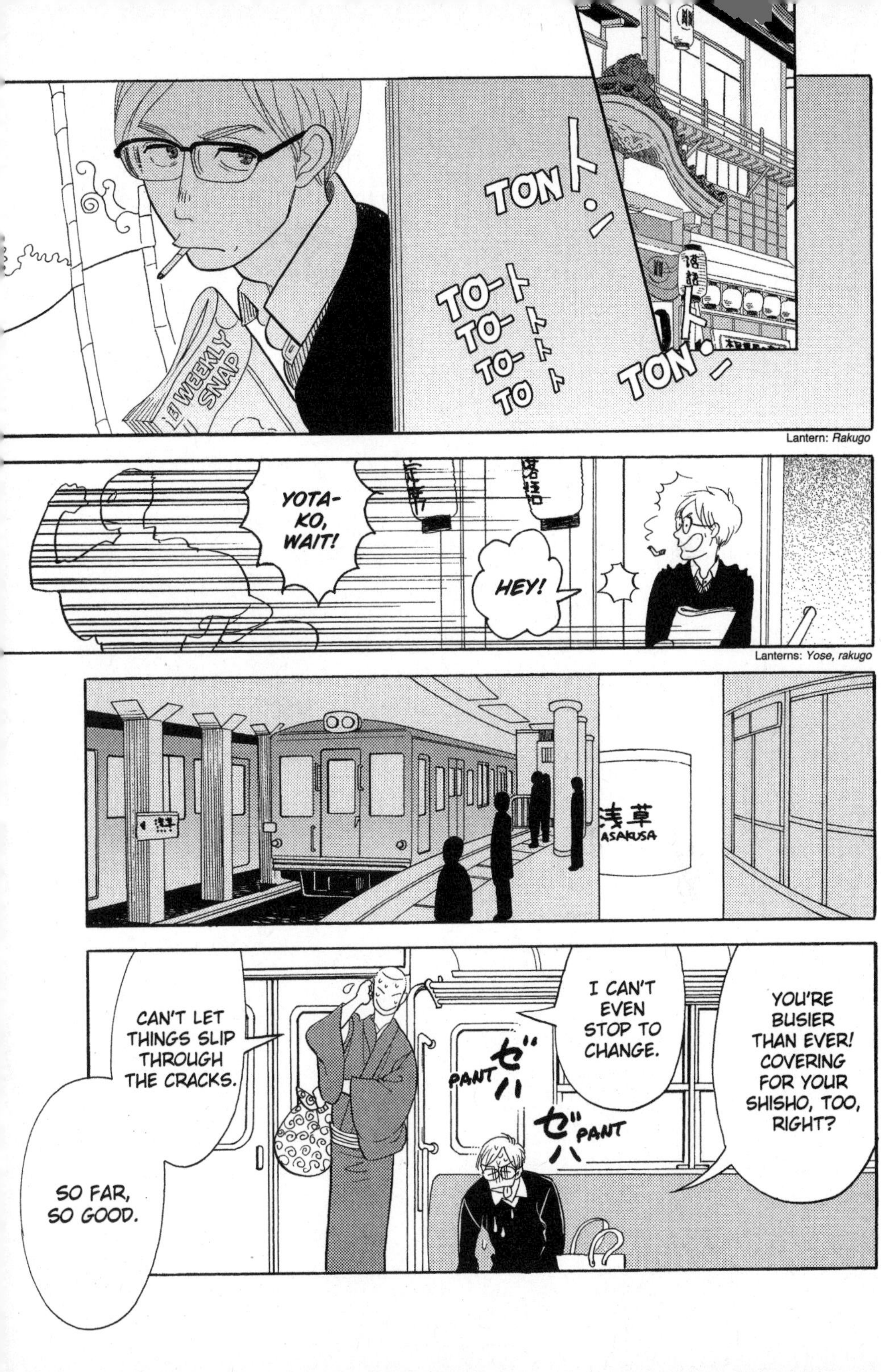
TON トン
TO— TO— TO— TO トトトト
TON トン
WEEKLY SNAP
Lantern: Rakugo
HEY!
YOTA-KO, WAIT!
Lanterns: Yose, rakugo
浅草
ASAKUSA
YOU'RE BUSIER THAN EVER! COVERING FOR YOUR SHISHO, TOO, RIGHT?
I CAN'T EVEN STOP TO CHANGE.
ゼハ PANT
ゼハ PANT
CAN'T LET THINGS SLIP THROUGH THE CRACKS.
SO FAR, SO GOOD.

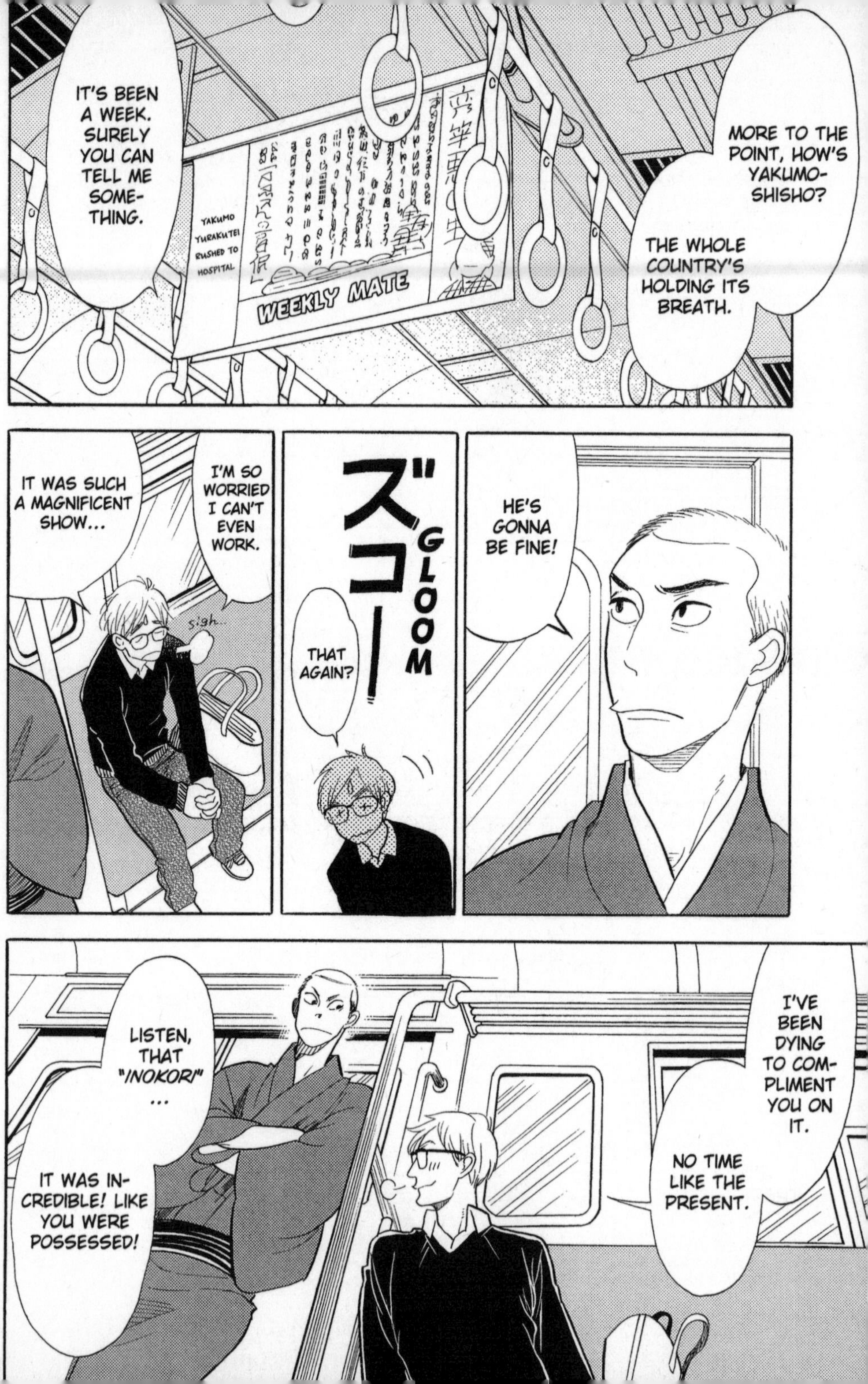
MORE TO THE POINT, HOW'S YAKUMO-SHISHO?
THE WHOLE COUNTRY'S HOLDING ITS BREATH.
YAKUMO YURAKUTEI RUSHED TO HOSPITAL
WEEKLY MATE
IT'S BEEN A WEEK. SURELY YOU CAN TELL ME SOMETHING.
HE'S GONNA BE FINE!
ズコー
GLOOM
THAT AGAIN?
I'M SO WORRIED I CAN'T EVEN WORK.
IT WAS SUCH A MAGNIFICENT SHOW...
sigh...
I'VE BEEN DYING TO COMPLIMENT YOU ON IT.
NO TIME LIKE THE PRESENT.
LISTEN, THAT "INOKORI"...
IT WAS INCREDIBLE! LIKE YOU WERE POSSESSED!

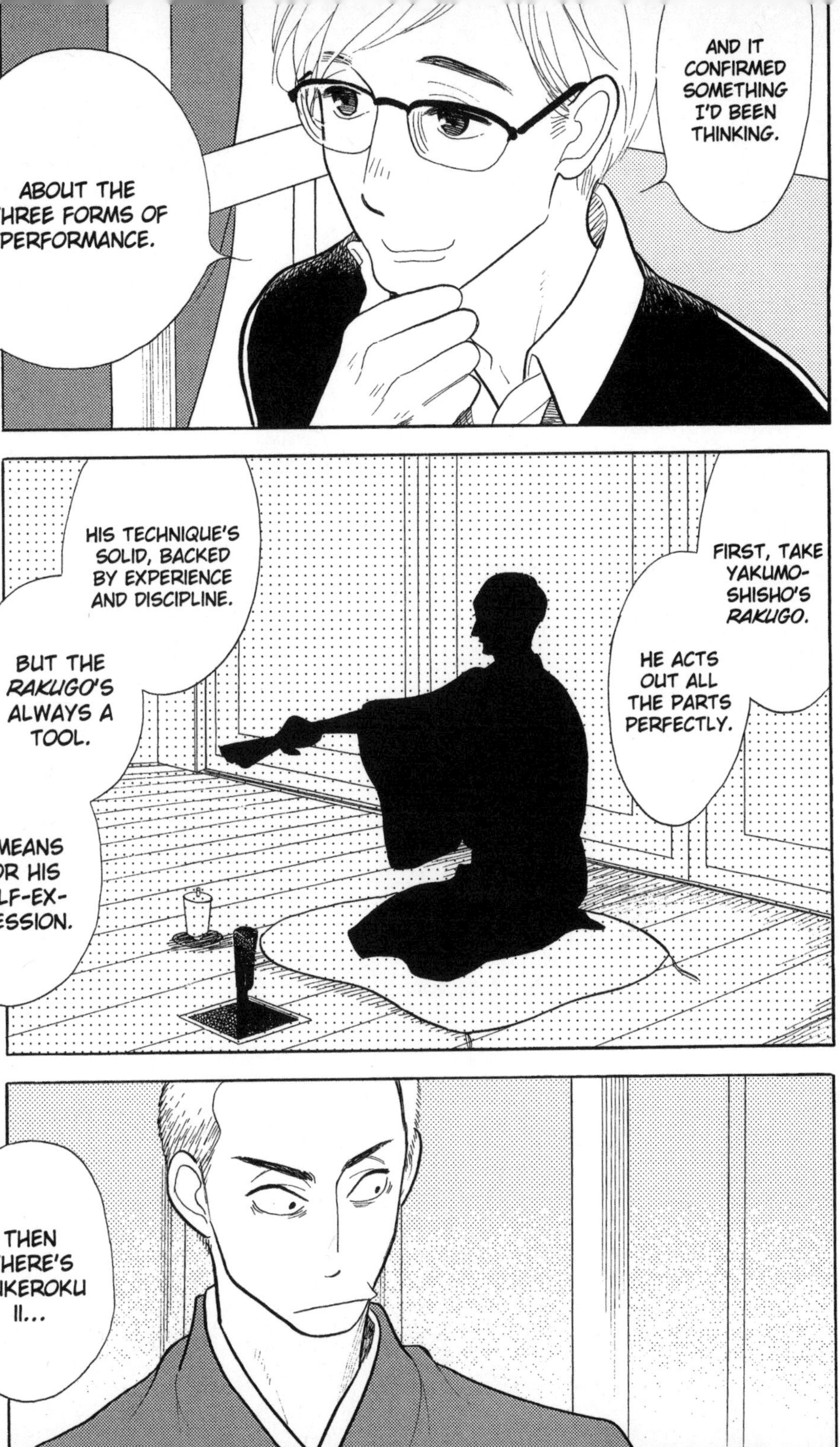
AND IT CONFIRMED SOMETHING I'D BEEN THINKING.
ABOUT THE THREE FORMS OF PERFORMANCE.
FIRST, TAKE YAKUMO-SHISHO'S *RAKUGO*.
HE ACTS OUT ALL THE PARTS PERFECTLY.
HIS TECHNIQUE'S SOLID, BACKED BY EXPERIENCE AND DISCIPLINE.
BUT THE *RAKUGO*'S ALWAYS A TOOL.
A MEANS FOR HIS SELF-EX-PRESSION.
THEN THERE'S SUKEROKU II...

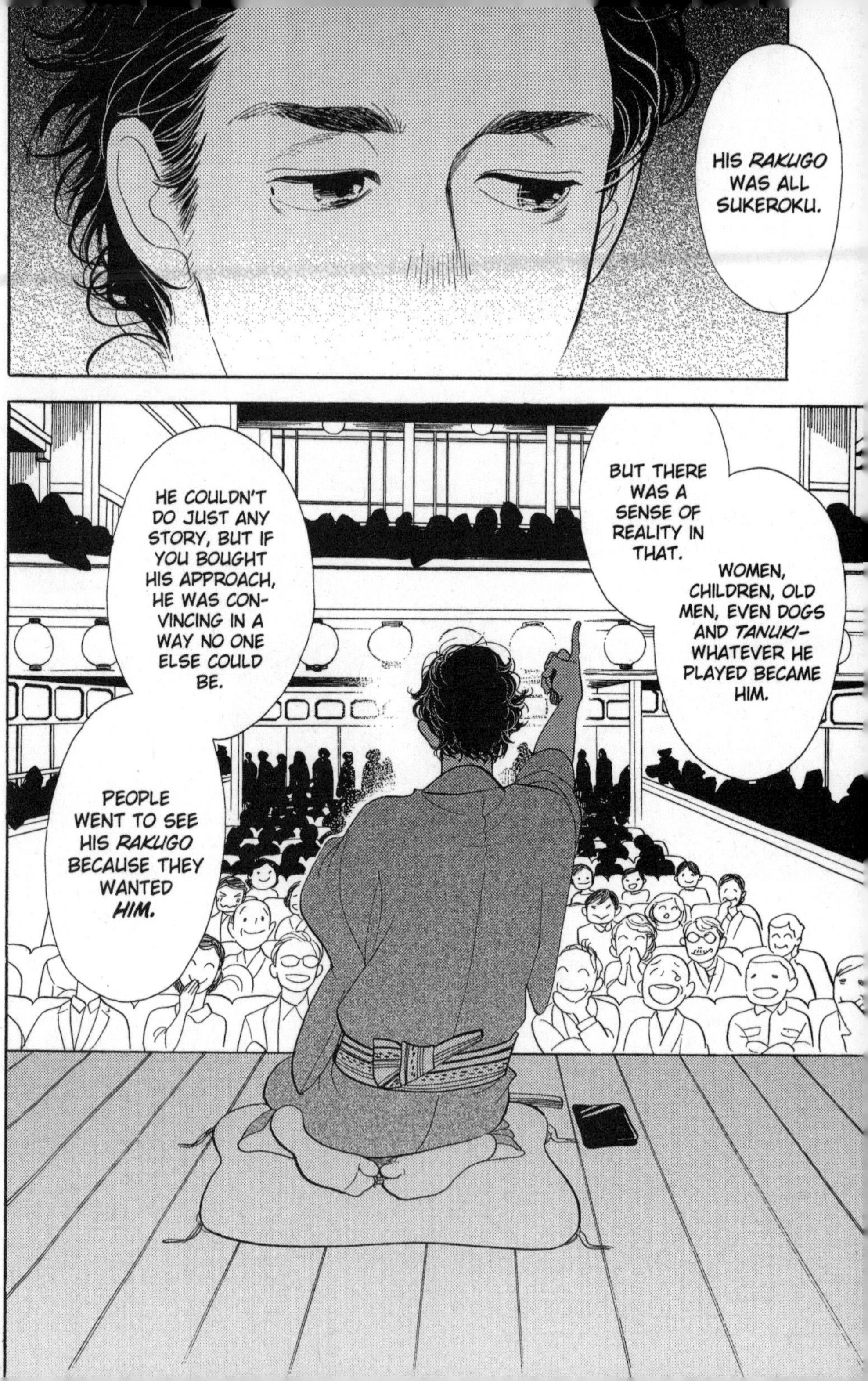
HIS *RAKUGO* WAS ALL SUKEROKU.
BUT THERE WAS A SENSE OF REALITY IN THAT.
WOMEN, CHILDREN, OLD MEN, EVEN DOGS AND *TANUKI*—WHATEVER HE PLAYED BECAME HIM.
HE COULDN'T DO JUST ANY STORY, BUT IF YOU BOUGHT HIS APPROACH, HE WAS CON-VINCING IN A WAY NO ONE ELSE COULD BE.
PEOPLE WENT TO SEE HIS *RAKUGO* BECAUSE THEY WANTED ***HIM.***

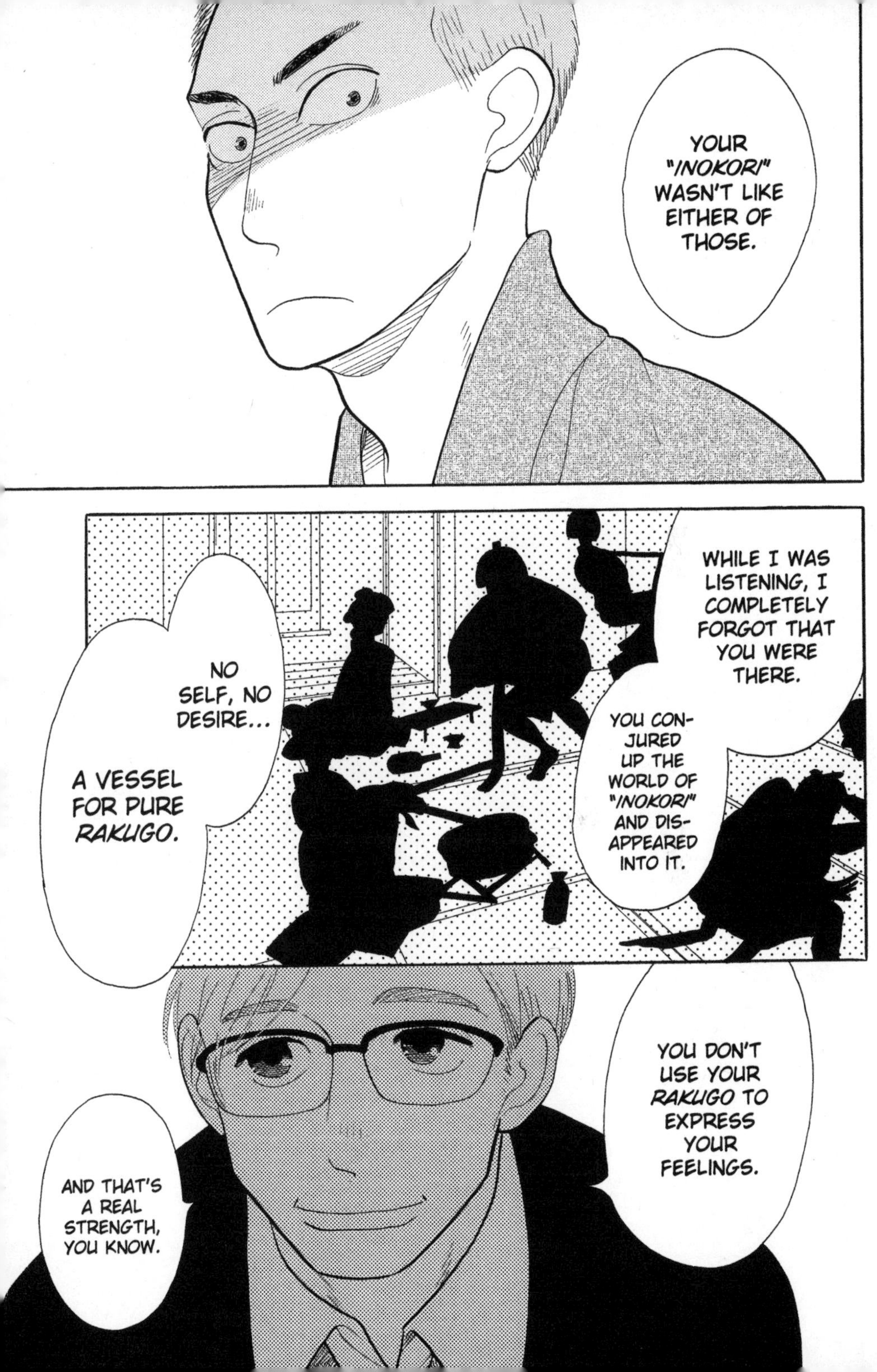
YOUR "*INOKORI*" WASN'T LIKE EITHER OF THOSE.
WHILE I WAS LISTENING, I COMPLETELY FORGOT THAT YOU WERE THERE.
YOU CONJURED UP THE WORLD OF "*INOKORI*" AND DISAPPEARED INTO IT.
NO SELF, NO DESIRE...
A VESSEL FOR PURE *RAKUGO*.
YOU DON'T USE YOUR *RAKUGO* TO EXPRESS YOUR FEELINGS.
AND THAT'S A REAL STRENGTH, YOU KNOW.

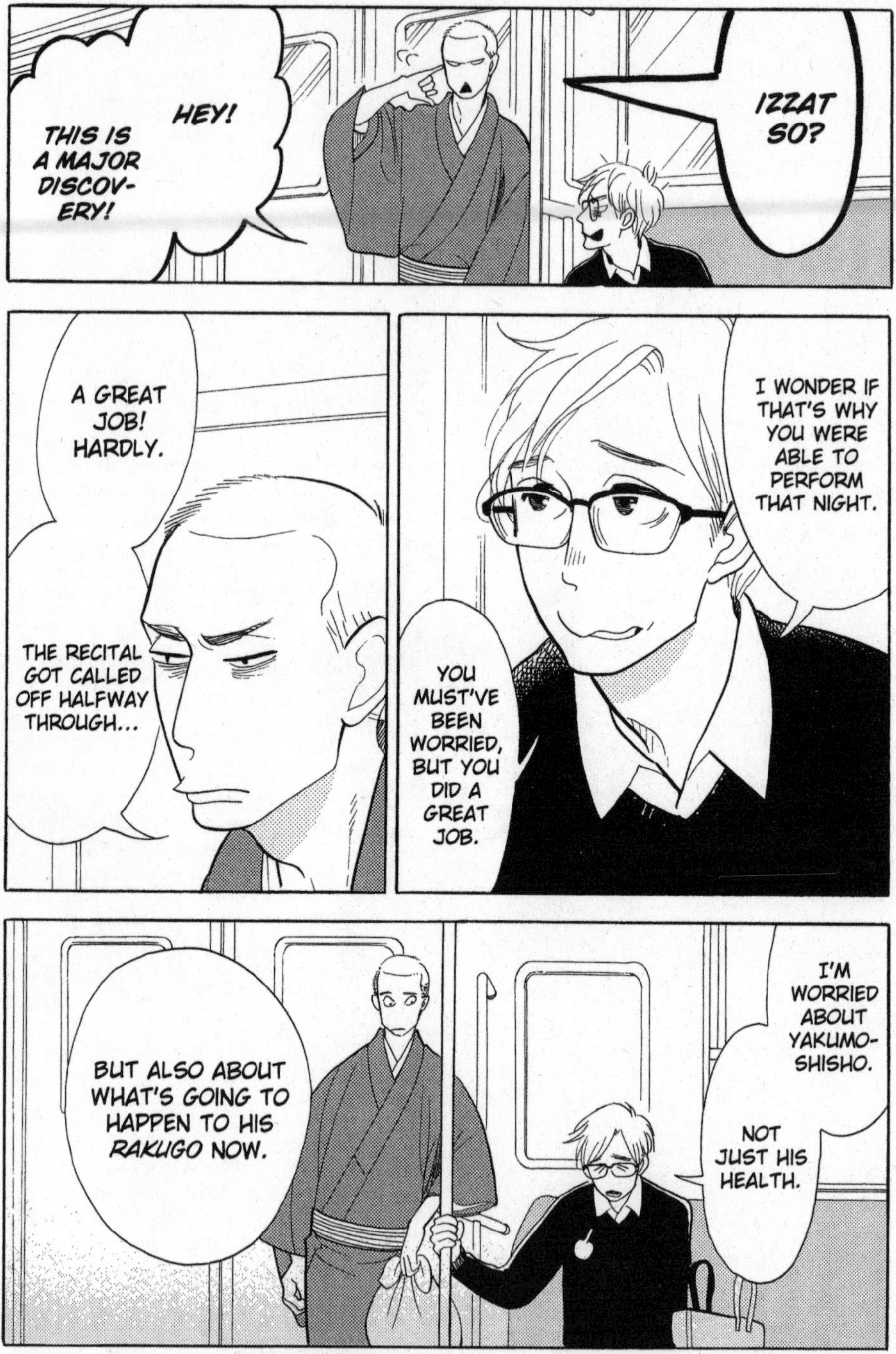
IZZAT SO?
HEY!
THIS IS A MAJOR DISCOVERY!
I WONDER IF THAT'S WHY YOU WERE ABLE TO PERFORM THAT NIGHT.
YOU MUST'VE BEEN WORRIED, BUT YOU DID A GREAT JOB.
A GREAT JOB! HARDLY.
THE RECITAL GOT CALLED OFF HALFWAY THROUGH...
I'M WORRIED ABOUT YAKUMO-SHISHO.
NOT JUST HIS HEALTH.
BUT ALSO ABOUT WHAT'S GOING TO HAPPEN TO HIS *RAKUGO* NOW.

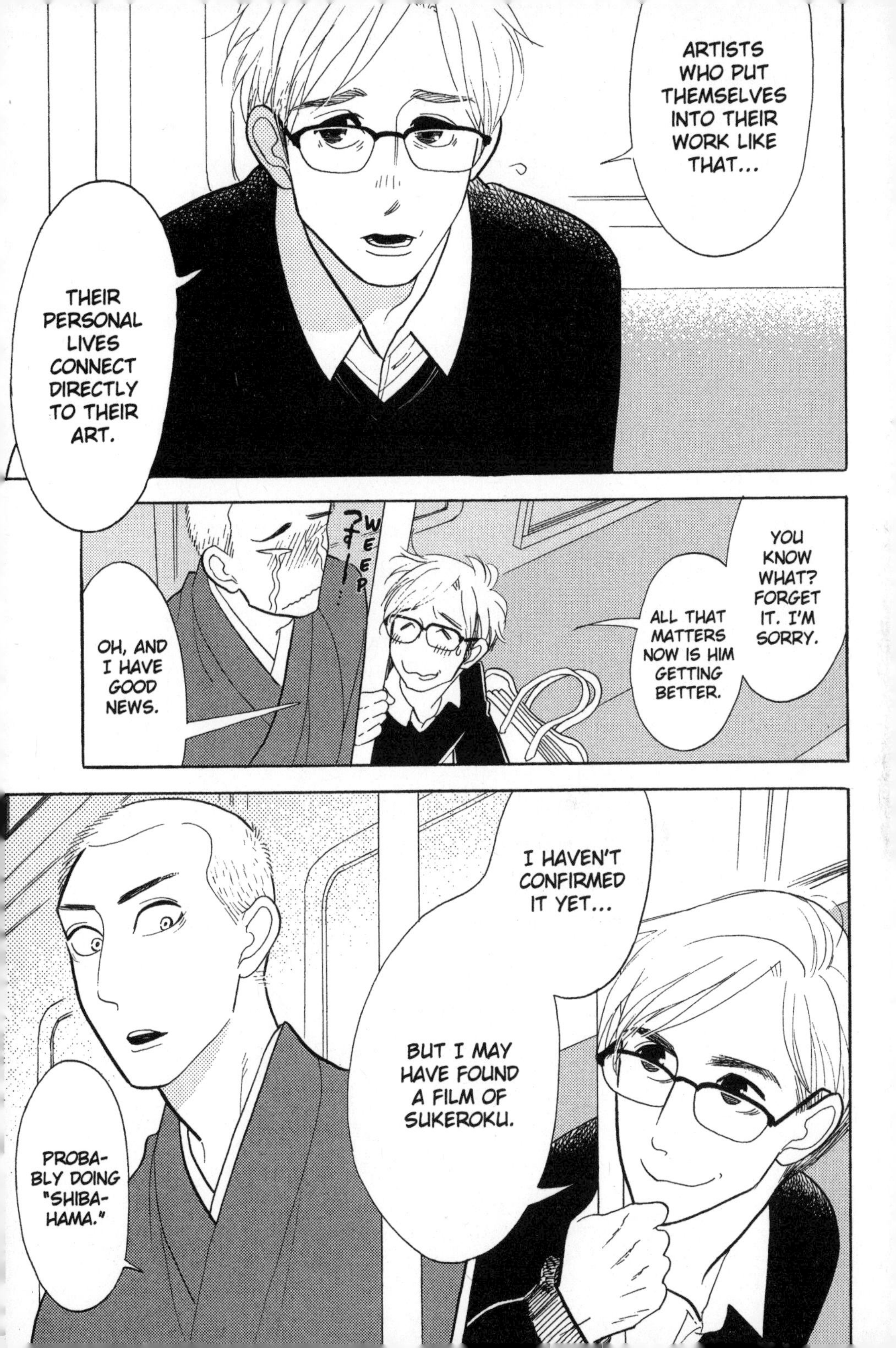

ARTISTS WHO PUT THEMSELVES INTO THEIR WORK LIKE THAT...
THEIR PERSONAL LIVES CONNECT DIRECTLY TO THEIR ART.
WEEP
YOU KNOW WHAT? FORGET IT. I'M SORRY.
ALL THAT MATTERS NOW IS HIM GETTING BETTER.
OH, AND I HAVE GOOD NEWS.
I HAVEN'T CONFIRMED IT YET...
BUT I MAY HAVE FOUND A FILM OF SUKEROKU.
PROBA-BLY DOING "SHIBA-HAMA."

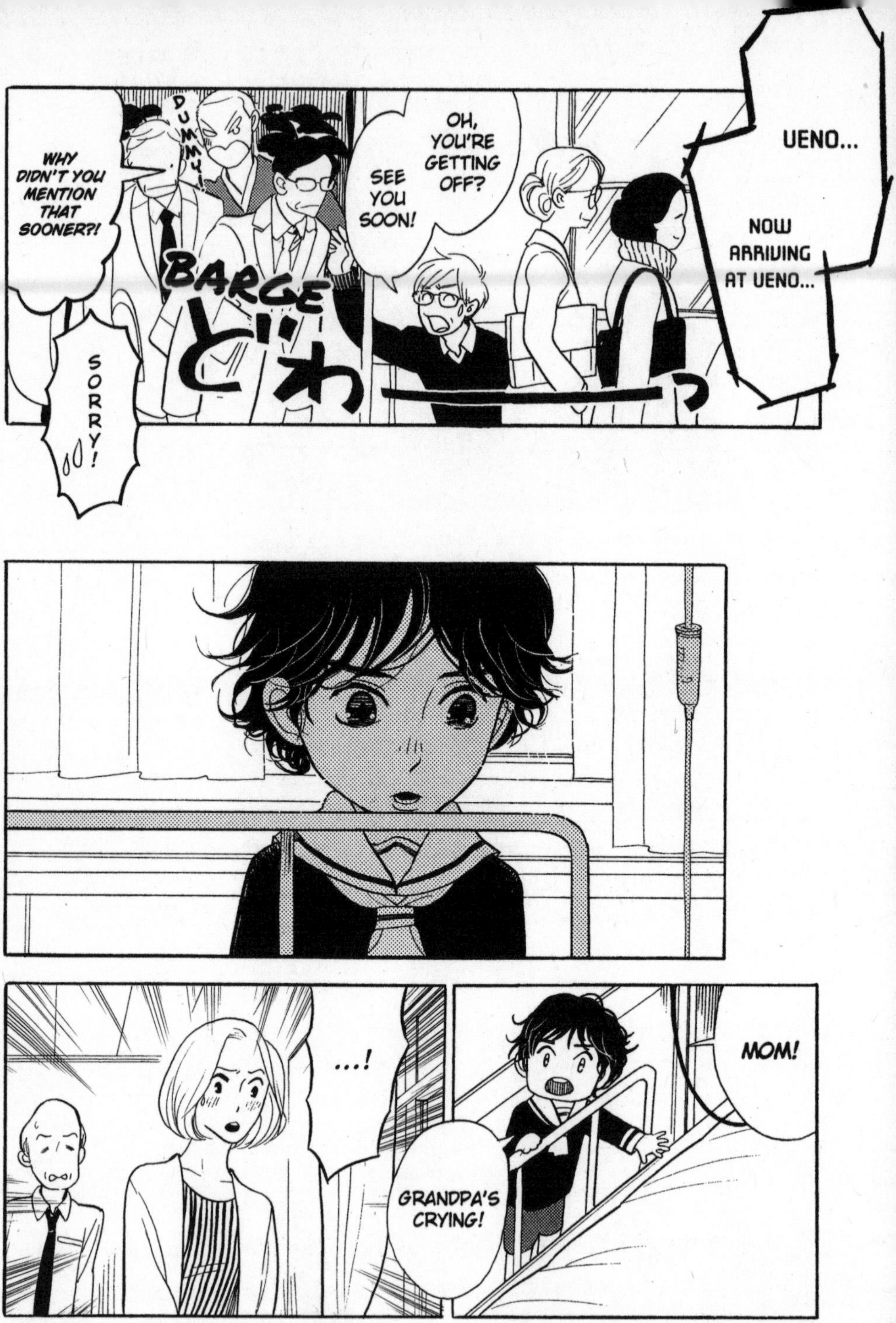
UENO...
NOW ARRIVING AT UENO...
OH, YOU'RE GETTING OFF?
SEE YOU SOON!
BARGE
どわーっ
DUMMY!
WHY DIDN'T YOU MENTION THAT SOONER?!
SORRY!
MOM!
GRANDPA'S CRYING!
...!

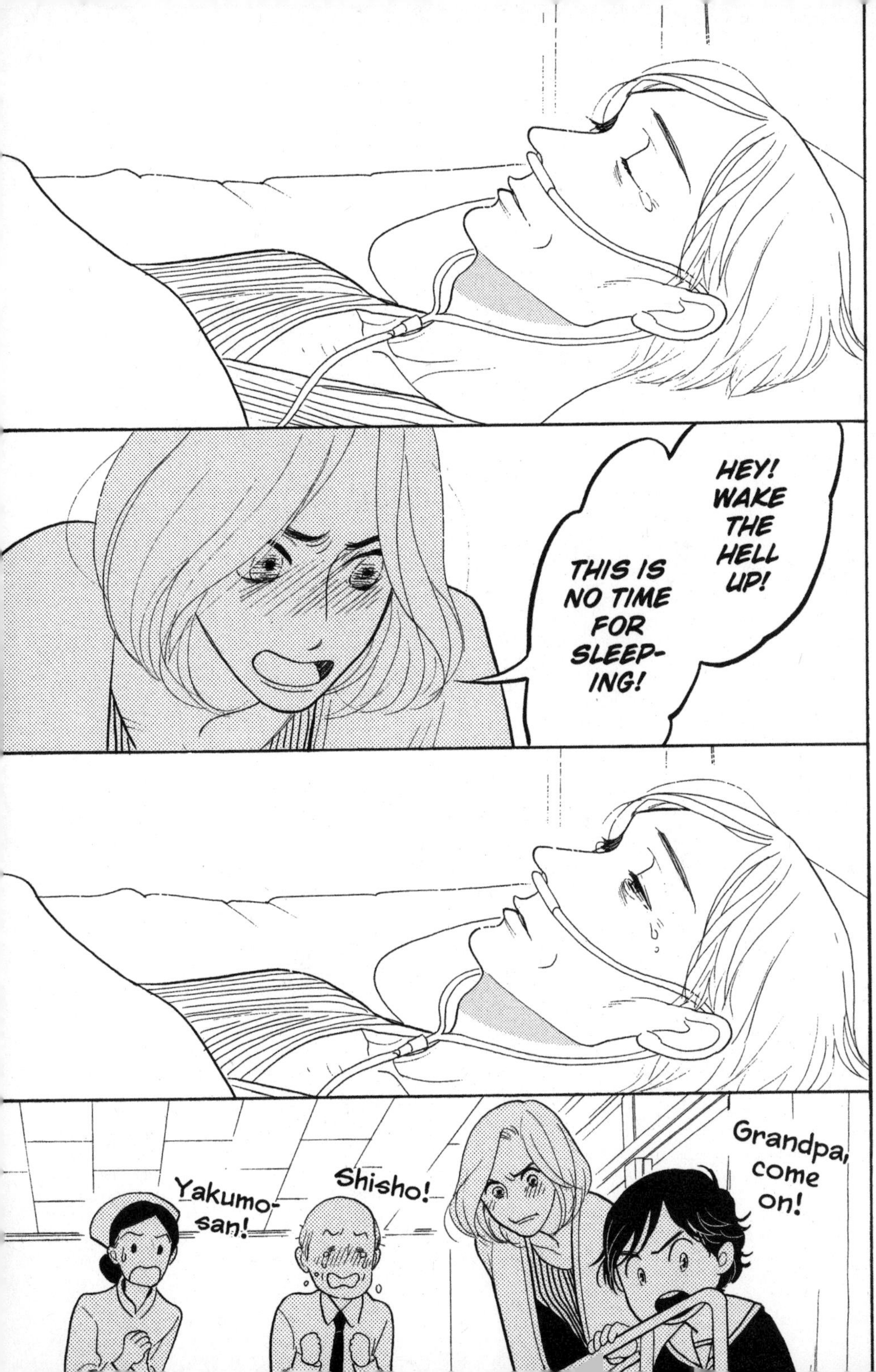
HEY! WAKE THE HELL UP!
THIS IS NO TIME FOR SLEEP-ING!
Grandpa, come on!
Shisho!
Yakumo-san!

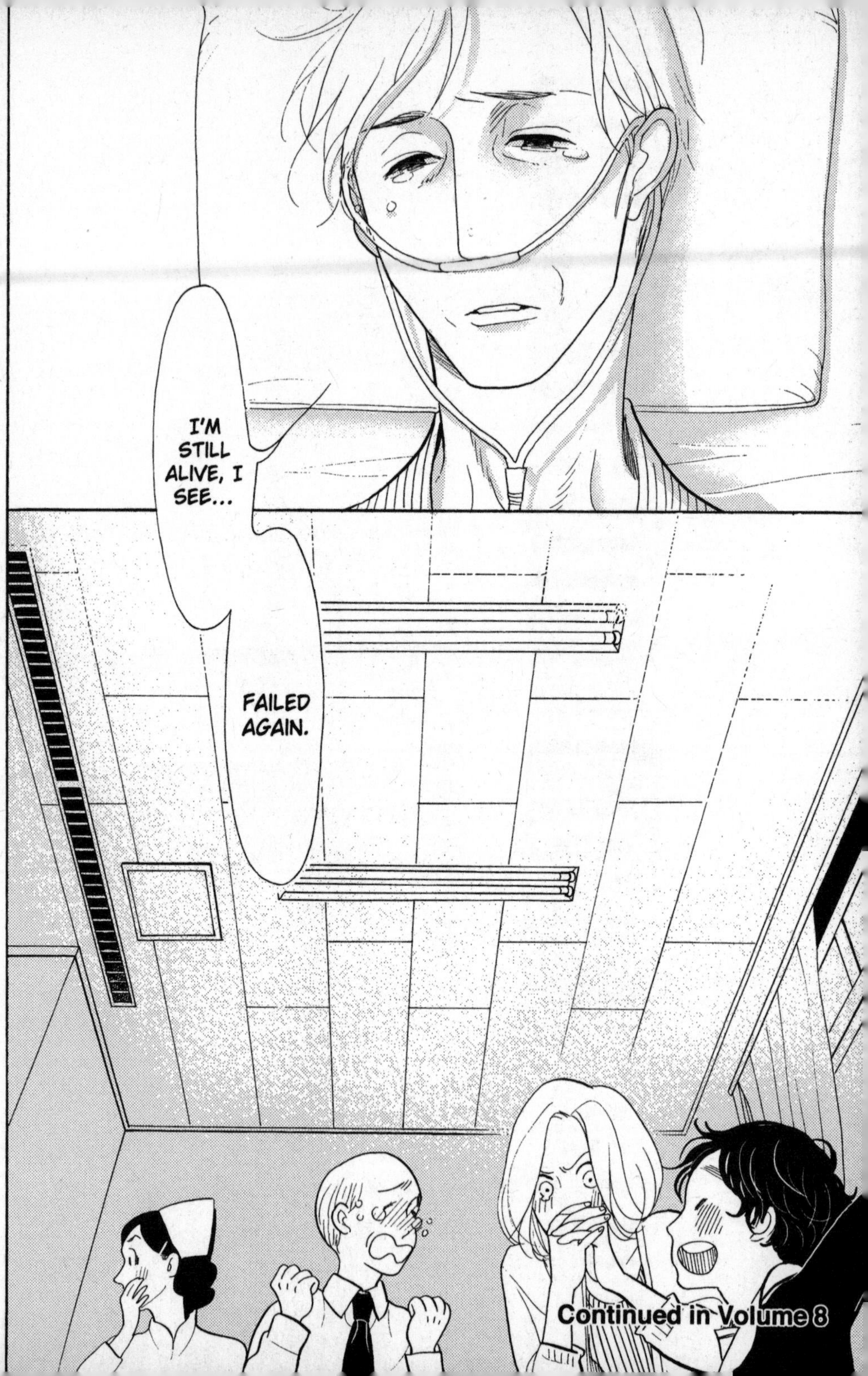
I'M STILL ALIVE, I SEE...
FAILED AGAIN.
Continued in Volume 8

Sources

Rakugo Hyakusen: Aki (One Hundred Rakugo Selections: Autumn) / Chikuma Bunko: Chikuma Shobo

Rakugo Tokusen (Special Rakugo Selection), vol. 2 / Chikuma Bunko: Chikuma Shobo

Shinpan Ensho Koten Rakugo (New Edition of Ensho's Classic Rakugo), vol. 1 / Shūeisha Bunko: Shūeisha

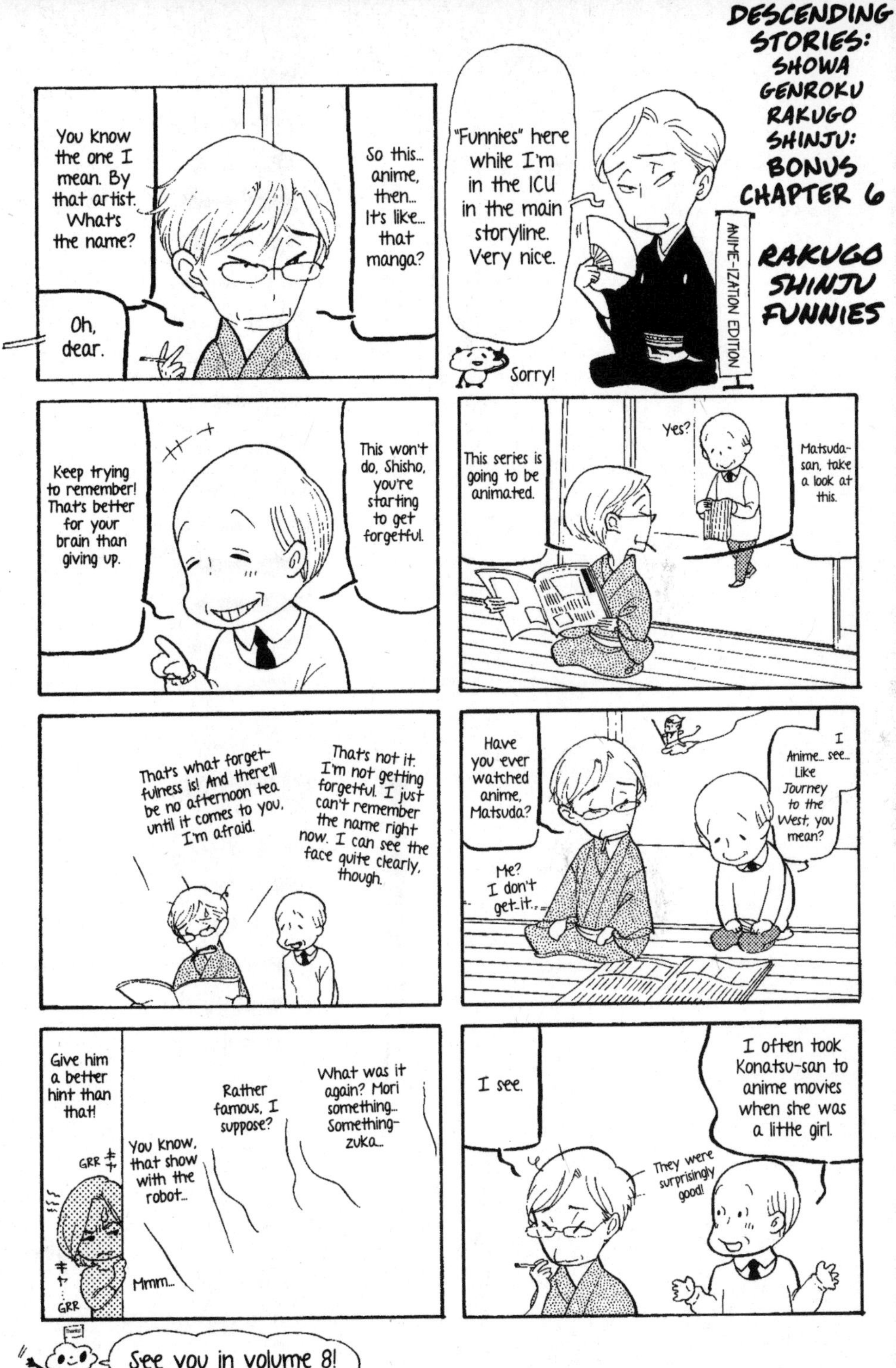

Descending Stories: Showa Genroku Rakugo Shinju: Bonus Chapter 6
Rakugo Shinju Funnies
Anime-ization Edition
"Funnies" here while I'm in the ICU in the main storyline. Very nice.
Sorry!
Matsuda-san, take a look at this.
Yes?
This series is going to be animated.
I Anime... see... Like Journey to the West, you mean?
Have you ever watched anime, Matsuda?
Me? I don't get it...
I often took Konatsu-san to anime movies when she was a little girl.
They were surprisingly good!
I see.
So this... anime, then... It's like... that manga?
You know the one I mean. By that artist. What's the name?
Oh, dear.
This won't do, Shisho, you're starting to get forgetful.
Keep trying to remember! That's better for your brain than giving up.
That's not it. I'm not getting forgetful. I just can't remember the name right now. I can see the face quite clearly, though.
That's what forgetfulness is! And there'll be no afternoon tea until it comes to you, I'm afraid.
What was it again? Mori something... Something-zuka...
Rather famous, I suppose?
You know, that show with the robot...
Mmm...
Give him a better hint than that!
GRR
GRR
See you in volume 8!

Translation Notes

Jugemu Jugemu Gokou no Surikire..., page 6
Shinnosuke is reciting a part from the *rakugo* "Jugemu," which is about a boy with a ridiculously long and auspicious name.

Bite right through my tongue, page 10
Japanese slang for "flub" (a verbal performance, etc.) is *kamu*, literally "to bite."

Five, six, seven, eight—by the way, you got the time?, page 12
Yotaro is performing "Time Soba," a *rakugo* about a noodle shop scam that involves confusing the owner by mixing coin-counting and asking the time. The shop keeper unwittingly fills in the next number in the count, and is thus shortchanged.

Mon, page 12
A fairly small unit of currency. For example, in this *rakugo* story, the price of a bowl of noodles is 16 mon.

The club to your oni, page 14
Oni were fearsome *yokai* similar to ogres. The club was their weapon of choice, and they are rarely ever pictured without one.

Debayashi and Kuromisu, page 14
The *debayashi* is the entrance and incidental music played at *rakugo* performances. Each *rakugo* artist has a different "theme." *Kuromisu* are musicians who play accompaniment for *rakugo* and other forms of theater.

Let's Play with Rakugo!, page 16
A play on a popular Japanese children's TV program, "Let's Play with Japanese" (*Nihongo de asobo*).

Good morning, page 17
Entertainers in Japan traditionally greet each other with "Good morning" (*ohayo gozaimasu*) no matter what time of day or night it is.

"Benkei and Komachi/Sure were dummies/Don't you think, honey?", page 22
This slightly risqué *senryu* is based on the popular legends of Benkei and Komachi having died virgins.

Kuruwabanashi, page 22
As mentioned in the Volume 2 translation notes, a *kuruwabanashi* is a story set in the pleasure quarters, usually the Yoshiwara.

Husband-and-wife manzai team, page 34
As mentioned in the Volume 1 translation notes, *manzai* is a form of comedy involving fast-paced banter between two people.

Zokkyoku, page 36
Popular songs performed at the *yose* as one type of attraction between *rakugo* performances.

Seventh night, page 46
A child's seventh night after birth. This was often when children were first given a name, as is the case in "Jugemu."

Out behind Kannon Temple, page 62
As referenced in Volume 2, "Kannon Temple" is another name for Asakusa's large Sensoji Temple. Behind the temple lay the old red light district.

Kabuki-za, page 66
Tokyo's oldest kabuki theater, much larger and more formal than a *yose*.

Bucho-san, page 68
A department head. In this case, apparently head of Advertising or Public Relations for the Edo *Rakugo* Association.

Narimono, page 73
Literally, "things that make noise." General term for backstage music and sound effects at the *yose*.

"Hangonko Incense," page 83
The name of a *rakugo* story. "*Hangonko*" literally means "Incense that calls spirits back."

Mokugyo and dodoitsu, page 86
Literally "wooden fish," *mokugyo* is a hollow wooden percussion instrument shaped like a fish and associated with Buddhism. *Dodoitsu* are cheerful, often bawdy songs with the moraic pattern 7-7-7-5.

Namu ya namu namu/Namu Amida..., page 86
A mantra recited by believers to Amida Buddha.

The Pine-covered hill of Sue, page 88
A reference to an ancient poem, used to invoke the idea of eternal love.

Toyama, Etchu... Hangontan, page 91
Hangontan was a famous digestive from Toyama in Etchu province (modern-day Toyama prefecture).

Heaven? ... Or hell?, page 105
Literally *gokuraku* and *jigoku*, a rough equivalent of the terminology from Buddhism.

No makura, page 116
The *makura* (literally "pillow") is the introductory banter to each *rakugo* piece, carefully crafted to lead the audience into the main story.

Shinagawa sounds perfect, page 121
Shinagawa is an area of Tokyo right on the edge of Tokyo Bay, which would have been more obvious in the Edo period than it is in modern-day era.

Lamp closet, page 123
Where the teahouse stored its lanterns and lamps during the day. Often used to hold deadbeats temporarily.

RAKUGO STORIES IN THIS VOLUME:

Jugemu (じゅげむ) - Jugemu (pages 6, 45)
Toki Soba (時そば) - The "Time-Noodle" Con Game (page 12)
Akegarasu (明鳥) - The Morning Crow (page 22)
Kajikazawa (鰍沢) - At the Kajika River (page 74)
Nishiki No Kesa (錦の袈裟) - The Brocade *Kesa* (page 83)
Hangonko (反魂香) - *Hangonko* Incense (page 83, 85)
Inokori Saheiji (居残り佐平次) - Saheiji is Kept Behind (page 83, 115)
Shinagawa Shinju (品川心中) - Double Suicide at Shinagawa (page 83)

DESCENDING
STORIES

SHOWA
GENROKU
RAKUGO
SHINJU

Haruko Kumota

It is said that the roots of the current *Rakugo Kyokai* Association can be traced to the Tokyo *Rakugo Kyokai* formed thanks to the efforts of Ryutei Saraku V following the 1923 Great Kanto Earthquake. Yanagiya Kosan IV was later appointed its chairman and established it anew as the *Rakugo Kyokai* Association. It received permission to become an incorporated association with the Agency for Cultural Affairs acting as its competent authority in 1977, and its stated goal was to "advance the spread of popular performing arts with a focus on classical *rakugo*, contributing to the cultural development of our country in the process." It later became the general incorporated association it is today in 2012. It conducts performances in four theatres (*yose*) in Tokyo, as well as in halls, assembly spaces, schools, and more around the country.

For an overview of the *Rakugo Kyokai* Association, please visit: http://rakugo-kyokai.jp/summary/

Clockwise from far left: May it be a big audience turnout; Shinnosuke, son; Longevity (on fan); Yakumo Yurakutei VIII; Matsuda-san; Sukeroku Yurakutei III; May it be a full house; Showa Genroku Rakugo Shinju; Konatsu, older sister.

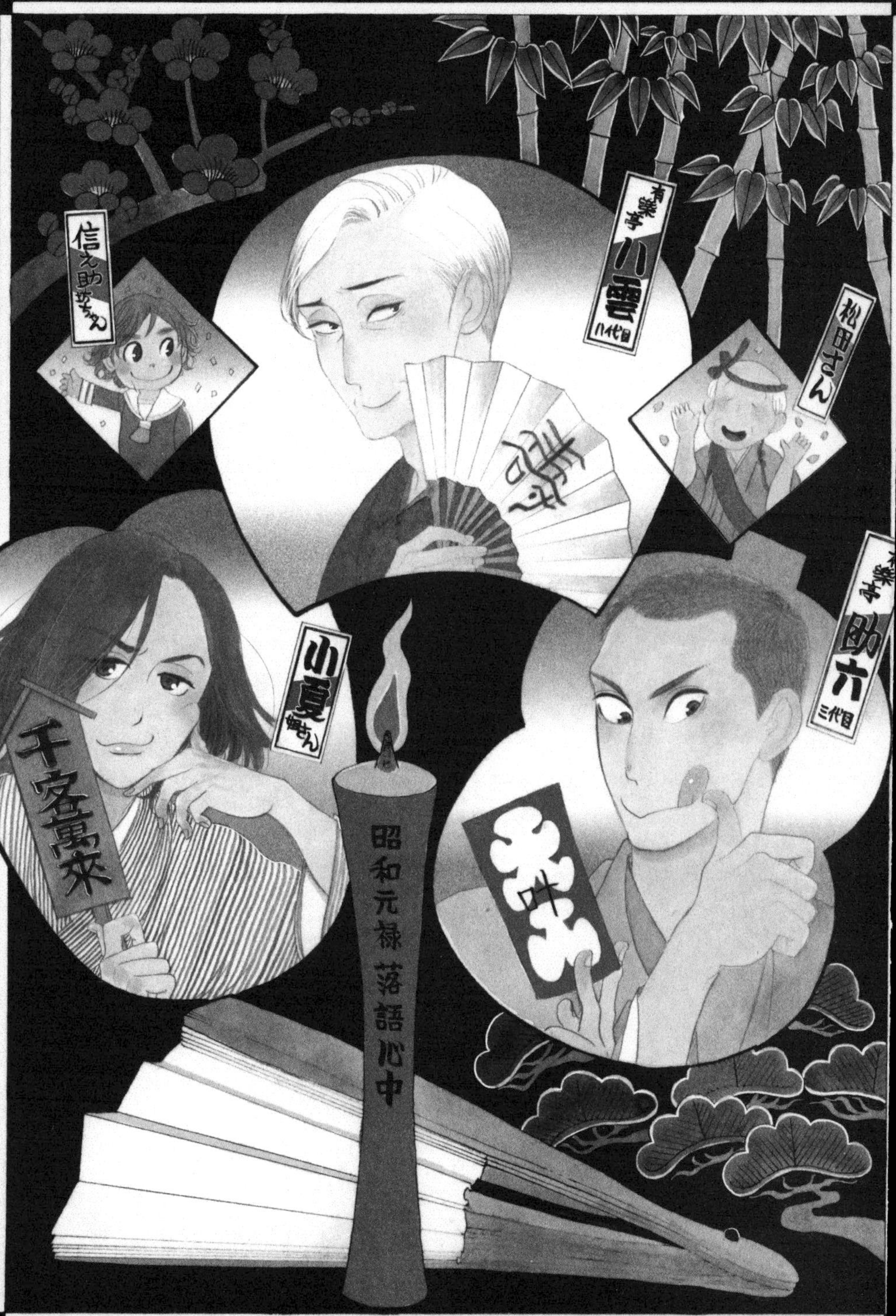
有楽亭 八雲 八代目
松田さん
信之助坊ちゃん
有楽亭 助六 三代目
小夏 姐さん
千客萬來
昭和元禄 落語心中

From the creator of No Game No Life

Naoto is a brilliant amateur mechanic who spends his days tinkering with gears and inventions. And his world is a playground—a massive, intricate machine. But his quiet life is disrupted when a box containing an automaton in the shape of a girl crashes into his home. Could this be an omen of a breakdown in Naoto's delicate clockwork planet? And is this his chance to become a hero?

CLOCKWORK PLANET

Praise for the manga and anime

"Immediately fast-paced and absorbing." - *Another Anime Review*

"A compelling science fiction world... Wildly fun and dynamic characters...T' ... who have read it all."

Now digitally!

New action series from Hiroyuki Takei, creator of the classic shonen franchise Shaman King!

In medieval Japan, a bell hanging on the collar is a sign that a cat has a master. Norachiyo's bell hangs from his katana sheath, but he is nonetheless a stray — a ronin. This one-eyed cat samurai travels across a dishonest world, cutting through pretense and deception with his blade.

STRAY CAT SAMURAI

By
Hiroyuki Takei

Descending Stories: Showa Genroku Rakugo Shinju volume 7 is a work of fiction. Names, characters, places, and incidents are the products of the author's imagination or are used fictitiously. Any resemblance to actual events, locales, or persons, living or dead, is entirely coincidental.

A Kodansha Comics Trade Paperback Original.

Published in the United States by Kodansha Comics, an imprint of Kodansha USA Publishing, LLC, New York.

Publication rights for this English edition arranged through Kodansha Ltd., Tokyo.

First published in Japan in 2015 by Kodansha Ltd., Tokyo.

ISBN 978-1-63236-545-3
Printed in the United States of America.

www.kodanshacomics.com

9 8 7 6 5 4 3 2 1

Translation: AltJapan Co., Ltd. (Matt Treyvaud, Hiroko Yoda, Matt Alt)
Lettering: Andrew Copeland
Editing: Tomoko Nagano
Rakugo term supervision: Rakugo Kyokai Association
Kodansha Comics edition cover design: Phil Balsman